MAJOR PRAISE FOR

In School

Frank McKenna, Premier of New Brunswick: "At a time when parents and educators alike are concerned about creating a safer and more responsive education system in our country, Ken Dryden gives us an accurate inside look at the Canadian classroom of the nineties, and at where we might focus our attention to achieve these goals. If you are interested in the learning process, you will find this book compelling and thought-provoking."

Atom Egoyan, Canadian filmmaker: "An important journey into the heart and soul of our society – through the story of one school in one year. Ken Dryden vividly presents a multitude of personalities and events that weave into a compelling portrait. *In School* does a remarkable job of making the reader look forward and back with anger, compassion, and hope.

Claude Ryan, former Minister of Education for Quebec: "Ken Dryden took care to observe, listen, and talk to kids, teachers, parents, and school administrators. The result is a penetrating description of interaction between all dimensions of students' lives, and a persuasive call for a deeper rapport between teachers and students."

John Evans, Chairman, Rockefeller Foundation, and Torstar: "A rare insight into the larger lives of students which colour and complicate their class-room experience.... We are reminded that each of the participants in the learn-ing process is a highly individualistic expression of a variety of influences and tensions in our complex, cosmopolitan, and rapidly changing society. The book is clearly a labour of love – love of young people, and love of learning."

Peter Herrndorf, Chairman and CEO of TVOntario: "Ken Dryden's book is critically important in understanding the learning process that our kids go through, and in shaping our educational agenda over the next decade."

Alan Mirabelli, Executive Director of the Vanier Institute of the Family: "Before joining forces with any of the camps on the educational battlefield read Ken Dryden's *In School*. His diary of observations gathered from the classroom tells us much, perhaps even more than we wanted to know, about today's stu-dents and their teachers and society's expectations of them both. This is required reading for those who truly care about their children."

John T. McLennan, President and CEO of Bell Canada: "How are we preparing our children? In place of the criticism and finger-pointing that too often dominate the debate, Ken Dryden offers a lively, wise, and empathetic account of the secondary school experience. Here is the foundation for a more thoughtful, less strident discussion of the problems and prospects of our next generation and its capacity to make a place for itself in the world.... An important book."

John O'Leary, President of Frontier College: "[Ken Dryden] has written the book that I always wanted to write! He looks at the real challenge facing schools today – how to educate the entire population. He provides the context, asks the right questions, and goes about answering them in the best way, by spending a year in a real classroom, meeting students, parents, and teachers and listening to their stories as they deal with the realities of learning and learning how to learn. None of the studies, seminars, or conferences that I am aware of is as effective as *In School* in helping the public to understand what schools are really dealing with."

David Strangway, President of the University of British Columbia: "Truly excellent.... I couldn't put it down. Unlike so many recent reports on our schools that purport to analyse the problems and offer solutions, this book provides an explicit view of the inside of the classroom.... Ken Dryden gives us a remarkable view of the nature of the teaching and learning process of the 1990s, and helps us to understand the joys and frustrations. *In School* is essential reading."

Albert Shanker, President, American Federation of Teachers: "In this journal of a year spent in an Ontario high school, Ken Dryden creates an intelligent, often moving portrait of the day-to-day interactions between students and teachers. Dryden is a parent and a writer, not an educator, but his insights about the frustrations and triumphs of teaching are on target. He captures the essence of how hard the teachers work, and with how much hope and inventiveness, to connect with students and connect students with learning."

Charles E. Pascal, former Ontario Deputy Minister of Education: "This book will make some education reformers excited and others nervous. Dryden's role as former Youth Commissioner in Ontario, his experience as an involved parent, and his 'see for himself' and reflective spirit has generated a very important book...."

Ralph Nader, consumer activist: "What is unique about Ken Dryden's *In School* is that he directly observes what is happening on the ground – in school and its classrooms.... A first-rate educational ethnography that should help thinking about the future of education."

IN SCHOOL

IN SCHOOL

Our Kids, Our Teachers, Our Classrooms

KEN DRYDEN

M&S

Canadian Cataloguing in Publication Data

Dryden, Ken, 1947-
  In school : our kids, our teachers, our classrooms

ISBN 0-7710-2869-5 bound   ISBN 0-7710-2868-7 pbk.

1. Education, Secondary – Canada.   I. Title.

LA416.D79   1995   373.71   C95-932201-9

The publishers acknowledge the support of the Canada Council and the Ontario Arts Council for their publishing program.

Typesetting by M&S, Toronto
Printed and bound in Canada

McClelland & Stewart Inc.
The Canadian Publishers
481 University Avenue
Toronto, Ontario
M5G 2E9

1 2 3 4 5   00 99 98 97 96

To *T.L.K.*

Nullius in Verba

("Take nobody's word for it; see for yourself.")

– motto of The Royal Society

Contents

Introduction

I hadn't been inside a high school classroom in nearly thirty years. I had been to our kids' parents' nights, their drama and music productions, their games and graduations. I had talked to gatherings of students on career days. But it's not the same. When I was Ontario Youth Commissioner in the mid-1980s, responsible for the province's youth employment and training programs, I had addressed high school assemblies. Unemployment, especially youth unemployment, was high. Most kids who were unemployed had dropped out of school. There was only enough money to put some of them into training programs. It seemed the best thing I could do was work from the other end: talk to these kids, get them to stay in school, keep them from becoming unemployed now, so they'd have a better chance later.

I used to put on a skit at these assemblies. I would choose twenty kids from the audience, ten boys and ten girls, and bring them on stage with me. They were to represent the typical grade-nine class of the time. I took them quickly through a scenario of their high school years, their early worries and growing ease, their tragedies and triumphs, their anxieties about a beckoning future. The twenty grade nines turned into twenty confident grade tens, but by the end of grade eleven, only fifteen were left, I told them; five had dropped out. Together those five moved to one corner of the stage and stood by themselves. Then more joined them. The group and the audience grew edgy.

I gave out diplomas to the graduates, then a few graduates went into the community-college line, a few more to the university line. Most joined the job line, which by now extended from one corner of the stage to its middle. I gave a name and name card to one kid in each line, and continued their stories. Nicole has dropped out. What will her life be like a year from now, I asked, in three years, five years? What about George? He has graduated from high school; where will he be living, what will he be doing? What job, if any, will he have? Will he have the sound system, car, and clothes he always imagined? An apartment of his own? And Jeremy, who has graduated from university, what about him?

The message was clear, and the kids knew it. Stay where you are and do what you're doing. There are no guarantees, but school remains the best, surest, most constructive route to a job, to the job you want, to the life you want.

I gave that speech many times for more than a year. I received many more invitations to give it; in time, I gave it less often, then finally not at all. My reluctance didn't evolve out of boredom; it came from a feeling I couldn't ignore. I knew I was right in what I was saying, and the kids and teachers knew that too. But for those who really needed to hear my message, it was already too late. They had stopped listening, just as they had in class. Falling back a little grade by grade, they were finally so far behind they couldn't imagine a way out. Hope, opportunity: for them, these no longer resided in school. They knew what another school day would bring. They also knew in theory what dropping out would mean, what jobs they would get, if any. But they knew these consequences only second-hand, from the unasked-for words of parents and teachers. Maybe things would be worse. But *maybe* they wouldn't. For them, infinitely better than the devil they knew was the devil they didn't know. Leaving school was the only hope left to them. For me to tell them to stay in school was like telling a dying man who knew he was dying that things would get better. It was a cheat. Just being right wasn't right.

What had happened to bring these kids to the brink of dropping out? The message of the future was so clear, to parents, teachers, kids, *everyone*. Why did doing better seem so beyond them? Standing on that stage, I knew I would never know. I had to go inside a classroom, forget my appointment book, watch and listen. When that skit ended this book began.

A few years passed. The education debate, which normally seems to heat up for one or two years during every decade, now refused to go away. We had gone from recession to boom to deeper recession to recovery; our insecurities heightened. Economic globalization had brought new competition, from who-knows-where, from people who did things who-knows-how, for who-knows-what price. Always somebody somewhere was willing to work a little harder for a little less. The competition had become intense but unknowable. What might that phantom "other guy" do? Can we do it first? Companies strove to be endlessly, blindly better: If it ain't broke, fix it anyway. And if outputs were to improve, so must inputs. Workers must be better trained. They must arrive at the office door from high school or university ready to contribute. But they didn't.

Fuelled by these anxieties, the education debate continues to rage, but goes nowhere. Positions have hardened, become routine and predictable. The debate has become a monologue, multi-sided, stalemated, full of anger, politics, and complication. The only message emerging from it is that parents must do better, and teachers must do better, for kids to do better. Which is the

chicken and which the egg? The question of who bears more of
the blame and responsibility has become a paralysing preoccupation. The irony is that this is a battle of educators, people who in
their own lives have been successful learners, who in their roles
as politicians, business people, lobbyists, academics, journalists, and
teachers are charged with instructing, informing, and educating
their audience. Yet if these parties were in a classroom, and the
state of schools was the day's lesson, this class would be as bad as
any cited as evidence of the problem. In the front row, politicians,
academics, educational bureaucrats, a handful of parents, monopo-
lizing the class; at the back, media and interest groups, disturbing,
interrupting, sniping one-liners like smart-ass kids; in the middle,
parents, teachers, kids, most of the class, dozing off, hiding.

Those at the front of the room have forgotten the very lessons
of teaching. Good teachers don't teach subjects, they teach
people. But to teach people, they must know them, spend time
with them, care about them, believe in them. Those teachers
who don't teach the way they should, kids who don't do their
homework, parents who are never there, are not evil people.
Theirs is no conspiracy to undermine the system. Rather, they
are flawed, they make mistakes, like all of us, and in this lies the
crucial story. A reason why. Something in the way they live their
lives, spend their time, in what they think and do; in what
matters to them most. A why that sends a life hurtling in one
direction and not another. A good teacher uncovers those whys
and teaches to them, and makes them work for him or her.

The education debate has abandoned the whys. It has abandoned the story, retreating to the easier, nastier, unthinking,
unfeeling, black-and-white ground of issues and policies. A
fruitless ground. As always, the problem, the solution, is people.

I decided to spend a year inside a school. I wanted it to be a high
school. Even if the stories and habits of a life are set in motion
much earlier, with a ten-year-old they can seem only temporary,

reversible. There's still so much time ahead, there are still so many experiences to be had, so much that can change in a young person who is still so unshaped. Whatever is today can be different tomorrow. Whatever I do as parent and teacher can be easily undone – or so it seems. But not so with a fifteen-year-old. In him or her, you can see the future. You can see the consequences of past and present, what has been done and not done. I wanted the implications of a good school and good home, or a bad school and bad home, to be undeniable.

I wanted to choose a school in the suburbs, because most North Americans live in suburbs, a school that wasn't the best and wasn't the worst – one like most kids attend. At first I was concerned that even an objectively average school might have some exaggerated feature that would make it *seem* average. I came to realize, however, that the most fundamental distinction between students is not their race or sex or religion or family income, but between those who *get* it and those who don't, and kids like these are present in every school, in every classroom. I wanted to focus mostly on kids not new to high school or about to graduate, but on those beginning to experience fully the complications of teenage life: independence; physical, intellectual, and emotional maturity; part-time jobs; money; cars; alcohol; drugs; sex; friends; relationships. On grade tens, I thought. But to know them better, I wanted to spend the first semester, from September to January, in various grades, to see how kids changed from year to year, how the tone and presentaion of classes and subject matter changed, to see where these grade tens had been, and where they were going. I wanted also to see different teachers in action, dealing with many of the same kids in the same circumstances, to see how they handled both, and with what results. I wanted kids in the regular academic stream, because that's where most kids are, studying the core subjects of English, Math, Science, and History.

I wanted a class of kids that second semester, not the best and not the worst, that stayed together, but that wasn't possible. Today in most high schools, there are no classes. There aren't even large groups of kids that remain as a unit for most of their four courses a day. Every new period is a new mix. As it turned out, fifteen kids were in two of the courses I followed, six were in three, the rest I saw only once a day.

I wanted most of all to get to know these kids and teachers. Who are they? What do they like to do? What do they think about? What matters to them? How do they spend their time? And how does school fit into that time? What do they bring with them into the classroom every morning at 8:40? What do they return to at night? How important *is* school in their lives? And what happens each day when these kids' and teachers' stories come together in the classroom? Why does that happen and not something else?

The rest was sitting and watching.

I arrived my first day in a sport jacket and tie; by the end of the second week, I was wearing a sweater and casual shoes like most of the male teachers. I sat at a regular student desk, usually on an outer aisle near the back, though those desks filled quickly. The first few days, I felt a nearly uncontrollable urge to raise my hand, finally able to answer most of the questions. But answering inside my head, sometimes I found I wasn't right, and the urge passed. Gradually, I just settled in. I knew that in time almost anything (even an attention-seeking camera, as news reporters have noted) will become unseen. I was amazed at how quickly I was just there. A few teachers might occasionally glance at me to see my reaction to something they had said, but they soon got over that. The kids, so preoccupied in their own teenage worlds, seemed undistracted by me almost from the beginning.

I was there day after day, class after class, because in that daily routine lies the school experience. But once I had to be reminded. One Monday morning, the Toronto area was hit by a howling winter storm, one of many that year. I knew the roads would be bad, it would take me double my usual time to travel

the twenty-nine kilometres from my home to school, so I
skipped. The next day, in the halls, in the staff room, I was asked
"Where were you?" I was asked again and again, even by teachers I rarely saw. "I thought you wanted to know what a school
was like, what it's like to be a teacher," they challenged and
teased. "It means being here on good days *and* bad days, when
you want to and when you don't." Later, when asked, I learned
to say that I was at the school almost every day, "not quite as often
as most teachers, but more often than most kids."

Perhaps I could seem like just another body in the classroom
because I was comfortable there. I was amazed at how the feeling
of a classroom never really leaves us. The good and bad of it;
the fear and boredom and pleasure. Sitting at a student's desk, I
felt like a student. Older, but not the three times older I was. I felt
enough like them that it never occurred to me they wouldn't see
me as I saw my self. And there were other timeless feelings, as
well. Once I was called to the office. I had arrived very early that
morning to talk to the head custodian. No one else was around.
No other cars were in the parking lot. A dusting of snow had
covered the painted lines on the pavement. I had to make my best
guess as to where my car should go. By noon, someone in the
office realized whose car was causing the problem, and called me
over the PA. It was as if I were ten years old again. *I didn't do it.
It wasn't me.* When I looked out the office window, I saw the long
rows of perfectly parked cars, and my car, nose-to-tail, tail-to-
nose, to all the others, perfectly blocking any way in or out.

Another day, a history teacher was arranging his class into
teams for a game, and was one player short. He asked me to fill
in. I had grown quite at ease in that class and had no interest in
the pressure of a game, yet saying no seemed inappropriate. Like
my teammates and opponents, I was to prepare answers to questions given us as homework and have them ready for the game.
When I went home, I felt a surge of resentment at this intrusion
on my night, forgot the questions, and didn't do them. As I was

walking to class the next day, I suddenly remembered. I searched for a quiet place, quickly scanned the 120 questions, divided 120 by the number of kids in the class (and the number who would likely be there), looked for the easiest ten questions, and prepared them, figuring I could always work ahead on others during the game if I had to. Some instincts never die.

When the school year began, the principal asked certain of the teachers if they would mind my being in their class. Within days, other teachers approached *me*, asking when I would be coming to see *their* kids. It became a kind of competition that went on the whole year. I had only one teacher, out of more than one hundred on staff, tell me he'd prefer I not sit in. He had a particularly difficult group, he said. He was going through a bad time; he didn't want to take the risk. As for the others, it was as if building up for years inside them was a story they were bursting to tell, one they needed to get off their chests, in the hope that others might understand. They seemed happy for another set of eyes in the room. They had heard so much public criticism for so long that even the most secure carried a heavy burden of doubt. Am I teaching this the right way? Am I getting through to him/her? How can I do better? The kids proved wonderful collaborators as well. Kids love to talk about themselves (except sometimes to their parents), if someone really wants to talk to them. Like the teachers, they asked only that I have an open mind. If I didn't pretend to have all the answers, they wouldn't either, and they would be willing to explore with me wherever exploration, wherever the whys, took us.

The teachers' real names are used in the book, as are those of the principal, vice-principals, and other staff. The kids' names have been changed, but no other details about them have been altered.

This is their story.

Chapter 1

Thomas L. Kennedy Secondary School,
Mississauga, Ontario

**Semester Two; Day One
Friday, February 4, 8:32 a.m.**

Today feels different from the first day of school in September. There was so much energy then. Everyone on the edge, so excited to be back, so anxious about the unknowns of the new year. Friends who had scattered far and wide for the summer together again, new clothes out of the closet, a bigger, smarter, prettier, three-month-older version of everyone, back to begin something new. All the possibilities. Clean slates for everyone. Last year's 65 in math might become a 90, a girl who didn't know you existed might now clutch you to the centre of her world. Yet also gone were all the comfortable certainties of an old dirty slate. For this might be the year things come apart. A teacher who doesn't like you, best friends who find someone else. For teachers, a class they can't handle.

Now five months into the year, on this first day of the second semester, it is more calm, more routine, almost just another day. Not so hopeful or fearful, grim or committed. Not a day that will stand up long to whatever reality presents itself in the days to come. For better or worse, by now the stories of most of these kids rushing to their day's first class have a familiar ring. Last semester's 65 will *not* be a 90. An 80 perhaps; sure, why not, for this is a first day after all.

Nelson has been wandering the halls since eight o'clock, anxious not to be late for anything, slowing at each gathering of kids he passes, smiling, hoping to be invited to join them. It hasn't happened yet. He was at a neighbouring school in the fall, and at two different schools last year in grade nine when he was living with his mother. None turned out well for him. He was always in trouble, not for his marks – he passed everything except last semester's English – or his attendance. Most kids like Nelson, who just scrape by academically, hate school and find in any imaginable symptom of illness an excuse to stay away. Yet every day he was there, occasionally a little late, but no more so than most of the other kids. In fact, he likes school; he likes learning. He gets excited when he comes upon something new. He vibrates with a child's pleasure even at math equations and metaphors, things that aren't supposed to be interesting to a kid his age, with his marks. Other kids his age, their eyes already seem harder, partially shut by their fifteen years of experiencing the world. His eyes, big and brown, joyous, guileless, with only a squint of doubt, seem always to see something new. It's wonderful, his teachers gush, that pure puppy-dog exuberance of learning, until a few times each day, every day, it becomes too much. Nelson, settle down. Nelson, get out in the hall. Nelson, go to the office!

What is he doing that's so wrong? he wonders. Why does everyone like me, then not like me? Even the kids. He's good-looking, wears the right clothes, likes the right music. At his old school, John Fraser, all the black kids played dominoes in the cafeteria at lunch; he got his uncle to teach him how to play. He's willing to like what they like, at least some of the time. Yet they turn him away, shake their heads. *Oh, Nelson.* He keeps crossing a line he just doesn't see.

Now if he can only find a friend, he thinks, as he looks around the halls of his new school. If his new teachers will just let him be him. Already he likes what he feels. A lot more black kids than he expected, and not the "snobby" feel he found at Fraser. *Maybe it will be different here. Nobody knows me. I have no history, no story others will insist on. Maybe I can be what I really am.*

Nelson looks for a seat at the front of the classroom as the others compete for seats at the back. Then he spots Julie, a tall, pretty, dark-haired girl, and sits down in front of her. Maria Cheung, their math teacher, passes around a seating plan; nothing is final, she assures them with a smile in her slightly Chinese-accented English. She will change them around as she comes to know them better. Several kids, having found themselves in the wrong room, get up and leave; others drift in.

Maria distributes copies of the course outline to Nelson and to the four others in the front row seats. They pass the sheets back over their heads without looking, all except Nelson. He turns and hands his pile to Julie. Quentin brings his copy up almost to the tip of his nose and squints to read it. Maria begins going through the course units they will cover. She has their attention, loses it, then gets it back when she mentions marks. The kids have heard all this before, and will hear it again in their other three classes of the day. The final exam counts for one-third of their semester mark. Results from frequent short quizzes and occasional longer tests account for most of the rest. Participation marks will also be given for attendance, punctuality, and preparedness for class. That means homework. Any missed test must be explained by a note from a parent or guardian, and made up after school on the first day of one's return. A mark of zero will otherwise be given. She asks for questions and gets no response.

Less than half an hour into the seventy-six-minute class, Sophia looks up at the clock and groans. Fifty minutes later, as announcements over the PA signal the class's end, she mutters, "Thank you, God." In between, she watches Maria Cheung with the concentration of someone for whom understanding in English is not taken for granted.

Sophia arrived in November from Belgrade, capital of the former Yugoslavia, now of Serbia. The civil war drove her family here, just as two years before it had driven them as Serbs from their home in Bosnia to the safety of Belgrade. She came with her mother and younger brother. They were taken in by her mother's sister and her family, who had escaped the war a few years earlier. Her parents are separated; her father will not be joining them. Since November, she has been monitoring classes, as counsellors and teachers try to assess her. She had had only four years of English in classes just twice a week in Yugoslavia, yet she understands written English well, spoken English not as well. She writes with the frequent grammar and spelling errors of translation. "Canada is for me like magic lang," she wrote when she arrived, "and I love her very muc."

Her real passion is science. Before she left Belgrade she had written special exams and been accepted into the stream that would lead to medical school. That had not been easy. Big classes, teachers who lectured and had no desire for personal contact with their students: for her the most vivid experience of survival hadn't been the civil war, but the fierce competition into medicine. The student next to her was not her friend. She had to answer faster, test higher. Now fifteen and in a new country, she feels the pressure of having a future to make and not much time, although there is little to suggest this urgency in her chubby doll's face, her gap-toothed grin, her round, dumpling body. Only her unbreakable attention.

She gets up and moves uncertainly towards her next class, science. No one goes with her. Julie heads to music; Nelson and Quentin to a different science class just a few doors away. Their teacher, Cathy Sylvester, welcomes them with a lively smile. She is in her mid-forties, not much more than five feet tall, even in her high heels, with a look and attitude not much changed since she was a teenager in the early 1960s. The teacher's pet has become teacher.

Cathy has no handouts for them, instead she has written the course outline on the board in her careful teacher's hand. She wants them to copy it down, she says, and instantly books come out of backpacks, pens and pencils start moving, the room goes quiet. She hates the "administrivia" of the first day. The kids have energy, the ones who are here, that is, but there is little they can do. They can't even look through the textbook together, because she won't give out the texts until Tuesday. Some kids who took science the first semester haven't returned their books, so there aren't enough. Some of these kids haven't turned in theirs from other courses and aren't allowed new ones until they do. Some kids spend the first few days of each semester shopping schools, not just classes. If they get teachers they don't like, they go somewhere else, and if they have been issued books, expensive science texts will be gone, and with them the taxpayers' money.

So Cathy creates something for them to do that looks and feels like schoolwork and breaks the whiteness of their binder pages. This is also her chance to come down from her riser at the front of the room, from behind her big science desk, and walk amongst them. Though her directions are straightforward and her writing is clear, there will be questions, she knows. She will hear voices, and in them tones, messages, attitudes, securities and insecurities, what she must work with, and get through these next twenty weeks, to teach them science.

Accents too, many more than when she began teaching here twenty-two years ago, and many more, she knows, that she will rarely hear, for most immigrant kids don't speak out in class. That's also why she walks around. She can see the kids doing their work, she will have something to refer to, to start a conversation, to get an idea of how they express themselves and how much they understand. Two Eastern European girls, probably Polish, sit in the middle of the middle row. One seems to speak well; she has probably been in Canada some time. The other smiles at everything, cheerfully, knowingly; nobody probes a smiling face. She's not understanding much, Cathy notes, yet her written English is good. She has taken down what's on the board and added things from what Cathy has said, all grammatical and spelled correctly. Still, Cathy thinks, she'll have to watch her carefully.

Two Oriental kids, a boy and a delicate, elegantly dressed girl, almost model-like, sit together in the front row opposite Nelson. Cathy notices their staccato writing style, so few adjectives, adverbs, conjunctions, their language stripped of everything but nouns and verbs, even in what they are copying from the board. She has some predictable partnerships: the Oriental kids, two Polish girls, two distinctly Canadian girls near the back, two South Asian girls at the back in the middle. Girls with girls, boys with boys, common races and languages together. Comfort more than ambition directs their choice, at least for most, and that has always surprised her. Especially in science where, with desk partners, you *have* to work with someone. Maybe the stronger wants nothing to do with the weaker, but the weaker, parasite to host, should surely try to latch on. To copy notes, benefit from an experiment done right, to get better marks. But comfort almost always wins out. Do yourselves a favour, she sometimes wants to scream. Grab onto the best student, hang on to him or her; it's your chance. But so few of them take it.

She allows these seating choices because the kids have made them for reasons important to them; because, she has found, many kids never get over a seating change they don't want, and turn against her. But miss, they say, we didn't do anything *really* wrong, so why did you move us? Because Cathy has power, she sometimes forgets she has it. Because the kids don't, they never forget. And if she uses hers arbitrarily, the kids will use theirs – *not* to be quiet, *not* to do their homework – arbitrarily too. Only if things get truly disruptive will she make a seating change. Then the class will understand, and so will the kids involved.

The class is working well. She overhears some of the kids' comments, some of them are even about science. She's got some good thinkers here. Nelson is certainly a live one. He's so eager and helpful, energetic and involved. He'll be good for the class. But he writes so slowly. She was standing near him as he took down her words from the board and his pen seemed scarcely to move, as if each word were a hurdle. And Quentin, squinting so painfully to make out the board just a few feet away. He's the only other black kid in the class, yet he and Nelson don't sit together, although they do sit across the aisle from each other. Interesting. Quentin said to her as she passed that he had taken and failed Science the first semester. He had missed a lot of classes, he said. That was the reason. He leafed through the experiments he had written up first semester so she could see them. Absence might not be the only reason, she thought to herself.

"Miss, what's that word after 'be'?" The voice comes gratingly from the back. Cathy looks up at the board.

"After 'be'? Where after 'be'?"

"After 'be'!" the voice wails again. It's Jody. She leans forward and squints as if trying hard to answer her own question.

"I'm sorry, but I don't –"

"After 'be'! On the second line –"

"Oh," Cathy brightens, "'calculated.'"

"'Calculated,' that doesn't look like 'calculated.'" Jody is still squinting.

"Are you having trouble seeing the board? Maybe you should sit up a little closer."

"No, I can see fine," Jody snaps, then mumbles, "It just doesn't look like 'calculated,' that's all."

Cathy had sensed trouble in that back corner. Jody, Jennifer, and Tracy. Jody and Jennifer together at one lab desk, Tracy by herself at the desk ahead, her body sideways on her stool, able to turn towards Cathy at the front, most often turned towards her friends at the back. From the moment they entered the room there was such resistance in them, such an edge. They've probably had a "bad experience" in science before, Cathy thinks. She hears it all the time: girls can't do science, we're not going to be doctors, what do we need science for anyway? *Besides, it's boring.*

Cathy smiles at Jody. I may have to do something back there, she thinks. But let's give it a few days. See if I can get through to them before then. At first a few, then all eyes turn to the clock – suddenly it flips to 11:22 – no bell goes off, but class is over. The kids jump up from their seats. Cathy is back on her riser behind her big science desk, the same lively smile on her face as they rush out the door.

Two periods down, for most kids and teachers it is lunch and two periods to go. Nelson meanders down the hall unseen, overhears some kids talking about Mickey's, a video games hangout near the school, but he decides to go to the Cafetorium, "the Caf," instead. The Caf is a large rectangular room with a stage at one end. Its eight lengthwise rows of long, collapsible tables and benches are nearly filled. He scans the room. He sees only a confusion of kids at first, then patterns emerge; the only one that matters to him is a half row of black kids playing dominoes. He squeezes in beside them, watching enough, interested enough, to belong, but no one asks him to join in.

Cathy Sylvester goes to the staff room. She checks for messages in her box in the wood honeycomb that covers one wall inside the door, and sits down at her usual table to eat. It's a comfortable room. The lunch tables, a sofa and some big chairs, a new rug, charcoal grey with red-orange flecks, very cushiony, so different from the old one; morning newspapers, strewn over tables and chairs; bulletin boards, wall dividers, the backs of doors all covered in announcements; a pop machine. An old school, Kennedy doesn't have department rooms large enough to meet in or work in, to give refuge, so teachers congregate here. About twenty-five of them now, the figure staying nearly constant as perhaps twice that number rotate in and out during the period. These teachers have mostly white, mostly middle-aged faces, what would have been next-door faces in most of Toronto only twenty years ago. A few more are women than men; the women are better dressed. They all seem happy to be here, so on the knife's edge of control in their classrooms, so exuberant among their peers. As if when they arrived in school this morning, they took in a deep breath, and expelled it just moments ago.

The talk is about the weekend, the weather – that with Toronto's record low temperatures this past month has been everybody's preoccupation – the Leafs in the midst of a rare good season, the Blue Jays about to go to spring training. About their spouses, most of whom are also teachers, and their kids, everybody by first name, familiar enough characters to everyone by now, though few have ever met. And especially they talk about their "kids," the students they teach.

"Who've ya got this semester?" says a voice at one of the room's three lunch tables.

"A grade eleven and a couple of grade nines. The grade nines are so good I can't believe it." Several arms reach out for some wood to touch. "Compared to last year's anyway." The heads at the table nod.

"I've got those grade twelve criminals. Remember that class?" Lots of eyes roll.

"Can you imagine them in ten years?" Noel Lim, an English teacher, grins. "Mr. and Mrs. Canada," they all laugh, Noel louder than the rest. "They might be my neighbours –" he yells. More screams of laughter.

"– maybe our boss." More screams.

"Hey, anybody got Willy?" There is laughter. Finally, one reluctant nod.

"Ah, he's not that bad," a voice says timidly. Eyebrows rise, Noel's higher than the rest. More timidly now: "He's harmless, at least."

"Just a little scary. I asked my class last fall to create a fantasy restaurant. You know, menu, decor, theme. He called his 'Road Kill.'" More nods.

A hoot comes through the doorway from a smaller room behind. It's the euchre guys. Dave Arthurs, a history teacher, has lost. No one is surprised.

"Hey, Davey, snatching defeat from the jaws of victory again?" More laughter.

"I hate this game," he snarls, raising his right arm and, like Michael Jordan, airborne and descending to the hoop, slamming his cards down on the table.

"Davey, do a reverse three-sixty." More laughter.

Jimmy, ET, Wardo and Ronnie, the Sandman and five or six others: they rotate four at a time during the two lunch periods, sometimes before and after school. New semesters mean new timetables, new lunch periods, new euchre partners, but winners always seem to win, losers to lose, and the table patter rarely varies.

"Hey, Davey, no big deal, all that money you're winning on ProLine." They laugh again. ProLine, a sports betting pool run by the province, combines two of Dave Arthurs' passions, and he is hooked.

"Yeah, but you wait," he laughs. "I can *feeeel* this one." Today, Dave came in with his latest ticket. Two nights' worth of games, six games in all; last night he won all three. "I already got the toughest ones," he says, pride rising in his voice. "I mean, San Jose over Calgary —" He waits for the appropriate buzz of respect, and doesn't get it. "And tonight, three sure things."

"Yeah, you got it made, Davey. Who you got now?" Dave hands him his ticket.

"Rangers over St. Louis, and they're at home. Edmonton over Ottawa —"

"— everybody beats Ottawa —"

"— the Leafs *at home* over the Mighty Ducks. It's a lock."

Mike Kozak, a math teacher, winks at the others. "Davey, tell ya what. I'll give you fifty bucks for the ticket. You paid ten for it; you pocket forty, free and clear."

"Are you kidding? This'll pay more than two-fifty. I'll give you something for fifty bucks — a sniff," he snarls, and laughs again.

ET, Ettore Palmeri, a teacher and guidance counsellor who does everything with full-throttle passion, looks strangely subdued. "Aw jeeezus, Davey, I mean I shouldn't bring this up," he says, pain contorting his face, "but you know Cujo [St. Louis goalie Curtis Joseph] can win a game by himself, and jeez, he plays well in New York, doesn't he, Sandman?" Dave Sands, the Sandman, looking suddenly just as worried, nods.

"And Ottawa, you gotta worry about a team that's lost ten in a row. I mean, you can't lose every game." He is now nearly in agony. "And — but no, no, no, Davey. You shouldn't worry. I mean, you're right. You got it made."

A large black cloud has descended over Dave. The others can hardly contain themselves. In ProLine, you have to get all six right to win. Dave Arthurs, who plays Santa Claus at every Christmas party, who as "Mr. Charity Week" spearheads the school's fund-raising drive every spring, is known as "old 5 out of 6 Dave."

◆ ◆ ◆

"Hey, Pat's here." Willy's cackle rises above the low-level din as the kids shuffle slowly to their desks. Willy, proprietor of "Road Kill," still in his winter coat, is short and skinny with a shaved, tadpole-shaped head. While Cathy Sylvester eats in the staff room, and Nelson in the Caf, Pat and Willy are down the hall in Rick Ray's grade ten History class, wishing they were anywhere else.

Rick starts right in, briefly describing the course. Last year as grade nines, these kids took geography; this is their first high-school history course, "Canada in the Twentieth Century." It is not about the making of the country, Rick says, but about its transformation: from the first great wave of immigrants in the early 1900s, to the awkward expressions of independence, first from the British Empire then the American Empire, to the two world wars and the Depression; from a mostly rural country of five million to a mostly urban one of almost thirty million. He mentions tests, the kids open their binders and begin writing – all except Willy who didn't bring his binder, and Pat who chooses not to write anything.

Rick knows about Pat and Willy from conversations he has overheard in the staff room. If he had wanted, he could have learned more from searching their records in the office, but he hasn't done that. To him, kids are what they are in *his* class, the rest doesn't matter. Maybe some transforming moment has just passed in their lives, giving them a new take on the world and their place in it; ahead for them a new future. If they want to change their lives, rewrite their stories, he must not stand in their way.

Nevertheless, Rick doesn't like what he sees. He stands at the front of the room, hunched over his lectern, a short, paunchy man in a tie, no jacket, glasses, his bald head rising like bread dough from a fringe of hair on the sides and a wavy, collar-length mane in back. He is in his late forties; to the kids he probably looks older. In front of him are fifteen students, a small class, ten in the regular academic stream called Advanced, five in the General stream, one of them an adult student. It's not their diversity that bothers him, but the way so many of them sit, their bodies angled away from him. Listening, but grudgingly, dipping only a toe in the pool of learning when they should be jumping in with both feet. In the twenty weeks ahead, Rick knows he must find a way to get those bodies to face him.

The smallness of the class will help. He will have more time. But in a mixed Advanced–General class, the gap between best student and worst is wide, and with so few students, the gradations between them are so broad. To run one's best race, everyone who is behind needs to be close enough to the one ahead to feel the pull to catch up. If contact is broken, there is no race and he has no class. Rick knows that kids drive other kids far more than he ever can.

He finishes the course description and hands out photocopies of two articles from the morning paper, one about figure skaters Tonya Harding and Nancy Kerrigan, the other about a Canadian Member of Parliament who lied about his academic qualifications. Taking each sentence of the stories, he asks them what is fact, what is opinion, what is argument? He wants them to be able to assess what they read and hear. Not just in textbooks, but in newspapers, and on TV and radio. He wants to introduce them to the historian's mind.

The lesson doesn't go well. Few hands go up, those he calls on react like restaurant patrons when a waiter arrives before they are ready: they pick the first sentence that strikes them, and describe it invariably as "factual." So used to expressing opinion and argument as fact, they can't see the difference. Yet they seem not to get discouraged, and have about them an "Advanced" level attitude, Rick notes. They get down to things, they work, they try. A learner's attitude is what he is looking for more than anything, what he wants to instil in them. An understanding, an expectation that in his class they must work. As class ends, to groans and a frenzy of (failed) negotiations, he gives them homework for the weekend. A regular assignment and a bonus question. The regular assignment to see who's dependable; the bonus to reveal ambition.

Nelson arrives after lunch for his English class with a blue bandanna around his head. He takes his usual right-front seat. One of the Polish girls from period two is also in the class. Everyone else is different. Some seem to know each other; most do not. They sit in a demoralizing straggle of occupied and empty seats. Teacher Noel Lim makes no comment and begins.

He writes the course outline on the board, holding his chalk in a metal holder, talking with his back to the kids as he does. He writes with quick, dancing strokes, as if playing with the words he puts down. He talks the kids through the outline, methodically, properly, so different in manner from that lively persona in the staff room. When he mentions that they will be reading *Romeo and Juliet*, he hears a groan from the back of the room. It is Ryan.

"Oh no, sir, not *Romeo and Juliet*. I've read it twice before."

Noel brightens, then catches himself. "Where?" he asks.

"In grade-ten English. Twice."

"Ahh," Noel nods. Then he asks what he's wanted to ask since he saw Ryan's name on his class list, "Are you Joey's brother?"

"Yeah."

He had taught Joey a few years before, a brilliant student, he remembers. Then Joey's girlfriend had a baby, Joey got involved in drugs and dropped out of school. Later, he came back, and is now in college, but the brilliance is gone.

Noel has gone over his class lists in advance, not just looking for names he knows, but for clues to the classroom he will face: a Chinese or Vietnamese name, a Sri Lankan name, a Polish or Bosnian name likely means someone new to the country and, already in his Advanced-level class, someone who has been rushed through English as a Second Language classes and who isn't ready. The Peel Board of Education allows immigrant kids to take five ESL courses before they must move on. ESL classes are smaller, usually eight to ten students, and expensive. If kids arrive in Canada at an elementary-school age, by the time they reach high school five ESL courses might be enough, but teenaged newcomers need more. These kids will work hard in this course, Noel knows, take their work home with them and grind away the night, but probably no one at home speaks English; they will have no one to practise with. They are good students, probably as far ahead in math or science as they are behind in English. With more time they will learn. But a semester passes quickly, and Noel has standards he will not bend.

He passes out a short story called "Guess What? I Almost Kissed My Father Goodnight" for the class to read aloud. Most kids read haltingly, out of adolescent shyness or something more fundamental, Noel doesn't yet know, but he does know his speculations are not far wrong: at least four of the kids are straight out of ESL. Nelson volunteers to read, but his words jam up inside him, then explode past their impediments in a rush too fast for him to control. Grateful to give up his turn, he goes quiet, so different from the Nelson in his other classes. Maybe it's because this is English, which he failed at his other school last fall. When Noel asks questions of the class, Nelson seems too uncertain of himself to offer serious answers, to be funny or outrageous, to take on any of the roles that might be his. Maybe it's the hour after lunch. Maybe it's the other kids. His attempt at reading won him no audience. There are many more black kids here, more kids who seem to know each other, amongst whom roles and pecking orders may be set. Many were the dominoes' players in the Caf, and, as lively and exuberant as he is, Nelson seems not to know what to do. Or maybe it's Noel. Nelson keeps looking at him, but Noel's glance slides by him to cover the room. By class end, Nelson seems to have been swallowed up in his own hole.

After Rick Ray's history class, Pat spent his lunch period at Mickey's, playing Foosball and video games, hanging out with his friends. Pat thought about not coming back for his Enhanced math class – it's cold outside, it's comfortable at Mickey's; nothing ever gets done on the first day of a semester anyway. It's been years since the promise of a first day meant much to him; he likes math, but he doesn't like this class. He has been dropping his Enhanced courses little by little, this is the only one he has left. He tried dropping it too, but his guidance counsellor wouldn't let him. Yet, to his own surprise, something did make him head out of Mickey's door. By the time he walks the few hundred metres back to the school, picks up his books at his locker, and arrives in class, all the other kids are in their seats facing teacher Sue Lishman. Pat goes to the back of the class. If he has to attend on someone else's terms, *how* he will attend will be on his.

Sue Lishman, tall and blonde, looks younger than her twenty-eight years. She arrives with a headache. It began period two with her big grade-nine math class and has persisted all day. Luckily, she had her lunch and preparation periods immediately after-wards; luckily she has this Enhanced period now. She has heard about these kids, mostly from Cathy Sylvester, who taught them science in the fall, and they are good, though demanding in their own way. They were identified as gifted in elementary school and many have shared the same classes since. At Kennedy, they are together for two Enhanced courses each semester, and take two Advanced courses apart. Their Enhanced classes follow the same curriculum as Advanced-level classes, and according to school policy tests are to be set at Advanced level, though Sue intends to make hers a little harder. Her approach will penalize these kids in one way, she knows, and a few years from now, applying to university, they will discover just how much every mark counts. Still, they should be challenged. If some adjustments seem nec-essary at the end, she can make them.

She knows, with few exceptions, that these kids will be here every day, do their homework, read the textbook if they have problems. The basic material they will understand. But so little of math is really x's and y's, learning, recalling, applying theorems twenty days and twenty years from now. Rather, math is a training. It's learning how to find your way to an answer when you have none. Taking what you know and discovering what you didn't know you knew. On a page, in your mind, a muddle of nothing; then suddenly the answer is there! Like Michelangelo and a block of marble: chipping away, suddenly revealing what was in that block all the time. Magic – or so it seems to the math outsider. Math is really learning the techniques and state of mind that allow you to turn that magic into logic. To puzzle and stumble, to know what it feels like to be lost, to keep going, then to know what it feels like when you *do* understand, that vibration of excitement and pleasure, and the addictive need to feel it over and over.

She knows that, working within the Advanced curriculum, most of these kids will get the right answers and their grades will reflect those answers. But is learning just the snapshot of grades, or the rolling celluloid of a lifetime? Is it her job to see them through to their highest marks this June, or to higher marks some other June? These kids, like all kids, need to flounder in the unknown a while. If they don't, they will move on to the next step with only answers to apply, but at every next step the questions are different. So she will push at them, because the struggle they go through pushing back may be their most important math experience.

And they will push at her as a teacher, which may be her most important experience too. These kids always want to know what they don't know and what you may not either. Sue knows she can't teach them with just what she has learned before. She has to be willing to learn with them. To think again, puzzle again, not know again, be willing to embarrass herself again, all for the possible but not certain payoff of learning something new. She probably couldn't have taught this class last year, her first year of teaching. Then she had to appear to know everything, for fear someone would find out what she didn't know.

She takes the kids through the class outline, talking to them in the language of math. They will begin with powers, roots, and real numbers, she says, then go on to functions and relations, polynomials and rational expressions, later to co-ordinate geometry, three-dimensional geometry, transformations, Euclidean geometry, and so on. To other kids, these terms may seem like a foreign language, something if not to be understood then to be memorized. To most of these kids, the terms seem to flow comfortably into their ears, if not already understood, something that soon will be. She gives them a handout with some questions to do.

The room gets quieter, but not for long. Some kids work as if in their own personal soundproof booth, shut off from everything except the work in front of them. Some turn to others with questions. There seem to be no identified sages in this class, the students ask those closest to them. Rohita walks to the back corner of the room, turns an empty desk around, and begins working. Simran and Reba find two other empty seats, no more strategically isolated or socially appropriate than the two they left, just different. Simran drags a stool with her, sets it down and props a foot on it. They work, they talk, they work and talk. About math. About badminton: Simran might try out for the school team. About values: "People talk about values and it's those who don't have any who do the best," says Simran. "Yeah," says Reba, "like lawyers." "Yeah," agrees Simran.

"My brother said to me last night," Reba says, "'You're lucky. You don't have to do anything. You can just go off and get married.'"

"How sexist."

"Yeah." This triggers something else. "How tall are you?" Reba asks.

"I've hit the big five-four."

"I'm five-three. I have a friend whose dad is five-eight, her mom's five-six, and she's four-eleven. Life is full of genetic goofs."

"Yeah."

Casey moves up to another desk close by them, Donald turns their way, to listen. They start comparing eyebrows. Simran's are "weird," they decide, Casey's "pretty normal," then someone spots Corey a few rows over. His are so thin they're almost "bald," they laugh.

The time flies by; it's suddenly 3:10. No bell goes off to signal the day's end. It's just over. The kids gather up their backpacks and head out the door. The first day's rituals are done.

Nelson lingers at his locker until most of the school has cleared. He will go home and meet up with his older brother and drive twenty-five kilometres southwest to Burlington to spend the weekend with his mother, two sisters, and little brother, and with his girlfriend. Sunday night he and his brother will be back with their father. On Monday, the semester will really begin.

Chapter 2

Setting the Scene

Thomas L. Kennedy Secondary School opened in September 1953 to 460 students from rural Toronto Township just west of the city of Toronto. The school was named for a one-time minister of agriculture and, briefly, acting-premier of Ontario, who had lived and farmed in the area for decades. Most of the first students were descendants of British settlers, beginning with the United Empire Loyalists who came north after the American Revolutionary War for land and the chance to live out their British destinies. They farmed the rich loam of these formerly Indian territories, built a scattering of villages, and, for more than a century, as Fort Toronto became York became Toronto, population 500,000, not much changed. Then some brickworks were built, and during World War II, Italian POWs were brought in to work them. At war's end, many of these POWs chose to stay, creating a Little Italy just south and west of the school. When T. L. Kennedy opened its doors, most of its students had British-sounding names, a few had western European, a few others Italian, and there was one family of Chinese.

Today there are few more cosmopolitan places on earth than Kennedy. The colours of its students' faces, the shadings of those colours, their clothes and "look," from "homeboy" to Dallas Cowboys to Indian sari to heavy metal to Hong Kong Chinese "nerd," from baseball caps to Muslim *hijab* headcoverings: all under the same roof, worn by kids rushing down the same halls for the same classes, competing to meet the same standards. Yet far from unique, T. L. Kennedy typifies the public high school of today's urban North America, and offers a rare glimpse of our changing reality. A downtown office, too small and self-selecting, obscures these changes. So do most neighbourhoods. A stadium crowd, a subway, bus, or other public place is too anonymous. The public high school stretches across neighbourhoods, puts kids into the same box, and lets them loose for six and a half hours a day, for most of a year, year after year. If Canada is an experiment in multiculturalism, the public high school is its crucible.

Across from Kennedy's main office is a display case. Sixty-seven tiny flags have been arranged in rows, one flag for each of the countries represented in the school. No mere exercise in genealogy or geography, this display is a mini-course in Geopolitics 101. The count stopped before the Soviet Union broke up and Yugoslavia blew apart. Today's total would be higher. As one counsellor at the school says, even if we never open a newspaper, two months later we know what's happened in the world because it's on our doorstep. Kids just off the plane, from Southeast Asia, Eastern Europe, and the Caribbean, many with unimaginable stories of horror and strife. Many others, Canadian-born, with their own unimaginable stories of domestic turmoil. Kids of the 1990s. At T. L. Kennedy, nearly 1,500 of them.

The school lies just north of the crossroads of Dundas and Hurontario streets, highways 5 and 10, the corner of "nickels and dimes," as the cabbies used to call it. This was the original centre of Mississauga, now a suburban city of 500,000, beyond the western boundary of Metropolitan Toronto. In the early 1970s, the city's centre moved two kilometres north with the construction of a large mall, Square One, and a new city hall. Exploding growth was pushing Mississauga into its hinterland, away from the lake, towards Toronto's Pearson airport and beyond, along Ontario's main east–west artery, Highway 401. The election of a Parti Québécois government in Quebec had led to an exodus of English-speaking Quebeckers, many of whose businesses relocated here. Job seekers from other provinces came and found the abundant work. But it was the new generation of Canadian immigrants that transformed the city. European immigration, a tidal wave in the postwar years, was slowing to a steady trickle by the 1970s and early 1980s. The new immigrants were now Asians – "boat people" from Vietnam, Tamils from Sri Lanka, Sikhs from Punjab – and "Islanders," many from Jamaica. Most were young people, with ambition and hope, with school-age kids or families still to be.

They had to begin somewhere. With the city developing north and west, many moved into the low-rise apartments and townhouses that had been left behind near the old city core, near T. L. Kennedy. The school, once set back from the street by a long suburban lawn, brought forward almost to the sidewalk by repeated additions, is now nearly hidden by the jumble of strip malls around it. The area that was once near-rural, then suburban, is now suburban inner-city, with all the demographic patterns of an inner city. New immigrants move in with relatives who have preceded them here; as soon as they can manage, they find a place of their own. A year or two later, on the well-worn immigrant road to success, they move again, to something bigger or newer, and someone else takes their place. Now also competing for the same ground, a new generation of "immigrant," the native-born Canadian set loose by job loss or family break-up. He too needs a place to start again. Here too he finds it. Only about a quarter of the kids at Kennedy stay at the school from grade nine through to graduation, and most *do* graduate.

The city of Mississauga lies within Peel Region. Peel's school board is the second-largest public board in Canada, with more than 170 schools, elementary to high school, 90,000 students, and 6,500 teachers. Of these students, 24 per cent do not speak English as their first language, 33 per cent describe themselves as a "visible minority," 20 per cent were born outside Canada. The figures for Kennedy are slightly higher. While Kennedy is similar to most schools in most ways, offering the regular Advanced, General, and Enhanced level programs, these modest variations from the median are its defining features. Kennedy is one of two high schools in Peel with a "Reception Centre," where kids new to the country are tested and assessed, so that they may be placed at their appropriate grade levels – usually in the school nearest to where they live, for most schools offer some ESL classes, and occasionally at Kennedy, which offers more. About 300 kids at Kennedy are in ESL, 20 per cent of the student population. Many more, like some in Noel's class, have moved on into regular courses and go uncounted.

Special programs like ESL are now under some pressure. The taxpayer is speaking loudly. Only eight to ten kids in a class, why not ten or twelve or more? It's just a couple of more kids. And maybe a couple more over there, and a little less money here, and maybe there. Last fall, just before school began, the provincial government "negotiated" public-sector cutbacks, $425 million to be eliminated in education alone over three years. Under a program devised by the New Democratic Party government, and called the "Social Contract," teacher salaries have been frozen, 6,000 to 7,000 teacher jobs are to be cut by attrition, increasing class size by 5 per cent, and unpaid days off for teachers – dubbed "Rae days," after Ontario Premier Bob Rae – are being imposed. In addition, teachers in Peel have been without a contract since September and negotiations with the Peel Board have not been going well. Walk-outs, lockouts, and punitive offers were the buzz of the fall, but nothing has happened: the sky hasn't fallen, even the "Social Contract" has become a reality of life, and life has moved past it. Even destreaming, one more change brought down from on high, with all the teacher-time it requires, the committees, the time that could be put to other use, seems now to have been taken in stride. Even the ups and downs of a school year, all the things that can go wrong, and do – last fall's meningitis scare and a macheté incident in the parking lot – and all the things that can go right, and do – the Terry Fox Run raising $12,000, the school's fortieth reunion party: in the end, one school year goes pretty much like every other one. But the voices of discontent – from the public and in the media – are getting louder. And teachers and administrators are becoming more disquieted, more resentful. Education has risen to the top of the public agenda and emotions are running high in a debate in which sides are being drawn and positions are hardening.

What is it about school that does this to us? Why does it get under our skin, and never leave us no matter how old we are? A place where the good times always seem better, and the bad times worse. Perhaps because at school those times seem so much more our own, finally unmonopolized, unfiltered by our parents. But the power of school doesn't end at graduation. With our own children, we experience it again, except now enhanced by all the baggage of our own childhood memories. Knowing too much and, one step removed, not able to know enough. Left to wondering, imagining, investing in the routine ups and downs of our child's life all the urgency of our own telescoped memories, every secondhand hurt hurting more, every tight squeeze seen as a "no way out." Having seen the future, everything has meaning to us. Our kids circling, circling through the maze of adolescence; to us, everything they do on a straight line to heaven or hell.

In lives that don't change much, school has little importance. When existence had to do with coaxing grains out of the ground, with killing or subduing the animals about you, with merest survival, you could learn what there was to know and pass that on to your child. And what that child came to know would see him through another generation. For thousands of years and hundreds of generations, that was enough, until not so many years ago. Until it seemed as if life could be more than survival, for more than a privileged few. Perhaps not all time and energy had to go to meeting the most basic needs. Perhaps all humans, not just kings and nobles, could be more than just beasts of the field. Perhaps a new relationship with the world was possible, one that went beyond survival to *abundance*. Not slothful excess, just enough to free the body to free the mind. To explore and discover these human capacities. To generate new abundance – not just material wealth but creative wealth too.

Out of that transition came so many more things to know. So much more than a parent could pass on; more than anyone could experience directly; more than could be explained in one good book. More than any wise person could know. A knowledge explosion: books, libraries, information highways, experts. So much more for each new generation to know in order to ensure its continuing abundance. But how?

Not much more than a century ago, children en masse laid down their ploughs and walked into school. Not for long, at least for most. School was compulsory only until age fourteen in Ontario, then sixteen, and for most that was long enough. By that time they had in hand the tools they needed to explore the external world, the world beyond their direct experience. They had a grounding in the "3 Rs"; the workplace would teach them the rest. They could start at the bottom and learn/work their way up. More like workplace drop-ins than school drop-outs, they had their bosses as their teachers, their offices as their classrooms. In the less anonymous society of the time, a diploma mattered little. Cities and towns were smaller, companies were smaller, people rarely moved. They knew each other, their families, their reputations. Workers needed to learn, companies to teach them, everyone was in it for the longer run. Family as much as credentials got you in the job door; character kept you there; ability, drive, and performance moved you up the ladder. For generation after generation, most business and government leaders never attended university, most never finished high school. That began to change after World War II.

The postwar period was a time to remake the future. After years of depression and war, in North America there was money to spend and things to buy. A car, a house in the suburbs, a Mixmaster, power mower, wash-and-wear clothes; what only the rich could afford a few years earlier, the average person now could too. The miracles of science were now coming through our front doors. To keep them coming, science needed well-trained minds. Kids who were taught longer and better by better trained teachers in new and better facilities. With a booming economy and more public money to spend, new schools were built with new science labs, libraries, gymnasiums, and auditoriums. Public and private futures, it seemed, were entwined. If generations of high school drop-outs could do what we have done, our parents thought, imagine what these, our university-bound, children will do.

Now school was central to people's dreams of the future. Fewer kids dropped out; more went on to university. Not all jobs were at the end of the road of hard work and sterling character. Some required prior training, and a diploma or degree as evidence of this training. People moved, cities, towns, and companies grew, families no longer knew each other intimately. Some objective standard was needed to decide who got through the job

door, was given a chance, promoted, kept on, and rewarded. And
the rewards were unmistakable. Today, a university graduate earns
hundreds of thousands of dollars more in a lifetime than a high
school graduate, who earns hundreds of thousands more than a
drop-out, who is one and a half times more likely to be unemployed than the high school graduate, who is nearly twice as
likely to be unemployed as the university graduate. Educational
haves and have nots, economic winners and losers, and with
each year that passes, a story more chiselled in stone. And, as wit-
nesses to the drama, anxious, agonizing parents determined that
their kids would not fall by the wayside in a world where second
chances seem frighteningly scarce. To the master of suspense,
Alfred Hitchcock, "mystery" meant giving a story to an audience
reluctantly. "Suspense" lay in giving it to that audience in the
first scene: someone is seated in a chair, under the chair is a
bomb about to go off. The person doesn't notice. Now watch,
Hitchcock tells his audience, and live with it. In the life of a child,
for a parent, bombs are everywhere.

As the twentieth century winds down, the future doesn't look
quite the same as it did after World War II. Those university-
trained sons and daughters, today in positions of power, have not
transformed the world. The scientific mind has its limits, everything is not forever onward and upward. And keeping up with
the Joneses is no longer enough; we need to match the
Yakamuras and the Reinhardts too. A better product made more
efficiently in Japan or Germany matters in Toronto or St. Louis,
a better school in Kyoto or Munich matters too. The barriers of
distance, politics, and ideology have come down, our futures are
linked to those of others in distant continents, so much more
seems beyond our control.

Everything is changing so fast. New technologies invade our
lives, are obsolete before we master them; newer technologies
take their place. There is no comfortable resting place when
ambition tires, when what *is* already seems good enough. Where

is the solid ground? A decision taken over there is a bankruptcy here is a bank crisis somewhere else, everything swirling around and around. You do your job, work hard, be on time, do what you're told, be loyal year after year – all the things that had been tickets of safe passage to the future now may not be enough.

But as challenging as the new world is for us as adults, it is even more so for us as parents. We are older; we have only to run this race a few years longer. We have been trained, educated in the best schools with the best teachers – or so we remember. We are as ready and able as anyone to survive these challenges. But what about our kids? They are not tough like us, haven't learned all we've learned. What about *their* schools? What about *their* teachers? They will need to learn more, have to run faster. We can see it coming. Not only the Japanese and Germans, but Koreans, Chinese, and who knows who else. Capital owes no allegiance, technology moves where technology is earned; those others, *they* are hungrier, cheaper, *they* want it more. What about our daughters, our sons? What will become of them? As parents, we have one overriding wish, for some voice from out of the future to assure us: *your kids will be okay.* We can leave them our money, but tomorrow money can be spent or lost or inflated away. What can we provide them with to see them through the minefield of the future?

Education. Learning and the ability to learn. So when things change, they can change too. That is the greatest gift we can give. To help them onto the right path, well provisioned and ready for a lifelong journey, their wits to see them through. But what about their schools? we ask. What about their teachers? Are they up to it? Can they do it?

Since the recession of the early 1980s, since increased free trade, globalization and higher rates of unemployment, since the deeper recession of the late 1980s and early 1990s, since the "downsizing" of middle management, since the insecurities of the present have made the imaginable future seem even more insecure, the cries for educational reform have grown louder, more shrill and urgent.

In 1983, the National Commission on Excellence in Education, appointed by the U.S. Secretary of Education, released its report, "A Nation at Risk." The report was brief, only thirty-six pages, written in popular style, not so much an examination of schools as a cry from the heart. It began,

> [T]he educational foundations of our society are presently being eroded by a rising tide of mediocrity. . . . If an unfriendly power had attempted to impose on America the mediocre educational performance that exists today, we might well have viewed it as an act of war. . . . We have, in effect, been committing an act of unthinking, unilateral educational disarmament.

The report's goal was to make America sit up and take notice and it worked. "A Nation at Risk" generated a mood, an urge for examination and action, and an angle through which to do both. What has followed since, in the United States and Canada, has been more than a decade of intense educational reform.

Hundreds of millions of words in newspapers, books and magazines, TV series and specials, government commissions in nearly every province and state in North America, in most industrialized countries of the world: everybody's doing it. Sensing a new kind of future, anxiously we want to know if we are preparing our kids the right way. What is the real purpose of schools? What are kids learning? How are we teaching? How can we do better? For some in education, it has been an exciting time, for most it has not. The spotlight has been relentless, blinding; the audience's mood foul. Trees may have been falling in the forest for years, but no one had heard them so they made no sound; now their sound is deafening. *International test results show . . .* SAT *scores show . . . unemployment rates show . . . employers, colleges, universities say . . .* and if they don't say or show, our own instincts, our own memories, tell us: we aren't doing well enough. How can that be? All the time and money spent, the people, training, facilities, new technologies, the priority education holds, that we know it holds, that we say it holds. And because it is happening on our generation's watch, it's our fault.

It didn't take long for fingers to be pointed. It's the teachers, accused parents, employers, and media commentators. Teachers don't care any more. They arrive late and leave early. Once they were selfless, now they're in it for the hours and long vacations. And teachers pointed back. It's the parents. Parents don't care any more. They're never around, or are too tired or busy when they are. They marry, don't marry, have families, break up, do whatever they want and forget about their kids. But journalists, commentators, and employers are parents too, and able to point the most public fingers, they succeeded in making teachers the more popular target. Besides, parents said, raising my kids may be my responsibility, but educating them is your *job*. As a taxpayer, I am your boss. I pay your salary.

Teachers have fought back. To every charge, they've an answer, with statistics to back them up. We *do* spend more time . . . we *are* better trained. . . . But no matter how many arguments teachers have won in their own minds, they've lost with the vocal public, who share an unanswerable feeling: the system isn't working. Some teachers and teachers' unions, realizing that they couldn't stop being a target without doing something, have become active in the system's reform. Seen as part of the problem, they have tried to become part of the solution. A few business leaders have pushed hard at improving schools, but mostly, it's become clear, on behalf of those few students who will go on to university and fill their corner offices. Many parents, trying to improve the system in general, have found it too slow to change, too intractable, too frustrating, and have moved off to its margins, to private and charter schools.

What seems most remarkable after more than a decade of effort and study, and billions of dollars spent, is that the mood around education is so little changed. Lots of initiatives have been taken, many promising projects tested, their successful elements identified and implemented in individual schools and groupings of schools, so much is different, there is so much to point to, but the system *feels* the same. After all this time, there is still no common page to point to, no shared understanding: this is what our schools are about, this is what they are for, this is what we do and how we do it.

Listen to a group of parents, educators, business people, anybody, talk about education. The real problem is class size, one says. The others nod. Yes, class size, that's right, and they talk about class size for a while, passionately, urgently, with a common heart. They are getting somewhere, they can feel it. Yes, yes, class size, someone else agrees, and school size too. Yes, yes, school size, they all nod again, and talk passionately about that for a while. And school organization, someone else says, and issues of empowerment, and use of technology, and − the dam bursts. Safety, streaming, destreaming, length of school year, teacher training, bureaucracy, funding − anything, everything − until all the issues of education are equally, impossibly, hopelessly tangled together. A hundred different threads all wound tightly in a big ball. Where even to start? Television documentaries begin with freshness and end in muddle. Debates turn into monologues of the deaf. Political campaigns begin with education as a central issue; then party platforms can't quite explain what a party intends, voters can't quite understand, and, except for money or safety, education as an issue disappears.

Part of the problem is the nature of public forums. A public stage, with performers and audience, rewards the theatre of division and dispute, conflict not resolution. It wants its performers to be advocates, not conciliators. Deal-making takes too long, and prime time waits for no man. Put out education's story by ministry document, commission report, union newsletter, and who will bother reading it? Twisted into TV/newspaper format, the problems of education become a story of *whats* and *hows*, a story without *whys*. *Whys* take time, TV and newspapers have no time. So they skip from *whats* to *hows*. *What* is the problem? *How* do I deal with it? But the real story lies in the *whys*. *Why* does the school system matter? *Why* does everyone need to learn, and know how to learn? *Why* can't kids read better? *Why* don't more read books? *Why* do some kids sit always at the front of the room, some always at the back? *Why* are some kids always there, on time, ahead of time? To a scientist, the challenge is to ask the right question, because the question leads you to your answer.

Whats and *hows* are for insiders, *whys* are for everybody. *Whats* and *hows* focus on structures; *whys* on people, kids and teachers, on the only question that matters: *why* does this kid learn, and that one doesn't? The answer to this question is the answer to every question about schools. Maybe the problem isn't the school system, or not entirely. Maybe it's some parts of it, not others. Maybe it doesn't work only for some kids. Maybe *that* is the problem.

School twists the gut of our most basic insecurities as parents, as employees and employers, as politicians, as citizens of a democracy, and it's inside this feeling that the real story of school lies. Not in the number of students and teachers, not in the time they put in and the priority they give to it, not in the cost to the taxpayer. School has to do with the *future*, with optimism and hope, with how we see ourselves and what we want to be, with the most emotion-laden phrase in the language: *our children*.

Except for a few with highly specialized talent – athletes, artists, entertainers – today the path to success runs undeniably through high school and university. Every parent believes his or her child must be on that path. School success may not get them there, school failure almost assuredly will not. These are the stakes. This is the bomb *tick tick tick*ing under Nelson's chair, under Ryan's and Sophia's and Willy's and Pat's, all in full, open-mouthed view of their parents and their teachers, of Rick and Cathy and Sue and Maria and Noel, if they choose to see it.

Chapter 3

Monday, February 14, 7:34 a.m.

Terry Chaffe is not happy. He sits in the early-morning gloom of his wood-panelled office, talking into the phone, mostly listening. He nods several times, less conclusively than his words express, then puts down the receiver harder than usual, his eyes still rivetted on the wooden desk in front of him. He is fifty-four years old, now in his fifth year as Kennedy's principal. He wears a tie, no jacket, his shirt, neither executive white nor blue, has a sailboat on its breast-pocket. He is short, and, with his slightly thinning grey-blond hair, looks like a determined Henry Gibson from TV's "Laugh-In." Bridget Harrison, superintendent for his area, has just told him that three kids who are "real trouble" have been to see her and that he's going to have to take them this semester. They've already been at two schools he knows of, and who knows where else, but the law says they have a right to seven years of high school education. They live in this area and Terry has room, so he has no choice but to admit them.

He has already taken in a few just like them this semester.

Every kid he doesn't take is one more that someone else must, and though he can be as selfish as anyone, he is mostly a system player. He isn't looking to make Kennedy a perfect school, nor himself a perfect principal, while everyone else picks up the pieces. But he doesn't want more than his share of trouble either, more than his school can handle. In the week since the semester began, he has been careful about whom he has taken and whom he hasn't, but this call has thrown his balance off.

Last September, he faced a more complicated choice. The collective agreement between the Peel Board of Education and the teachers' union says there must be one teacher for every 15.126 students. ESL and other special courses requiring more individual attention are the exceptions. So Kennedy was staffed with 106 teachers for the 1,470 or so students who show up every year. In the early days of a school year, though, there are never enough students. Kids shop schools, or they just don't show up – 453 were absent that first day in September. Are they away or are they not coming at all? The staff in the office must get on the phones to find out. Too many kids, and teachers complain of large classes. Too few, and the school falls below staffing levels, then a teacher or more may be taken away from the school's allocation. Suddenly, two weeks into the semester, someone has to move within the system to address an unexpected bulge, and kids get shifted around in the giving and receiving schools. Sometimes, not often, Terry has found himself needing kids, at the last minute having to "haul them in," as his office staff puts it. He knows he won't have to put up with many of them for long. More than 170 kids left during the fall semester, just 53 transferred in. For this semester, about 100 more are gone, 200 are new. Kennedy is a semester school like most high schools in the Greater Toronto Area. Courses begin and end twice a year, in September and January, February and June. Nearby are two non-semester schools. Some of their kids need only a course or two to graduate and don't want to wait until next year to take it, so they come here. As of a few minutes ago, Terry's numbers were fine – "touch wood" – then his phone rang.

He knows these new problem kids well, although he's never seen them before. They don't want to be in school, they want nothing to do with school. Their parents say they have to be here, or student welfare tells them their cheques will be cut off if they don't attend, so they go to the superintendent asking to be admitted. There's nothing she can do. If Terry sees them first, he can try to discourage them, be tough, go over their records and make deals, "Okay, I'll take you, but only if . . . ," turning the screws tighter than he knows they will accept. They may have the right to seven years of high school education, but after the age of sixteen it is their choice whether to attend or not. If they want to quit, that's fine with him.

It used to bother him that he felt this way. He's an educator, how can he give up on kids like this? There's no such thing as a bad kid, he has always thought, only a kid in bad circumstances who has made bad choices. Change the circumstances, change the kid. Change *can* happen. Nothing is irrevocable, no one's destiny is engraved in stone. He was raised to believe this, it's part of why he went into teaching in the first place. After parents, he knows he is the next big destiny-writer in a kid's life. If he doesn't do something for a kid with problems, who will? And if no one does, what desperate, hopeless future is in store? Life on the streets, drugs, violence, decades of welfare and prison all at public expense. Better a dollar spent now, constructively, than thousands later – except now it's a dollar in *his* school.

He knows too that things never change for certain kids. Maybe it's their fault, maybe it's their parents' or his, maybe it just *is*. They could make it – "No kid ever fails because he can't do the work," Terry likes to say – but they don't. A handful will drop out, then a few weeks or months or years later, they will drop back in. No jobs to go to, outside more boring than inside, survival suddenly square in front of their eyes. They return to night school, to adult classes, maybe they come back to Kennedy, once they have found their own reasons to be here. But most don't drop out. They stay on and infect the classroom with their belligerent presence, disrupting, destroying.

Most classrooms can't handle this virus. Some Enhanced-level classes can, but in Advanced and General there is such a tenuous mix of kids, some who want to learn, some who don't, and most who can go either way. The difference between a good class and a bad class might be one or two kids, that's all, kids who are strong enough, persuasive enough, charming enough that other kids follow them. A teacher can move these kids, isolate them, use all his or her faculty-of-education tricks on them, but a semester moves fast and falling behind a few minutes at a time, day after day, always playing catch-up, everybody pays.

A school is such a fragile thing. More than bricks and mortar, more than the collected wisdom of ministries of education, school boards, teachers and time, it's a feeling. "Tone," Terry calls it. Something in the air that makes teachers teach their best and students learn their best. Something he can always tell is there or isn't but never quite knows why. He has been teaching for more than thirty years, has been a department head in history, a vice-principal, this is his second "experience" as principal. Yet this place, any school, he knows, is essentially beyond his control and he must respect its power. He has age, position, size, strength, reward and punishment on his side; he has custom, expectation, and culture. But a simple "no" from a kid or a teacher and these are nothing.

And today more students do say no. Homework: *But sir, I gotta have time for myself too.* Part-time jobs: *I need the money, miss (besides, you have no right even to suggest I stop working).* Arriving late: *But sir, I was tired.* Life in general: *It's my life, sir. I don't care how old I am and how old you are, I have my rights. What are you going to do anyway? Give me a detention? Maybe I'll fight it, maybe I'll go;*

maybe I'll skip it. So you give me two; maybe I'll skip them both. Give me four, eight, sixteen, after a while you know I'll never catch them up so I won't even try. Suspend me? Three days, because that's all you'll give me. I want ten extra minutes in the sack and you give me a three-day holiday. Think about that. And my mother's not going to like it. I'm late, so maybe I'll catch some heat for that, but she's got to work every day. What is she going to do with me those three days I'm home? Who's going to get more heat, you or me? She'll be on the phone to you so fast: "Why are you so hard on my son?" Then she'll call the trustee, and he'll listen, you know that. He's been hearing all about the sad state of his schools, blah blah blah, the cost to the taxpayer, blah blah blah. And the trustee will call the superintendent, and the superintendent will call you. Are you sure that's what you want?

And you can't kick me out; you and I both know what the law says. You can't suspend me for ten or twenty days unless I hit someone or carry a weapon. Besides, ten days is two weeks of classes, more than 10 per cent of a semester. That's seventy-six minutes a day, every day, of English, science, history, math, all missed. You know what a struggle it is for kids like me to catch up. So I fail my courses, lose a whole semester, all for being ten minutes late. Like swatting a mosquito with a nuclear bomb, don't you think, sir?

Terry wonders, what has happened to *not* being late? To being punctual because everyone else was? To feeling embarrassed if you were late? To a detention being a censure, a suspension a black mark on family and child? To assuming that the teacher knows something, and even if he doesn't, because he's an adult in a position of power, you do what he says anyway? Most kids are not late, they weren't before and aren't now, and most who are don't skip detentions. Very few are ever suspended. Nothing is that different, it seems. But those few who have called the system's bluff have made Terry realize his own vulnerability.

Terry is a doer. He grew up in St. Catharines, Ontario, a blue-collar town of about 50,000 in the Niagara Peninsula, his father a toolmaker, his mother a clerk in a clothing store; Terry the elder of two kids. He was a good student but not a great one; a good athlete, too small to be better, never a star. His first principal's job was at Britannia, "Coconut College," the teachers called it, the worst of Peel's vocational schools. It was for Basic-level kids, below Advanced, below General, kids who had never been able to learn with their heads. At Britannia, they were taught to learn with their hands – welding, auto body, cosmetology, fashion design. After four years, Terry was sent to Kennedy, not to a model school filled with model kids with upper-middle-class model parents. But he likes it at Kennedy, just as he liked it at Britannia. These kids don't take anything for granted, and neither does he.

For him, the worst time every year is the last weeks of summer holiday. The old school year is gone, the momentum of vacation is over, and there's time to doubt. To wonder: can I do it one more time? Then he starts to get himself ready. He believes in good starts. Every morning, school-year and summer, he gets up early. A good start is a chance at a good day, a good day at a good week, a good week at a month, a month at a semester, a semester at a whole year. Have a good year, *touch wood*, and your whole life might follow. Momentum. Keeping things rolling. Stumbling at times, but never stopping, for it's the stops that kill you.

Keeping things going was what he probably managed best the first semester. Fifteen hundreds kids, or most of them anyway, are now one semester closer to graduation, reasonably healthy, reasonably happy. The same with his staff. He was able to avoid the one big disaster that creates the buzz he cannot stop, the tone that will not change. Now, everything is in place for another good semester. He sees his job not to be an educational visionary, to see past the *what is* to the *what might be*, trying always to implement the latest wisdom he reads. In truth, he hasn't the time for visions; he isn't sure the kids, the teachers, the system could adapt to them anyway. Even if it is to those visionaries that the spoils seem to go – to superintendents, academics, government bureaucrats, commentators – he isn't sure that that's where they belong, or that the answer lies with them, if indeed there is an answer. His loyalty, his affection, his time, the drift of his mind is always toward the real world of Kennedy. This school. His school. This is where education happens or it doesn't.

Terry hears the dwarfs' marching song from *Snow White*, "Heigh ho, heigh ho, it's off to work we go," over the school's loud-speaker. He looks up at the clock over the door – 8:35 a.m. He concludes a phone call abruptly, puts down his pen, it's time to show his face again. He emerges from his office, moving slowly to the middle of the main hallway, like a jaywalker on an express-way. "Heigh Ho, Heigh Ho" turns to the "William Tell Over-ture," kids are still streaming through the front door, the first class is only a minute or two from beginning. His face tightens.

"Hurry up," he growls. "Gotta get to class."

By habit or circumstance, he spends most of his days helping others get through theirs. He is the enabler, the buffer. Re-flecting the reality of the outside world, its demands and expec-tations, trying hard to deflect its individual slings and arrows. So that teachers can teach and students can study, undistracted, undisturbed.

When the "William Tell Overture" ends, "O Canada" begins, then a thirty-second silence for meditation, prayer, or any other quiet personal purpose. With no school bells, the anthem and silence freeze anyone who is late, disrespect being a much less tol-erated offence than tardiness. He follows the kids down the halls towards their classrooms, his presence causing them to speed up. He watches them disappear into their rooms, the doors close, the halls go increasingly quiet. His job is done for the moment. Inside these classrooms, the business of education can begin.

✦ ✦ ✦

There is no rush to Sue Lishman's Enhanced math class. Andrea was already here at 8:15 when Sue arrived, then Reba and Simran, then Rohita about 8:25. All but Pat and Leah were in the room before the music even started, hovering around Sue's desk asking questions, writing out equations on the board; Philip, standing in the doorway, keeping his options open, flirting with any girl in the room or out who would pay him attention.

When the thirty seconds of silence ends, Sue begins right in. She takes them through a fifty-minute lesson on the Pythagorean theorem. She stands at the board, explaining in her clear, no-nonsense voice, turning occasionally to write the essential points crisply on its chalky surface, with her left hand, in big girlish loops, the palm of her right hand propped against her hip, her elbow out, like the Sealy Posturepedic girl. She is tall, about five-foot-ten, with short, swept-back Swedish-blonde hair; her maiden name is Carlson. Her manner, size, pacing, the timbre of her voice: she has presence. The kids ask questions, they answer them or she does. The lesson flies by. When she is done, she gives them the rest of the period to work on homework problems.

There is such energy in this room. It is exuded, escapes the skin, doesn't bubble away inside. It is loud, active, sometimes chaotic, sometimes uncontrollable, because that's what learning is. These kids *want* to learn, but they are not eighteen sit-up-straight goody-two-shoes. They slouch, wind lanky legs around, through, and into any space that's open; their eyes focus on Sue, their books, or each other, their bodies on a swivel, to the left, right, behind, ahead, ready to suck up learning from every direction. Like very young children, they welcome in the world, without the fears, attitudes, and baggage of repeated failure that, like high castle walls, shut others off. These kids are willing to let down their guard, lose themselves in what they are doing, get outside themselves, and that isn't easy, especially for adolescents who are preoccupied with their changing world, their changing bodies, their minds filled with new things they're supposed to understand and don't. So much about themselves still in the learning and making: what they are, what they want to be, what they can be, what they should be, what they need to do to be it.

On the outside, others see the face of that inner turmoil. Fear, confusion, more often an unreadable, unbreachable wall of sullenness. "Good," "Fine," "I don't know" grunted back at every unasked-for probe, while inside, the adolescent's own unremitting, eloquent dialogue goes on. What do you want from me, his or her face says to the inquisitor when "Good" or "Fine" seems not enough. *Everything that isn't bad is good. That's what I feel, that's all I know. With so many things to know, I don't know any more. So don't ask. When I have an answer, you will see it on my face.*

The kids in Enhanced have this internal world much more in hand. They have emerged from its cocoon, metamorphosed, ready to enter the outer world. Able to be preoccupied with something other than themselves, they find something of interest, throw youthful energy at it, school, sports, music, *something.* And they learn. So little self-absorbed because they can afford to be; able to relax their defences because there is so little to hurt them. Academically they can fend for themselves. More so than many adults, they are at the centre of their own lives, in control, in command. These kids have "got it together."

So different from Sue's grade nine class in period two. Every day she leaves that room with a headache. Despite nine years of schooling, these grade nines seem untamed to the classroom. Loud, active, easily distracted and disturbed. Too needy: *"Miss, miss . . ."* Always asking questions, never trusting themselves to sort things out. *"Miss, miss . . ."* Never sure. The class had started as a noble experiment. On the second floor of the school, there is one large classroom separated into two by several low dividers. It is the only such room in the school. Sue was timetabled to teach grade nine math on one side of the room, her colleague, Pam Sawyer, the same course on the other. The dividers are far from soundproof, whispers of her lesson would certainly carry to any distracted ear on the other side. Why not put the two classes together, the two women reasoned. Push the dividers over, move most of the desks to one side, then take turns giving the lesson with the other stationed at the back to keep control. Math lessons often don't last more than twenty-five or thirty minutes, the other forty-five minutes the kids are working on problems at their seats. Forty-eight kids, forty-eight desks in one room are a lot, but when the lesson is done, the kids can spread out and use both rooms.

This solution had seemed even more appealing in light of the "transition years" problem. Many kids have difficulty making the transition from elementary to high school, so steps have been taken to integrate the curriculum for grades seven, eight, and nine. Beginning this year, the provincial government has also decreed that streaming of kids into Advanced or General levels cannot begin until grade ten. Despite best intentions and a strong philosophical case – *not everybody can learn in an academic way. Some learn best with their hands and should be encouraged to do so. We don't have enough good tradespeople. Even with high unemployment, we import immigrants to work these trades, which pay very well. Have you paid a plumber lately?* – in North America, no good alternative has been developed to the academic stream that leads to university. The non-academic, or General, route is fine – for everybody else's son or daughter. In reality it is a dumping ground, piled high with the poor, the disabled, and the newly arrived. Because the system is so unforgiving, the government has decided to give all kids at least one year of high school – unstreamed – before they are slotted into either the Advanced or General streams.

Many teachers don't endorse the move to grade-nine destreaming. Kids differ in their abilities; some can learn and some can't, and by grade nine it is clear who falls into which category, they insist. They feel as if the system wants them to play God and remake these kids into something they're not. But it's too late, they say, God has already played God.

Whatever the debate's merits, the result is grade-nine classes with a broader range of kids. How does a teacher give both the Enhanced kids and the stragglers what they need? Perhaps, Sue and Pam thought, their double class might provide an opportunity to break the kids into smaller groups according to their abilities and give them the kind of instruction and support they need. But the results have been distressing. The off-the-wall energy Sue is used to from grade nines is many times normal, and her head has been pounding seventy-six minutes a day, sometimes longer, since the beginning of the semester. Today, she has them next.

As for her Enhanced kids, only two weeks into the semester and already Sue feels she knows them. At age twenty-eight, she is more than a decade older than they are. She grew up in the secure comfort of a 1950s-style white, middle-class family, her father a meteorologist, her mother a housewife, in Brampton, on Toronto's northwestern edge. The kids in this class might seem different from her in almost every way – age, colour, family structure, family income – but to her they are soulmates, people who share her love of learning. They are like kites and she is their handler. They are already well launched and in the air; it is up to her to keep a good, steady wind under them, a tight hand on their strings, offering little tugs of tension not to hold them back but to keep them aloft, to make them pull harder, to soar as high as they are able.

After the first quiz last week, she thought she might have given them too much wind. The results were disappointing, some very good, too many very ordinary. So she backed off for a few days, slowed down, assumed less, made no leaps over swaths of curriculum, gave detentions to three who were late, gave them all another quiz, and finally they seem to be hitting their galloping stride. There are a few black clouds. Pat, of course, who at least is here more often than in history, and without most of the attitude.

Attitude doesn't play well in this room. Leah, who sits beside Pat, but hasn't his instinctive math mind and might become infected by his habits; Casey, who seems a little overwhelmed. Donald, who seems smart and tries too hard to impress. Andrea, who was added to the class a few days into the semester, a good math student, who seems happy enough yet sits one seat removed from the rest. Philip, with his smiling face and irrepressible disposition – "I know, I know, I know," he always says, shooting up his arm whenever Sue asks a question, though he rarely does know. Asked his interests the first day, he wrote "women." But even these kids are more puzzles than problems, Sue thinks, at least this early in the semester.

Through their working and talking, most kids have finished most of the questions Sue assigned. They have only a few left for homework. Suddenly three or four voices, nowhere near in unison, start singing "Happy Birthday." The others join in, not sure who they are singing for, searching for someone not singing who looks embarrassed. It's Elaine. She is sixteen today.

As the kids move briskly out the door to their next class, Sue's feeling of dread returns.

✦ ✦ ✦

History teacher Rick Ray looks at the scatter of kids in their seats, notes who is missing, and decides to begin. He closes the door. This will be their last day on sentence identification, he tells them. Muted cheers go up.

The door opens. Pat walks in, crosses the room, and sits down. Rick stops; and starts again. The door opens. Willy and Chad walk in, Willy without his books. Rick stops and fixes his attention on Willy's big winter coat, which he still has on and, like many kids, wears to class every day.

"William," Rick says firmly, "could you please not wear your coat to class." Having thought about it all last weekend, Rick has decided not to call him "Willy" but "William," and Pat "Patrick" or "Mr. Wilkes."

"It's not a coat, sir," Willy says, so used to denying that even he looks surprised when he hears his own words. "I mean, I wear it all the time."

"Could you not wear it here, please." Willy nods; he is also used to nodding. Rick looks back at the blackboard; Willy looks at Chad and rolls his eyes. He has survived another awkward moment, but is unable to let well enough alone. "But sir," he blurts, "why can't we wear our coats?"

Rick stops and turns. "Because we don't wear coats in an office, do we, William? We'd get all hot and we couldn't work."

Willy nods, then when Rick turns back to the board, he shakes his head. *A coat isn't a coat, sir, it's an identity, just like a base-ball cap, which the school doesn't let us wear either, isn't worn to shade our eyes from the fluorescent lights of the ceiling. It's a look; it's me. Just as my shoes and socks and underwear are me, and you'd never ask me not to wear them, would you? Besides, it's cold outside. If I'm going to have time for a smoke between classes, I've got to wear my coat. Ha ha.*

It would be easy to give up on Willy. Most teachers have, it would be nothing new to him or his parents. It would bring no outcry from on high. Some kids you can't give up on because they contaminate a class. If you don't get to them, they will get to it. But Willy isn't like that. He is distracting and time-consuming, but usually harmless, so most teachers restrain him with a gentle hand and let him be. Rick is trying to change him, however, and Willy isn't used to that. Sometimes he responds, often he doesn't, many times he fights back.

After some difficult early days, there had seemed a break-through. Rick announced at the end of a class last week that the following day they would play a game. He'd divide the class into two teams, ask each team in turn, and each member in turn, to provide a factual statement, an opinion, or an "argument statement." If the other side thought an answer was wrong, it could challenge and offer its corrected version. For each correct statement or challenge, Rick would award points.

Some kids arrived game-day with pages of prepared statements; many, Willy included, did not.

"Okay, it's time to start," Rick said to them. Bodies straightened, smiles of excitement and competition appeared.

"What game, sir?" Pat asked.

Willy grinned. "If you'd been to class, Mr. Wilkes, you'd know, wouldn't you," he cackled; he couldn't believe his luck.

Before the game could begin, there was a knock. A pretty girl was standing at the door. Rick spoke with her a moment, the boys tried to lip-read her side of the conversation. Rick closed the door.

"Hey, sir, is she a student here?" Willy asked.

"Yeah," Pat interrupted.

"Wooo-ooo," Willy shrieked, still on his roll.

Rick chuckled. "She's only interested in guys who come to class every day," he said. The rest of the class laughed. Willy and Pat looked at each other. *Not bad, sir.*

Jamie had the biggest grin. An adult student, he is twenty-six years old, very thin and blond, no older-looking than the others. He sits at the back, one seat removed from everyone else, not to escape, but to concentrate. But he has been having trouble. As the most faithful attendee in the class, with Rick's comment he raised his arms and flashed a double-V sign for victory. Willy looked at him. "Hey, she wouldn't give you the time of day, man," he sneered.

The game went well. In the heat of competition, the kids forgot themselves. The sullen came alive, the smart became important, and the not-smart smart enough to know it. Willy, Rodney, Calvin, Pat went quiet; from the shadows of a week of quiet industry, Fahad, Charlene, and Monika emerged as the stars. Monika was her team's captain. Willy listened to her as she plotted their strategy. Charlene, captain of the other side, answered and got her points; so did Monika. When they were sure Rick wasn't looking, Chad read his answer from statements Monika had prepared, Willy from Fahad's. Both got their points. Willy pumped his fist in the air. Pat read from no one's list. He hadn't known about the game, he had nothing prepared, but he didn't need anybody's help. He can think on his feet better than anyone in this room, that's what street-smart guys like him are trained for. Pat got his points.

Jamie was enjoying the game, until his own turn came. He started and stumbled. He had spent all the previous night working on his questions, not finishing until 1:00 a.m. But his words always somehow get muddled. They start under his control, then take him in directions of their own choosing.

"Tonya Harding is allowable to take, um, take her place in the Olympics because they haven't proved, um, guilty." He paused, "Um, um," then blurted, "an argument statement." There was near silence. Rick jumped in.

"You're saying, Mr. Dixon, if I understand correctly," nodding vigorously as he went, "that Tonya Harding can skate because her guilt hasn't been proven, and can't be proven, before the Games begin. Am I right, sir? And that that is an argument statement?" Jamie nodded uncertainly, excitedly, the others said nothing. Jamie got his point.

The score was close, there was time for only one more statement. It was Charlene's team's turn, they could clinch victory with a correct response. Charlene made the response herself. She sounded decisive. "*Yes!*" her teammates shrieked in support. *It's over.* But Monika shouted out a challenge.

"That's not a proper argument statement," she said. The room was in an uproar. Rick turned to Monika, "All right, who will make the challenge on your team's behalf?" Three hands shot up, Monika's, Fahad's, and Willy's. The three of them looked at each other and squirmed. Charlene's team looked at the three of them and squealed.

"I can only take one," Rick said.

"*Wil-ly! Wil-ly!*" Charlene's team chanted.

"Shaddup," Willy yelled.

"*Wil-ly! Wil-ly!*" The chanting continued.

Rick looked at him. "William?" Monika and Fahad said nothing.

Slowly, Willy offered a new argument statement. "Nancy Corrigan —"

"— Kerrigan," his teammates whispered.

"— Kerrigan," Willy repeated, "doesn't want to practise on, um, the same ice as Tonya Harding because, um, she couldn't really, um, practise that way. She'd be too distracted."

"*Yes!*" Fahad, Monika and the rest of the team shrieked, and erupted into applause.

"I award a point to William's team," Rick announced. The game was tied. Time had run out, the tie-breaker would be held the next day.

The kids made for the door, Willy with a new strut in his stride.

"Hey, Monika, how'd you like that," he chirped. " 'Wil-ly! Wil-ly!' I just shoved it in their faces."

When the next day came, Willy wasn't there; the game was decided without him. The day after, he was back and, still in his coat, he explained. "I wanted to be here so bad yesterday," he said. Then throwing back his head he closed his eyes and began to snore. "Unfortunately, I was unconscious." Everyone laughed but Rick.

Rick informed the office the day Willy was absent, and the office called his home. Rick talked to Willy before class the day he returned, telling him that his pattern of being here and not being here wasn't good enough, that he must attend every day.

Willy nodded, then, walking to his desk, he grinned at Pat and Chad. Last Thursday, he and Rick had another showdown. Rick had given them a quiz; Willy, he noticed, worked at his for a while, then drifted, doing some parts, leaving others. Rick told Willy that if he didn't finish in time, he would give him more time after class. To Willy, this was not good news.

"There's no way I'm gonna stay, sir. You can't make me."

"I can keep you here as long as I want," Rick countered.

Suddenly Willy's attention focused. He started working harder and faster, but he had waited too long and time ran out.

"But, sir, I'm so hungry I can't stay. I've got to eat."

Finally Rick offered a deal. I'll let you go now, he said, but only if you come back at 3:10 when school is over and finish. Willy nodded.

He never showed up, and he wasn't there Friday, as Rick knew he wouldn't be. Friday, he'd have had to face up to Thursday. It is the same with Pat. On Thursday, Rick saw Pat in the hall before class with his coat on, heading out the door. He stopped him, took him by the arm, and talked him into the room. On Friday, when Rick saw him again, Pat told Rick he'd be in class, but he never came. Today Rick will give him a detention, but what good will that do?

Rick worries about Pat and Willy and kids like them. They think school is such a drag, but really, Rick thinks, school protects them. What will they do with their don't-care attitude when they leave here, when they are out on the streets? Who will tolerate them there? Their absences, their irresponsibility. They are setting out on a tough road and can't stop. It's as if there is something about them that has to fail, that can only handle failure. Failure, they know, they can control, they can live with. Success scares them. That's why Willy didn't show up that tie-breaking day. He *had* to sleep through that class and willed himself to do it. Willy didn't know what to do with his momentary success. It was uncharted ground, bringing feelings he wasn't used to, that he didn't understand. As with so many kids, if things go well for a while he's okay. Then he sabotages himself. He has to. They're all the same, kids like Willy and Pat, they hate themselves, Rick thinks. They hate how they are and hate what they cannot be. They've got no place to go. Rick tries to help them, gives up, tries again, gives up, tries; feels lousy when he does and lousy when he doesn't.

And what about the others, the ones who do work hard, play the game by the rules? Fahad, Monika, Charlene, they could do with some help too. Not to pass, or do well, they will do that without him, but to do as well as they can. Don't they have that right too? And Calvin, he talks too much, distracts Ahmed and himself, but he's a good kid. Deep down, he wants to learn, and *can* learn. Rick could make a real difference with him. But the Willys and Pats always get to him. It's instinctive. They're his challenge, his satisfaction. Part of being a teacher is the need to save lost souls, and here they are, his legacy, his self-definition, his identity. The ones who prove you to you, who prove that what you are doing really matters, that *you* matter.

It has been a hard ten days. He can sense a mood in the school about this time every semester. The classes get louder, crankier, more unsettled, as if the honeymoon of the new semester is ending. The new possibilities, habits, and patterns can no longer hold back the old. The first test results are back; disappointment has already set in. But soon that will change again, and then again. This is when the real teaching and learning begin. Let's see what happens *now*, Rick thinks.

◆ ◆ ◆

English teacher Noel Lim has finally had enough. He decides to move James to another seat. James, handsome, with big bright eyes, light black skin, and hair that rises from his scalp like a Shriner's fez, would be irresistibly charming if he didn't know it.

"But sir, why me?" he asks.

"James, you know why."

"It's because I'm black." Everybody laughs.

Noel moves Sheri as well, James to the front on the opposite side, Sheri to the middle.

"It's a conspiracy, sir," James snarls. He trudges over to his new desk and wanders back; Noel looks up and points. "Shit," James mutters and trudges back again.

"James, did you say something?" Noel asks with a trace of a grin.

"I said, 'I want to sail a ship.'" Everyone laughs. He sits, looks around, starts humming, gets up, looks around, then spots Tim's shoes. Tim sits behind him.

"Hey, you on the basketball team?" James asks. James *is* on the basketball team.

"James, sit down."

"Sir, I can't work up here."

Noel says nothing.

Sheri is moved behind Ragini. "Sir, it smells funny here." The room goes silent. She moves herself back one seat.

Two steps over, one step back; pretty much the way it has been since the first day of the semester. The class has moved ahead with its work – each day, Noel gives them a short writing assignment – but never without a struggle. Noel remains calm and unde-terred. When he is done his lesson, the kids begin writing at their desks. He has come to marking what they do before the end of periods as their "work in progress," just to keep them going. It hasn't been wholly successful. The problem is the class's two dis-tinct seating blocs. One is by his desk at the front of the room, the ESL kids, two Hong Kong Chinese, one Vietnamese, one Indian. They are quiet, concentrated, determined; here every day. They are a problem only because, with a scattering of empty seats between them and the other larger bloc, they look like an uncomfortable little island. They talk to each other and no one else; the others don't know enough about them to think they might be interesting to talk to. The written work they submit falls into what Noel sees as the wide chasm between ESL and Advanced, and is not good enough. It is hard to imagine that by semester end their work will measure up.

But it's a few kids from the other group who set the class tone. James is the group's guiding spirit, and even now, isolated on the other side of the room, he is still a presence. The first to fall in with him was Wesley, tall and thin, with a Bill Cosby-like lantern jaw and a shy, tight smile that draws back into dimples. Then Nelson. Exuberant in his other classes, here he is over the edge of tolerable. His engine running at just a few too many RPMs, cranked up to the point where loud becomes blaring, funny obnoxious, and likeable a nuisance.

Behind Nelson is Lydia, every day so fresh and clean and smart-looking. Today the bright red scrunchy in her hair matches her bright red sweat pants, her new bright red, white, and grey Nikes, and the red outline of the blue letters on the white background of her Howard University T-shirt, a crest on its left sleeve reading "African American College Alliance." She is friends with James, Wesley, and Sheri, and is getting to know Nelson. She takes great delight in their antics, but doesn't share their need for crowd attention. When the crowd lures them too far, she holds herself back.

Behind her is Wesley and behind him Shiva, who seems even more out of place than Lydia. The others are Jamaican blacks, he is from India. More than a week has passed and he hasn't said a word. The class's most invisible person, he is also its most curiously visible. What is going on inside that body, behind the face that conveys such calm, a face that is unmoving, not blank or distant? His eyes take in everything, and a tiny upward curl seems etched at the corners of his mouth. Sitting in the eye of the hurricane, he is somehow untouched by what is around him, able to hear through the noise to some sound of his own.

Once across the aisle, now one more row removed, is Sheri. She is smart, eloquent, angry, funny, charming, physically stunning, worldly beyond her years. She is a Star. She doesn't go in search of the spotlight like James, the spotlight finds her. So used to it, she seems not even to notice its presence. Yet there is a story that follows her around that her friends and some teachers know. Two years ago, Sheri was shot by a boy who was harassing her on the street. As jarring as the story is, more jarring is how remote it seems from that elegant being sitting there in row four, seat three. Yet there is something unsettling about her, something in her that can do great things, and that keeps her from them. She is away so much for someone so apparently healthy and strong. What does she do when she's not here? She seems to like it in this classroom, though she is definitely not of it. James amuses her; Wesley amuses her; Noel amuses her sometimes too; Nelson, as much younger than his age as she is older, annoys her. They are to her like younger nieces and nephews, just kids but fun to be around. Her point of contact with the class seems to be Lydia, as cool a presence as she is hot. As if Lydia knows her story and watches over her, keeping Sheri from becoming too angry, too contemptuous, too distant.

At the back are two girls, Simone and Sharifa, who never shut up. They whisper, giggle, make meowing sounds, they whine like Valley girls. Not quite part of any group, they are co-conspirators with anyone who will have them. Scattered through the rest of the room, Chantal, Josie, and Mai, Drew, Joanne. And Ryan, tall, handsome, in his leather, knee-high, calf-hugging jackboots, black pants, and T-shirts, today's bearing the message "Power Stems from the Barrel of the Gun." Twenty-one kids in all, with no collective class feeling, only sharing the same room.

As a first assignment, Noel had them write a character sketch about someone they knew or someone fictional, three paragraphs, one paragraph on the character's appearance, one on his or her habits, a third on personality traits. Nearly all the kids passed, but the highest marks, awarded to Shiva and Ryan, were only nineteen out of twenty-five. Shiva wrote about a friend, as most of them did. Ryan's subject was Lestat, the Anne Rice character, a vampire who has "shoulder-length blond hair and pale white skin with greyish-blue eyes that glare at you and study your neck." Pauline, one of the silent girls in front, wrote about her mother, who is fifty-four years old, from Vietnam, whose favourite TV show is "Wheel of Fortune," which she watches every night. Her mother is "very gentle and calm," Pauline wrote, "everytimes when I had done something wrong, she never told my father, but quietly she sat down and explained to me what I had done was wrong. She also a standard mother, for example, every day she always remind us of our homework, even about taking a bath. My mother is very worry about our family's future, she tells us never spend too much money on something because maybe we will need it in the future. My father said she's too worry and careness. Anyways, she always my best mother in the world." Pauline got eleven out of twenty-five; "Basic skills lacking," Noel wrote on her paper.

Nelson, who got fifteen, wrote about his girlfriend. "She twitches her nose when she is really happy, or really angry. Always has favorite sayings. Talks on the phone alot. She bites her bottom lip when she thinks, she shivers when she's nervous. She eats alot of chocolat." Lydia wrote about James. "He is attractive with his good looks and his muscular features." He has "big broad shoulders to go along with his big feet," and has "these sleepy, lazy eyes." He's a "daydreamer," she writes, "sometimes I'll be talking to him and he'll just drift off." He loves music and basketball, "his baddest habit is playing video games." He is "always telling jokes even about people. The only thing I hate is when he turns the joke on me." "I'm really glad to know him," Lydia concluded. "To me he's like my older brother."

James wrote about his friend, Chris. "Chris is a pretty much straight forward type of guy. At times he could be a bug, but for the most part he's an o.k. type guy." "One thing that Chris loves to do is play 'ball,' that's what 'we' call it refering to my friends and I. Basketball is an ok sport that Chris and I have been playing for the longest time now, at least three to four years now." James wrote on for six more paragraphs. Noel gave him thirteen out of twenty-five. In the margin, he wrote at various points, "untidy," "unnecessary," "very confusing," "this is padding"; at the end, "You did not follow instructions. You have over 6 paragraphs. It is unfortunate as you do have potential."

The kids' papers were filled with Noel's markings, circles surrounding spelling mistakes, slashing underlines for inappropriate use of colloquial language. Wesley too, wrote with his ear to language, but his ear seems out of some different time and place. Because the assignment was given near to Valentine's Day, he decided that his sketch should be "about my first love, whom shall be anonymous." He described her: "Physically she was as Black as sweet chocolate, 5'8 in height. Her hair was as black as the sky without the stars, and the moon at midnight. Her eyes were beautiful garnet stones, so crystal clear. Her voice was so tantilizing and smooth that whatever she said everyone wanted to hear. Her smile was gifted with teeth like pearls, and if she smiled at someone they would definetly ask 'who's that girl?' Her hands were as soft as the feathers of a dove, with one touch the average Man would be singing songs of love. She had long legs causing her to walk in elegant strides, and her beauty was so captivating that any mortal which saw her would immediately thank God to be alive."

"Far too many grammar mistakes," Noel wrote on his paper. Fourteen out of twenty-five.

Noel believes passionately in the value of proper language. He knows some teachers try to turn English into a "communications" course. If a student can't find the written words he or she needs, draw something to accompany the words you have, they say, use video, music. But Noel never forgets the essential point: there is such a thing as a sentence that is good, clear, and grammatical, and one that isn't. He doesn't care if someone just got off the boat, having run for her life from civil war, unable to speak a word of English, both her parents dead, and so on. Terrible writing is still terrible writing.

He knows English probably as well as any teacher in this school knows any subject. He is of Chinese background – "it gives me a different slant on things, don't you think" (loud laugh) – one of only three on the staff. A century ago his ancestors left China for British Guiana, now Guyana. There he was raised and schooled until university, when he came to Canada. He has been teaching seventeen years, first in Scarborough, an eastern suburb of Toronto, then Fort Frances in northwestern Ontario, in York Region just north of the city, and the last seven years here. He knows English the way an immigrant in his own native land comes to know it, has to know it. The language of Shakespeare, Keats, Shelley, and all the other incomparable writers of that incomparable, distant land, his colonial superiors, the mother country. For him growing up in Guyana, language was a gift, a way for a child into his own imagination, into so many unimaginable lives and places so distant. Into feelings. He could take their language, turn every period to a comma, every chapter end into never-ending space, and write on and on, a story of his own.

It was a privilege, nothing less, and it's a privilege he is extending to these kids. To lead them off into unknowns of their own, into books and words and ideas they've never experienced before. In every kid in every class who sits before him, that's what he's looking for. Someone who is willing to explore those unknowns. Who takes chances. He hates *safe*. So boring, dead and deadening.

What could be worse? He hates quiet, well-behaved classes. "Nice little boys and girls," he calls them sneeringly. But he knows chaos doesn't work either. It offers the sort of illusory freedom that becomes imprisoning. Everybody needs rules. Behaviour is like a personal grammar, know how to behave and when, and the rest is yours. Proper English isn't a straitjacket, but a tool of liberation. Get the grammar and spelling right and the freedom begins.

He will teach these kids the best he can to the extent they will allow. But he is only a teacher; it is not his job to motivate and explain. He is not their father, not even their friend. He tells his students that sometimes, to the older kids when they know him better. "I'm not your friend. I don't want to be your friend. I want you to learn," he says. "To be able to read and write. To use language. To love language." *It may be human nature to want to get close, but the fuel is you.* You *are the only one you can count on, the only one who can deliver the passion that's needed each day. I will try to help you, but you must drive yourself.*

The noise level in class seems to have risen even from the first day. Last week, Noel had to be away for two days at a literacy conference. One substitute teacher quit after her first day. When Noel got back, he read the riot act and things seemed to improve, until today. Now James is up and wandering again. He tries to get Noel's attention; Noel ignores him. James keeps at it.

"I'm sorry, James," Noel says finally. "You've got me so upset I don't want to talk to you." The unflappable Noel has flapped. The class sits stunned to eerie silence. Nelson tries to get Noel's attention; Noel ignores him too.

"He's too upset to talk," someone mutters. The room goes quiet again and stays that way. A few minutes pass; James raises his hand. Noel, still busy not noticing, ignores him. James drops his hand. Normal noises pick up: breathing, the turning of pages, clacking of binders – no words. Almost every head is down at his or her work, James's included. Sharifa starts writing in tiny letters on the blackboard beside her. "I sit here," she writes, and draws an arrow down the board towards her. "She sits there," drawing another arrow towards Simone. Below that, "Note: For a good time, call 1 800 9-CROTCH!!!"

At period end, Noel calls James outside into the hall and tells him that he has had enough. What happened today will not happen again. James appears contrite. Noel turns back into the room as James walks away. "Sometimes it's so hard to keep a straight face," Noel laughs. "When in doubt, act hurt," he says, and laughs again.

✦ ✦ ✦

Maria Cheung ploughs ahead. She has a math lesson to give and a course to cover. She speaks and writes on the blackboard for thirty or thirty-five minutes, for the second half of the class she gives the kids problems to do, enough for homework, then wanders up and down the aisles peeking over shoulders to see how each is doing, checking last night's homework, waiting for urgent hands to go up, "Miss, miss, I don't understand." It never takes long.

It is a big class, twenty-eight, about six more than average, yet crammed enough into this room to appear to be more. Perhaps it is the clutter of winter coats and bookbags that does it, maybe it's kids two generations taller than kids were when the school was built, and used to slouching and spreading themselves out. The room would be much more crowded if everyone were here – which never happens. Today, twenty-four are present, more than 85 per cent of the class, about average.

Maria Cheung came to Canada fourteen years ago from Hong Kong, to study at McGill University. She met her husband there, he was a graduate student. They have a nine-year-old son; her husband is a mechanical engineer at Pratt & Whitney, the airplane engine manufacturer. This is her second year at Kennedy. She doesn't have a permanent position, she is called an "LTO," a "Long Term Occasional" teacher, replacing another teacher who is on a lengthy leave of absence. He will almost surely never come back. Terry Chaffe, the principal, would like nothing more than to be able to remove him from the staff roster entirely and hire someone permanently, but he cannot. So Maria, who doesn't want a permanent position, fills in, and every June is without a job; in mid-August she is hired back again on a new contract. While her status on paper seems shaky, her commitment to her job is strong.

Tiny and lively, she still speaks English with enough of a Chinese accent that twenty years ago she might occasionally have been laughed at in the classroom, not understood at other times. But twenty years ago, like so many others in this room, she might not have come to Canada. Travel outside North America today, offer a few words in the native tongue of the country you're visiting, even a close approximation of the real pronunciation, and no one will understand you. In Canada today, especially in the big cities, do the same in English and almost everyone will understand. We are a country of accents, our ears trained so that almost any pronunciation will do. And in this school, because so many kids have accents, people seldom mock how another speaks.

A few days ago, Sophia had a question. It was about her eighth of the day; there was still half a class to go. Maria had been doing a lesson on square roots. Sophia didn't understand. Slightly ahead of her raised hand, she growled, "Miss, miss, what is 'hrrroot'?"

"Square root?" Maria asked. Sophia nodded. "It's the number which times itself gives the larger number inside the sign. For example, the square root of 4 is −?"

"Two or minus two," Sophia answered.

"Right," said Maria.

" 'Hrrroot'?" said Sophia, repeating what she thought Maria had just said.

"Right," said Maria, repeating what she thought Sophia had just said. It had the makings of "Who's on First?" The others laughed.

"Yes, 'hrrroot,'" Sophia repeated again, growing exasperated. "But what 'hrrroot' is?!" They all laughed again.

Language barriers are broken down by math. The immigrant, just off the boat, dropped into a grade ten English class, is lost; in math, confronted by symbols as familiar to Sophia in Belgrade and to Maria in Hong Kong as to anyone here, he feels the excitement of a little bit of home. But it's more than the symbols, it's the logic of math, the mathematical syntax, which links the symbols together. Often immigrants, especially Asians, do well in math, and science too, because they don't feel as if they are starting so far behind, they feel immediate achievement and reward. Because in maths and sciences there are no hidden cultural assumptions, no vast spaces between the lines where idiom and nuance, and trouble, reside. Because math can be a solitary study, just you and a piece of paper, a calculator, a computer, no one has to be patient with your endless errors, there's nobody to embarrass you; you can fail alone. And years later, many immigrants go into maths or science because, looking for a job, facing imaginable prejudice, they feel more secure entering the more objective, right-or-wrong world of maths or science, where reputation and assumption are on their side.

Maria's class moves at a crisper pace than a history or English class because math, like science, is highly visual. It may seem abstract, but symbols and letters can transform concepts into something you can see, can follow on a blackboard, on an overhead, like a video, like TV. This is a generation of kids much more used to watching than reading, to symbols, short-cut messages and the minimal time and patience they require. Speaking and listening are okay; reading and writing take too long. Except for the precision of mind it requires, math is in tune with its 1990s audience.

Maria uses all the languages at her disposal – letters, numbers, symbols – to communicate. What she still hasn't been able to get across, however, is for the kids to be on time, and to do their homework. She tells them how important both are, but they have heard all this before. Day after day, the same three or four kids hang around the door when class should be beginning, and a few seconds are lost unnecessarily. The door closes, minutes pass, the door opens and Peter walks in, eyes half closed, head averted, stumbling into his seat. Maria stops, the kids stop; more seconds lost. Then Jessica, then Ashley, then Sheri the days she comes, not a hint of embarrassment on their faces. These kids have learned: meet in-your-face challenge with in-your-face challenge. Betray nothing, show anger that is beyond what any teacher can comprehend, make teachers wonder about all those things they're not certain they understand – kids of the 1990s, immigrant kids, kids from broken homes, kids and drugs, part-time jobs, peer pressure. Make them start thinking: there must be more to this than just being late. Then you've got them.

Priya breezes in twenty-five minutes into class. She swings the heavy classroom door shut. Maria jumps, heads pop up; she stops writing on the blackboard, turns and stares at Priya. Priya stares back. When Maria's lesson is done, she checks homework; most have done all of it, a few, including Priya, have done half; only Quentin, squinting into his book, has done none.

✦ ✦ ✦

Lunch time. The question in the staff room these days is always the same, "Do you ever remember it being this cold this long?" No one can. From a conversational ice-breaker, weather has become the conversation itself. Teachers have taken to watching the Weather Channel on TV: it's the only news that matters, one explained. And because relief is so desperately hoped for, tomorrow's weather becomes more important than today's. Yet nothing seems to change: another prairie-like high sits over the region, which brings another day of bright blue skies, sun, wind, and shrivelling temperatures. On and on. Behind it, a storm that is hammering the midwest. On TV screens, endless shots of cars in ditches, transports overturned, traffic in a snarl, and in a few days, everyone knows, that is us. First the lightning; then the thunder. The kids know too. The day before a big storm is to hit, the energy in the school picks up. "Shouldn't you cancel tomorrow's test, miss? Have it next week instead?" Teachers go home right after classes to make sure the refrigerator is stocked. Everyone waits.

The Voice of God is the morning radio. "School cancellations today include all the schools in York Region, in the Halton and Wentworth boards, in the Dufferin–Peel Separate School Board . . ." It almost never happens; only once this year. There needs to be enough snow hitting late enough in the morning, about five or six o'clock, that road crews don't have enough time to at least partly clear the routes; and not too late that teachers and students are already on the road and there is no turning back. For teachers living east of the school, who go against Toronto's traffic and with Toronto's more favourable weather patterns, there isn't much problem. Live to the west, in Burlington or Hamilton, to the north in Milton or Georgetown, far enough away to escape the worst of Toronto's inflated housing prices, and you run into the worst of weather. When the first snowflake falls on Manitoba, as one teacher who lives west of Mississauga puts it, our forty-five-minute drive is thirty minutes longer.

Today at the lunch tables the only other talk is of the Olympic Winter Games in Lillehammer, and of the film *Schindler's List* – the Academy Award nominations just came out, the first and only sign of spring. As usual, most of the noise comes from the euchre room. Last week, the big news there was Dave Arthurs and his ProLine ticket: six picks made, the first three all winners; three to go and $278 was his. He spent that night at home in front of his TV, watching his beloved Leafs, and the out-of-town scores.

The Rangers went ahead early as he knew they would, and won. Four for four; only two to go. In the Leafs' game, the Sharks scored early, 1–0 – ugh! – then 2–0, then 3–0. He slammed off the set. A few minutes later, he turned it on: 3–1, 3–2, 3–3. The game went into overtime. Leafs' sniper Dave Andreychuk was wide open in front of the net, the game and much more than he knew riding with him. He shot – and missed the net. The game ended in a tie. Lowly Ottawa, who never wins, beat lowly Edmonton. The next morning, Dave's euchre buddies tried to soothe him.

"Hey, Davey, don't let it get you down."

"Yeah, you gave it a good run."

"What would you do with the $278 anyway?"

Old "5 out of 6" Dave isn't taken in.

"But hey, Davey, you sure fooled 'em," the Sandman chirped. "Only 4 out of 6 this time." They laughed.

◆ ◆ ◆

Yesterday, Cathy Sylvester's science class did a lab on magnetism and some kids were away. Today, Cathy asks Quentin and Andrea to help them out. Quentin says okay, Andrea, Cathy's top student, Sue Lishman's too, says she is confused by too many things and asks not to. Quentin begins by helping her. He took this same material five months ago in the first semester, and reviewed it just days ago for his exam, which he failed. He did well in the physics part of the course, his previous teacher told Cathy, but later in biology, where more reading was required, he had trouble. Then there were all his absences, some explained, some not.

Quentin has had to deal with so many assumptions. Triggered by his colour, his size, his clothes, the curiosities in his manner. On one level, everyone else in the room seems a variation of everyone else. Bigger, smaller, more or less good-looking, but not very far from the median. Only in some inner story might any of them show themselves unique. Quentin needs only to sit in place for a scanning eye to stop. His dreadlocks, his long, thin body with long, thin arms and hands and fingers, always in motion to a rhythm no one else can hear, as if a Walkman were embedded in his ear. Today, he has on a pair of black jeans with a portrait of Martin Luther King, and the years "1929–1968" hand-painted on the right leg; on the left leg, below three vertical stripes – the green, yellow, and red of the Guyanese flag – the words, "Let's Make It More Than a Dream." And then, of course, his eyes, the windows to his soul, squinted nearly shut.

But today Quentin is the reigning class expert on magnetism. After helping Andrea, he moves on to Erin and Kimberley near the back. He lays a bar magnet on their desk, places a piece of acetate on top of it, then sprinkles iron filings on the acetate. He asks them what they see.

"The filings concentrate at the poles –" Kimberley begins.

"– and the ones not at the poles kind of just go around the magnet," Erin finishes.

Quentin nods. "And what about the pattern of those filings?"

"They're kind of in lines –"

"– in circles."

"Yes, and –" He wants more. He pushes at them patiently, to uncover the answer themselves.

"The lines don't cross."

"Right," he nods.

He folds the acetate and funnels the filings back into the bottle, puts two bar magnets on the table, end to end, north pole to north pole, slightly apart. He places the acetate over them and pours on the filings. They snap onto each pole, leaving clear space between them, and arrange themselves in thin force lines around the magnets.

"My God, they're repelling!" Kimberley shrieks.

"Right," Quentin smiles.

He does the same procedure for two south poles together, then a south and a north.

"What do you see now?"

"They look the same," Kimberley says.

"But one thing's different."

"They attract across the middle."

"Right," he says again. "Well, that's about it," he smiles, beginning to clean up, his head now angled away from them. "Except to do the readings in the book and the questions."

"Thanks," they say; he smiles and walks back to his desk.

Minutes later, Cathy asks the class what gives magnets their strength. Quentin raises his hand. He explains about the "domains" of the magnetite within a bar magnet, how they can get misaligned and scrambled, and go in different directions. Align and straighten those domains, he says, and the magnet gets stronger.

"Wow," Cathy exclaims. "My job is in jeopardy." Quentin grins.

A hand goes up at the back.

"Do we have to take down this Domain Theory stuff?" It's Jody.

Cathy has been trying to get them to ask more questions. That's what science is about, after all, she tells them. Two north poles repelling each other – *but why?* Force lines around the magnets not crossing – *but why?* Such simple, obvious questions that would leap into anyone's mind. Why not theirs? Or maybe they do think about them, but are too shy to ask. Because they are awkward adolescents, shy about lots of things, because asking will show they don't know, because it will take up time that other kids and teachers may think wasted, or because school seems a place for answers not questions. But science is nature's magic show – "My God, they're repelling!" – how can you *not* ask? Don't you want to know how God/Nature did it? What's inside its top hat, up its sleeve? Every little child wants to know that. Some people stay curious, but what about the rest? What happens to them?

Why doesn't Jennifer have her hand up? Why doesn't Simone? Since the first day of this semester, why haven't most of them had their hands up even once, for a question, an answer, anything? Why is Nelson's hand up all the time, his arm and fingers stretched out straight, his body almost out of his seat?

Cathy can encourage more questions, she can break down the barriers that are the reasons *not* to ask; but can she, can anyone, generate reasons *to* ask? She wants them to really think, she says. To wonder. Because out of wonder, she knows, will come delight; it has to. There are so many incredible, fascinating things around us. And once wonder is present, we're hooked, lined, and sinkered. But where does wonder come from? The great literary critic and educator Northrop Frye once said that the purpose of school is to instil a love of learning. Because once you love learning, you can't get enough of it, can't spend enough time at it – the rest follows. But how do you learn to love learning? We often hear that what we really need in schools is for kids to "learn how to learn," and to carry that fundamental skill over a lifetime. But how? Is there a course you can take? The answer lies not in technique, but in attitude. But where does that attitude come from, and how?

"They've had some bad experiences," Cathy says often about this class, the girls at the back – Tracy, Jennifer, and Jody – especially. Something has happened. They feel "stupid" in science. Their minds were already closed when they walked into class the first day. As for Jody, at least she's asking questions, Cathy thinks. You have to be listening to ask, you have to think you might know something to bother. At first, Cathy thought the class had real promise; after the first lab results, she thought it might be one of the weakest she has had. Two repeaters, other kids who don't have the language skills for Advanced level, one boy from Sri Lanka, Prideep, who seems utterly lost. When he comes to class, which isn't every day, he sits stiff and still at his desk as if he understands nothing. Yet when she looks at his written work, some ability is evident. But not enough. His words seem just to peter out, as if he can do Advanced work but not at the speed he must. Cathy has talked to Jan Coomber, one of the vice-principals, about placing him somewhere else. But this morning there was a notice in the staff room that Jan's mother had died in England, so she will be away for a few days. And it will be a few more days in a short semester, before he will be dealt with.

The second lab was better and now Cathy thinks the class will be all right. They have fallen a little behind as she pushed them to get more involved, and this week's disruptions haven't helped. A number of kids have been called out of class for routine counselling appointments, and none of them can afford to lose class time. Nelson hasn't been himself the last few days, however. He's asking too many questions, as if he doesn't trust himself to have any of the answers and wants her to hold his hand. He didn't do well on his labs, maybe that has brought back all his insecurities, maybe there's something else. Today, when he isn't asking questions he seems lost in himself. He begins playing with the tap on his science desk, turning on the water, letting it run, turning it off, watching drops form at the end, watching them stretch slowly downward, then bringing his finger close to each drop, nearly touching it, watching as somehow it is drawn to his finger, like metal to magnet. Then tapping the tap to see more water run out, waiting for the next drip. An experience in pure science, perhaps, but not what he needs to be doing now.

When class ends, the girls at the back are first out the door. Nelson and Andrea hover around Cathy at the front, asking questions, and so does Doug. He tells Cathy he won't be around next week, and wants to know what will be covered so he can work ahead. Cathy is concerned. Doug is having trouble keeping up even when he attends class. What is he doing next week, Cathy asks. I'm going out west, he answers excitedly, to ski with my aunt and uncle.

Chapter 4

Tuesday, February 22, 12:04 p.m.

It has been a bad day for Rick Ray in his history class. It started with Willy and Chad coming in late, noisy, paying no heed to the class or to the lesson he had already begun. Then it was Marv and Pat, then Rodney, who had had such a good week last week. Then Chandra. She at least was as quiet as usual, but he had to reprimand her, another disruption to a class that was still not under control. That's the way it went all morning. Stops and starts, no flow, nothing easy; the lesson punching up against them, nothing penetrating. Just unconnected moments. He's lost Calvin today, lost Rodney, even Monika. She's had her worst day. He's even lost Jamie, who is always so constructive, willing to struggle through the confusion of his mind. He never pushes, never tests the patience and goodwill that are his saviours. But today he's been loud, even obnoxious. Yesterday, they had watched a movie on immigrant America in the early 1900s. This morning when someone described the illness of one of the characters as "pneumonia," Jamie yelled, "It was double pneumonia," and when no one seemed to hear, or think the distinction important, he yelled again, "Double pneumonia. I know from personal experience."

More than anything else, it's their disrespect that bothers him. They know you don't act like this in a classroom. You don't treat people this way. Why do they do it? The son of an air force corporal, he has lived a lot of places in his forty-nine years. He has taught twenty-seven years. And what he knows better than he knows anything is that people are good. Kids are good. They do bad things, we all do, but they are fundamentally good. So why are they being this way? The edge of outrage in his voice every time he corrects them, this is where it comes from. And the kids respond because they *are* good. Willy, Pat, these tough "who-gives-a-shit" kids who refuse to care about anything because caring never got them anything but pain. "You're right, sir. I'm sorry, sir"; he can see contrition in their faces. In a few minutes, of course, things change again. They have other needs, other roles to play. But a fundamental decency is there. He believes it as a teacher; he believes it as a human being.

How can you teach if you don't believe in people, Rick wonders. His wife tells him he lives in a "never-never land." She is a guidance counsellor at another high school in Peel. Every day, all day, she sees kids with problems: abused, abandoned, kicked out of class again and again. Are they kids with problems or problem kids? After a while it's hard to know. As a teacher it's so much easier not to believe, then the problem is them, not you. You did your best, that is your absolution, except something bubbles up from deep inside you that poisons your well. In the collision between what you are and what you want to be, you turn hard, cynical; the kids fight you, so you fight them back. You outwit them, outquick them, outmean them. Unable to win the way you want to win – by teaching them something – you win any way you can. But the victory is hollow. Too often he has seen them, teachers who get out of bed every day just to be one day closer to retirement.

What is he really teaching in this classroom? The course is called "Canada in the Twentieth Century": life amidst the British and American empires, immigration, the growth of the West, the wars, the Depression? Sure, but names and dates important in March will be erased from kids' minds by August. Why do these kids need to know any of this anyway? It's past, gone, over and done with. It's *history*. But it isn't gone, and a few days ago, for a brief moment, the kids seemed to realize that.

He had dropped them back into the 1890s, to the time of the Boer War. He wanted them to feel the complications of Canadian nation-building and British imperialism. Canada is barely thirty years old, he told them, the British Empire extends around the globe. Then he stopped himself, and gave to them a phrase he had once heard and has never forgotten: "The sun never sets on the British Empire," he intoned, the words rolling out of his mouth in the patriotic tone of the time. In Europe, he continued, Germany is rising as an imperial power. It has moved into southwest Africa. The British have pushed the Dutch from the South African coastline into the interior, where the Dutch have discovered gold and diamonds.

"Let's say we're in London," he suggested to them. "We're members of Joseph Chamberlain's Cabinet. What do we do?"

"We're afraid the Germans might extend their empire into the interior," said Fahad, "and with all the gold and diamonds –"

"– they'd get richer and stronger," Monika said with a sudden nod.

"Okay," Rick mused, "but what can we do? We're a democratic country. Can we just march in and take the land from the Boers?"

"No!" the kids exclaimed. "That's not fair."

"But if we don't, and the Germans move in," Rick was beginning to bait the hook, "and if their empire grows, and with their newer, stronger navy in strategic locations, like South Africa, it might put in jeopardy India and Australia. Even Canada. The whole English–speaking world –" his voice rising higher with every phrase.

The realities of geopolitics seemed suddenly very complicated. The kids fell into confused silence. All except Fahad. He has been around history's block before. "The British should shoot themselves and say the Boers did it. Just like the Germans did with the Poles."

"Maybe," Rick smiled, "but let's talk about that later. I want to know about Canada. About Laurier." When Rick had first shown them a picture of Prime Minister Wilfrid Laurier a few weeks ago, he had asked them who it was. Someone important in Canadian history, he hinted. The guessing began:

"Abraham Lincoln?"

"Napoleon?"

"George Washington?"

Not even Fahad knew. (Noting Laurier's very bald head and wavy, collar–length mane in back, Rick joked, "Particularly handsome man, don't you think?") Now they all know who Laurier is, though Willy still calls him "Laurelle."

"Chamberlain tells Laurier they need Canada's help," Rick continued. "To save the English–speaking world. You're Laurier, what do you do?"

There were mumblings, but nothing else. He tried again. "This is Canada in 1900. Who lives here?"

"People who were British."

"Okay, and what are they going to feel?"

"That we gotta help out."

"Sure," Rick said, getting more excited. "The Empire's in jeopardy. Remember John A. Macdonald in 1891 in his last campaign: 'A British citizen I was born; a British citizen I will die.' And he was the *Canadian* Prime Minister!" He took a breath. "But who else lives in Canada?"

"Lots of immigrants."

"No," Rick said, "not that many yet. Remember, this is 1900. But who does live here?"

Silence.

"Remember, the province of Quebec . . ."

"The French," several voices cried.

"Right, French-Canadians. And what are they going to feel?" Rick waited, and sensing no answers, went on, "Have they ever had any experience with British imperialism?"

No answers. Fahad's hand was up, Rick looked around and over it until he couldn't ignore it any longer. "Fahad?"

"The conquest. Something about Wolfe and Montcalm." Fahad has been in Canada from Kenya only a year.

"That's right. The French settled parts of Canada and were defeated by the British." Again Rick grew excited. "They were put under a government not of their choosing. *A conquered people.*" Rick let the phrase echo. "So how are they going to feel?"

"Like the Boers," Pat said, getting involved in spite of himself. "That the Boers are like them."

"So, are they going to say to Laurier or Chamberlain, 'Sure, take my men. I'll fight your battles. I'll die for you'?"

"No way," yelled Willy.

"They're gonna say, 'That's not my war.'" Chad this time.

Rick smiled. "So what does Laurier do?"

Fahad, wrapping himself in Laurier's cloak: "This might bring unity in the Empire," he said, "but it would bring disunity at home."

"So what do you do now?" Rick asked.

The discussion picked up even more. Fahad, Pat, Rodney, even Jamie. The boys, but none of the girls. Rick tried to bring them in. He asked Monika a question; she answered. He asked Sandee her opinion; she hemmed and hawed until he cut her off to save her embarrassment, and asked someone else. If he had asked her something right out of the book, he knew she'd have the answer. She'd have read the passage and written the answer as homework. Not many of the boys would have known. Why do girls resist expressing an opinion aloud? Do they feel less worthy, or less worldly, as if they don't know about things like power, corruption, and greed? As if they don't have the street smarts, the instincts, the insight into this kind of human behaviour? Boys act so much more aggressive, more competitive, as if putting on a show is instinctive to them. Everything a contest, and the more often you play, the better you play. Of the girls, the worst is Karen. Rick decided to ask her a question –

"Well," she began her reply, "like Laurier had, uh, you know, like, to listen to, um, Chamberlain, or whatever –" Her voice so quiet, her posture so uncertain, her expression as tentative as her answers, as if she were waiting for a voice to say, "No, you're wrong. That has nothing to do with what we are talking about." Karen drifts on until Pat cuts her off.

"The British Empire supported Canada," he said. "Canada must do the same." It's the loyalty of the streets. Rodney and Jamie agreed. Fahad did not.

"If the British got into this for gold and diamonds," he said, "Canada should get gold and diamonds in return."

Pat said you need strong leaders who should do what *they* think is right. Fahad said a leader is "only a voicebox of the people. He amplifies what we say to him."

Street-smart Pat, the idealist as imperialist; strait-laced Fahad, the scheming pragmatist. Rick providing many of the details, the kids providing fifteen years of experience in human behaviour. Together, acting out, understanding history, discovering something in common.

That's really what Rick has been trying to teach them: the historical mind, and as many of history's details as are needed to tell that story and develop that mind. To see things as related, connected, to understand themselves as history's most recent chapter. Not history as past, gone, over and done with, but as an ongoing story, which if known can shape them and they it, which can change how they live. To see history as the story of people: a time, a place, a set of circumstances – now here's what happened. History repeating itself because, facing similar circumstances, people repeat themselves.

To discover that the mystery of history isn't names and dates, but the mystery of human nature, and they all know something about human nature. Much of what Willy has learned has come from the streets, from hockey arenas and lunch periods at Mickey's; Fahad, from books. Sports, clubs, summer jobs, all offer a direct window on human behaviour. History and literature, timeless and universal, offer the same window but indirectly. Indeed, Willy, who gravitates towards trouble and who, not big or strong, forever jumps into things without measuring the consequences and gets pummelled for it, would be a lot more street-smart if he knew more history. Faced with the next big scrap of heavyweights at Mickey's, if he knew his "Laurelle," he might sit it out.

Rick knows that most of school isn't about specifics. The kids must learn specifics, they are tested in specifics, perhaps learning has to seem that way. Yet when school is over, it is ways of thinking, not specifics, that stick. A science mind, a math mind, a history mind, perhaps a human mind too. For it's in school, not just at home, that kids learn about fairness, decency, civility, and Rick tries never to forget that. Like it or not, he is a model to them. He is part of their lives seventy-six minutes a day, five days a week for twenty weeks. He is with them more than many parents are. So *how* he teaches them, *how* he treats them, matters. He can be tough, easygoing, funny, serious, almost anything, and probably he needs to be almost everything at one time or another. But at the very least, he has to be fair, has to care, and he can't give up.

Rick almost quit teaching after his first year at Kennedy. He had a grade-nine General-level class: Kennedy was then a non-semester school, so he had the class for the whole year. A few days into the term, some new kids were added. Kids on welfare, kids from the court system who had to be in school, kids who really didn't want to be there. From twenty-two, the class swelled to nearly forty. Every night, Rick went home and planned what he'd do, three hours for every hour of class time, but nothing really worked. If I have to spend all night at this and still lose, he thought, maybe I should consider another career.

Little can humiliate a teacher more than a class that doesn't work. Teenagers, so much younger, smaller, less experienced and knowing, bringing a teacher to his or her knees. Be tough, be nice, be funny, be patient, scream, yell – all for nothing. There were days when that class would move ahead, other days when it was like the first day all over again, as if, useless and irrelevant, he'd never been there. About halfway through the year, the class was dead in the water. Towards the end, it got better because most of the kids who were there for other reasons voted wants over needs and left, with only the original core remaining.

Rick learned a great lesson in humility, one every teacher must learn. He has a teacher's need to help kids, perhaps even to save a few. He has the urge to personalize every kid's success and failure, feel the highs, suffer the lows, but by now he knows he is no saviour. So much is going on in each kid's life, every story is so complicated. He is just one small brush stroke on a large canvas. But he *is* one small brush stroke, and that he must never forget. They matter, and he matters too.

He has a hard time remembering any of that today. He will feel frustrated the rest of the day, and the feeling might last all week. Tonight, as he eats dinner and watches TV, he'll be thinking about this class, about what he can do tomorrow to make things better. Should he come down on them, make them work so hard they have no time for distraction or disrespect? Punish them for his sake and maybe for theirs? It is not the answer, he knows, but as he watches them rush out his door to lunch, joking, laughing, he is tempted.

✦ ✦ ✦

Wednesday, February 23, 11:22 a.m.

They are hardly in the door and not yet in their seats.

"I'm very disappointed the way things have gone lately," Rick begins. The stragglers suddenly pick up their pace. Rick's hands are on his lectern, his head bobs gravely with his words. "I like this class very much," he tells them, "but we've got some problems." He cuts off his words abruptly, walks to the blackboard and starts to write. "Take this down in your binders," he tells them. Willy doesn't have a binder; he borrows a sheet of paper from Pat. Rick writes "RULES" high on the board, and five headings underneath. His chalk *clack clack*s at the board. For lateness, a first-time offender must give him the same number of minutes that he's late, *after class*, during the lunch period. Willy spits out a breath; his eyes fly open. "There's no way," he mutters. With each subsequent offence, the penalty doubles. As for coats in the classroom, a ten-minute penalty will be served after class, cumulative for each offence. The same for disruptions, lack of equipment (pens, notebooks, and so on), and absences without a note.

There is grumbling, but Rick isn't finished. He has a new seating plan, he tells them. When Rodney and Chad stumble noisily to their new seats, he explodes.

"Move now and move quietly!" he shouts. No one has heard him speak like this before; they are startled. The room goes quiet. Those who have experienced little censure in their lives are embarrassed, contrite. The others know what to do. Their faces go blank, their bodies rigid. Unable to protect themselves by doing better, *presto*, they stop caring.

Except that feeling doesn't last long either. As the lesson goes on, bodies loosen, the kids forget themselves. They have a lively discussion about immigrant life in a big city, now and at the turn of the century. Near the end of class, Rick returns to what he was saying more than an hour before. "To believe in yourself," he tells them, "you need self-respect. Part of that is hard work. And today, you worked hard. Tomorrow, be on time."

When the other kids are gone, Jamie approaches Rick, still shaken. "Don't yell like that again, sir," he says, his eyes pleading.

Rick has taken a chance and he knows it. He has drawn a line and put himself on that line far more than he has put them. What happens if the coats come back tomorrow? If the pattern of lateness and disrespect continues? He has set out the challenge, now he must meet it.

Chapter 5

Thursday, March 3, 1:05 p.m.

This may be the hardest time of every semester. It comes after the organizational disruptions of the first days, after the next few weeks of calm, after the first assignments have been done and returned, and the first test results are in. After explanations and excuses have been made and tried, and answers reluctantly found; when things just *are*. All that this kid or class a few weeks ago *might be* now *is*. Fifteen more weeks to go. For everyone, the same question: Do I ride it out, or fight?

Noel Lim and his English class have just finished reading Act I, scene iv, of *Romeo and Juliet* aloud. Noel has given the kids a writing assignment, and most of them are working quietly at their desks. Nelson is playing with his pencil, staring off into who knows where. He had wanted to play Romeo, Noel chose Ryan instead, Nelson complained louder than he should have, Noel yelled at him, Nelson slunk away. He looks discouraged. The ghost of Nelson past has caught up with him these last few days. He thought he had left it behind at his old schools where it would never find him, that maybe the old Nelson had to do more with them than with him, that at Kennedy he could write a whole new story. But now Kennedy is getting him wrong too. He fights back, but awkwardly, annoyingly, demoralizing the very allies he needs. He doesn't make things easy for Noel or for his other teachers, and with so many kids competing for a teacher's special attention, the kind that goes beyond professional duty and expectation, easy may be necessary.

Sheri sits two rows away from Nelson. It's hard to know how she feels. She is so often away, and when she is in class, she doesn't sit at her desk with the trepidation of other poor attendees, feeling guilty, behind in their work, trying to hide until tomorrow when they can stay away again. She lets everyone know that she is PRESENT. The past few days the kids have been acting out *Romeo and Juliet* in class; it has not been a pretty sound. Most of them seldom if ever read on their own time, so they don't read well. Add the pressure of reading aloud and acting out a scene, the unfamiliarity of Shakespearean English, and the result, even for those whose first language is English, is a series of disconnected words, spoken without inflection, context, or hint of meaning. All except for Sheri. When it's her turn to speak, she is loud and commanding. She speaks in complete, meaningful passages, as if the role – today Juliet, yesterday Romeo – is hers.

Sheri was born in Montego Bay, Jamaica, the second of four children. In 1987, when she was ten, her mother sent her to live with her aunt and her aunt's family in Scarborough, Ontario. The product of a conservative, churchgoing family, she was the special child, a brilliant student in Jamaica, the favourite of her aunt. Sheri's first few months were awful. She dressed and talked differently, even from the other Jamaican kids at her school. They made fun of her singsong island cadences and quaint phrases. Always so special and proud, she felt humiliated. She decided that she wouldn't leave her house until she could speak properly. So in her room she practised, shedding old speech rhythms, taking on new ones, and emerging with a full-blown British accent. If they are going to make fun of me, she decided, I will put myself on such elevated ground that I can make fun of them. In time, she developed many accents and languages, using whichever seemed the most appropriate to meet her purposes.

At home things were stormy. She was so different from that quiet, brilliant kid her aunt knew in Jamaica. So headstrong and disruptive, so much older-seeming than kids her own age, with problems only older kids had. This wasn't what her aunt had bargained for; just trying to make a life for her own family was hard enough. Everyone had to go in the same direction, the one she and her husband, as the adults in the family, had set. But Sheri wanted to go her own way. *Imagine, deciding not to go to school until you can speak properly. Think of the trouble you're causing us. Life isn't easy here and you're making it harder.* Worse still, Sheri was the oldest of the kids in the house. Her two younger cousins looked up to her; she was a bad influence on them. In good times, the blood tie between Sheri and her aunt would have seemed unbreakable. In bad, neither of them was ever more than a breath away from the thought: *she is only an aunt/a niece; if things don't get better, I can always leave/kick her out.*

Sheri returned to Jamaica for three weeks in 1989, then for six months in 1991. The relationship with her aunt had worsened, she wanted to go back to her parents. But in Jamaica, there was no life for her but the one her mother and her mother's mother had lived for generations, so she went back to Canada again, to Mississauga, where her aunt had moved.

By now she was fifteen. It was May 1992. She and a girlfriend decided to take the subway across the city to Scarborough to meet up with some old friends. It was a school night. They spent the evening wandering around a mall, and were walking to the bus that would take them to the subway home. A bunch of guys started harassing them. Nothing too bad, but there were so many of them, and they wouldn't stop. Sheri and her friend just kept walking, trying to ignore them. They tried banter and put-down, but the guys kept it up. She was very patient, she recalls, much more so than she is now. Finally, she said "two more words" to them, still walking away towards the bus. Suddenly, a sharp, quick sound exploded in her ears. She threw up her hands to cover them, still walking. The next few seconds seemed to take minutes to pass. The sound, her hands over her ears, then a feeling of wetness and warmth. When the sound went away, she lowered her hands, and looked where the wetness was. Her right hand was covered in blood. Her girlfriend screamed. Sheri still didn't understand what had happened, couldn't understand, wouldn't understand. The sound had nothing to do with a gun, with a bullet, the warm wetness with blood, the blood with her. The guys ran off. The two girls stumbled into the street and stopped a car.

Sheri left hospital a week later with a wound in the back of her neck and an exit wound on her jaw line, about halfway between her ear and her chin. The bullet had missed her spinal cord by a centimetre. She returned home on painkillers she would need for several weeks, permanently shaken by the knowledge that her life had nearly ended.

She needed comforting. A voice to tell her that everything was going to be okay. But her aunt and family needed comforting too. *A gun! Can you believe it? What is this girl bringing into our life, our home? What about our kids? How do we explain this to them? What was she doing there that night anyway, a school night? What did she say to those guys?* Inside Sheri was a different voice: *the shooter hasn't been caught, he might come back and finish me off.*

She decided that she had to get away. She was too weak to leave by herself, so a friend carried her to another friend's, where she stayed until she got stronger. Then she went to New York to live with relatives; later she moved in with other friends. She was there six months. After that, it was back to Mississauga, to live with a cousin, then with friends, returning to T. L. Kennedy, finally this year moving in again with her aunt and uncle. She can never forget what has happened, but they have changed enough, or she has, that somehow they will manage together as long as they must.

Now, with a little breathing space, Sheri is beginning to put together her life. To connect what she has been with what she wants to be. If she doesn't do that soon, she is now realizing, the two will never join. She has found new friends. Her old friends had been nearly old enough to be her parents, too old to want to bother with her unless she found a way to fit in. That's how her drinking started. She would be talking and drinking with her friends, get so absorbed in what she was saying, and the alcohol would hit her. This went on for a few years. Then one day, as if waking from a stupor, she saw things a new way. Her friends suddenly looked old. There was nothing really special about them. In ten years, they would only be ten years older and still going nowhere. She wanted none of that. For her, life meant so many places to go, things to do, people to be. You either go ahead or go back, she likes to say. If she stayed with them, they would drag her down with them. Nobody was going to do that.

Her new friends are just out of university, working, making something of themselves, full of possibilities, ambitions. She doesn't see any of her Kennedy classmates outside school. When 3:10 comes, she exchanges one life for another. Yet she likes the kids here; she plays dominoes or crazy eights with them at lunch in the Caf. With James, Nelson, and Wesley. She likes dominoes best. "You gotta see right through people to be good at that game," she says, "and I'm good at it." Lydia is the only one she feels close to at school. So down to earth, so self-contained, so wise. As for the rest, Sheri feels almost nothing in common with them. In math and especially in English, she watches with gentle bemusement, with a mixture of patience, envy, and delight. She sees in her classmates somebody she has never been. "Whenever I see myself as a child," she says, "I'm always in Jamaica. When I was nine or ten; that's when my childhood ended."

Her favourite subject is French because it seems so wonderfully incongruous. A Jamaican kid speaking the language of Molière. In New York, she had met a Haitian and spoke French to him. "But you're Jamaican," he said. She loved it. In French class, in the midst of kids too self-conscious to open their mouths, she can overact to her heart's content. She also loves reading. Not boring school books, but romance novels, bodice-rippers, full of overblown emotions that allow her to push her own emotions even farther. Put her down at a table, she says, set a good meal in front of her or a good book, and she'll take the book every time.

Now is a good time for her, she thinks. It has been many years since her life has been so stable. She did miss most of the first two weeks of the semester, her doctor thought she might have cancer, she had an operation, but now she's fine. Life with her aunt and uncle is good. Every Sunday, she goes to church. She's a Seventh Day Adventist; very conservative, very straight, not much rollicking around there, she laughs. She likes church music especially, and, even if her mind drifts during the sermons, in the quiet she feels what she wants to feel. She takes four courses at Kennedy, another business course at a neighbouring high school Tuesday and Thursday nights from 6:30 to 10:00. It is a lot, but she likes the concreteness of the business course. She has missed three classes, in night school four absences and you're out, but she's no fool. She won't miss another.

She misses too many classes at Kennedy and is pathologically late, but now, she insists, she is serious and ambitious. She is going to "change her life." She worries at times that her past might haunt her future. She is seventeen; but only by the calendar, she says. In her mind, she's past thirty; in her body, who knows. "I've screwed up so many things," she says. "I used to sing, but not any more. I was a runner, but if you don't use it, you lose it." Not long ago, she attended a conference called "Change Your Future," organized by the new part-time counsellor at Kennedy who works with visible minority kids. The conference affected her greatly. Its speakers were all blacks – a lawyer, a businessman, a teacher – who told the one hundred or so kids present how they had made it. As she listened, she realized they weren't any smarter than she was. They talked about doing what had to be done every day, never missing, about commitment and dedication, qualities that have long been absent from her life. But that wasn't the point. Not to her. *They weren't any smarter*, they didn't talk any better, and if they could be dedicated, she could too. She could make it just like them.

She wants to be a lawyer. She thinks that, with all the experiences she's had, if somehow she can earn the degree to get her in the door, with her ambition and style, her spirit, with all the roles she's learned to play, she could really be something.

◆ ◆ ◆

For Kelly, the slide has begun. She sits one row over and one seat back of Sheri in Noel's class. Quiet, attentive, she appears immensely capable, but Kelly is missing classes again. She has mild asthma, is smart enough to pass most of the time without attending more often, and feels no need to do better. But there is something else as well, some complicated broken-home game she and her mother feel the need to play out. Kelly's father is gone, he left several years ago, Kelly is unhappy, her mother feels guilty. Everything that goes wrong is her mother's fault; everything that goes wrong makes Kelly more unhappy and eager to punish her, her mother more guilty and willing to accept punishment. Every morning, Kelly awakens with that licence in her hands: feel sad, feel mad, feel anything she wants to feel, stay home from school if she wants. And every next morning, *write me a note, Mother, say how sick I was, lie, so I won't get mad and you won't feel guilty and we won't fight – except I'll fail another course and make you feel even worse.*

After repeated absences, vice-principal Jan Coomber called Kelly's mother, and yesterday she came to see Jan. She looks very much like her daughter, except, while Kelly appears composed, her mother is on the edge. She appears several years older than she probably is.

"Were you surprised by my call?" Jan asked her, as she asks every parent who comes to see her.

"No," Kelly's mom stuttered, "not really."

It is Kelly's attendance, Jan told her, but it's more than that. "Kelly is nineteen years old," Jan said, her voice rising slightly, "and she is still taking some grade ten courses."

Jan glanced at her computer screen, and together they looked at Kelly's profile. Somewhere along the line, Kelly's train went off the tracks. She is a smart girl, all her teachers say. She can do the work; she can excel. But something happened. It doesn't matter which teacher, which course. The problem lies with Kelly, and both her mother and Jan know it.

She was always a little different, her mother related to Jan, always kept me on the fringes of her life. Even when she was younger, when we did things together, there was a part of her she wouldn't expose, wouldn't let me touch. Her mother doesn't know why, or if she does, she doesn't want to think about it. Living under the same roof, the father gone, mother and daughter inhabit separate worlds. Kelly's younger brother, who also attends Kennedy, has the same attendance problems, but he is new to the school. Like Kelly's mother, he is bothered by change; with him there seems an answer. But what about Kelly?

How much can a mother do? Kelly's mother asked Jan. She works at a day care, does volunteer work, and goes to school as well. There's only one of her. She knows there was so much more she could've done, but that time is past. Jan interrupted her and brought her back to the present. She suggested her mother have a talk with Kelly, and that perhaps Jan should too.

Kelly's mother nodded, then stammered, "Maybe it'd be better if you talk to her because I don't know what Kelly's going to say to me." She shook her head. "Probably nothing, then I'll get mad and she'll shut herself off even more, and – "

Jan interrupted her. "Kelly is nineteen," she repeated. "We've got to start looking at her situation realistically. She's *not* going to graduate. Even if everything goes right, she'd be at least twenty-one." Kelly's mother nodded. "Yes, she could go to summer school," Jan continued. "But is that the answer? That and everything else is just more of the same." She paused, then went on more softly. "You know, maybe everybody needs a change. Maybe she should get a job, go to night school, be on her own. Maybe she should be away from you." Kelly's mother nodded again. Maybe that's it. Maybe that's the answer. She will talk to Kelly, she told Jan, and Jan, of course, should talk to Kelly too. With a tiny jolt of hope, she left.

✦ ✦ ✦

Leah sits in front of Pat in Sue Lishman's Enhanced math class. For the first time in her life, she's unsure of herself. She is tall and athletically slender, with long brown hair and saucer eyes. She plays on the school's volleyball and baseball teams; she plays the piano, flute, and now the guitar. She is an honours student, and has been in gifted classes most of her school years. But she has failed the first math test, passed the second, and failed the third. Last year, she had the highest mark, higher than Reba's and Simran's, higher than Rohita's. What is happening, she wonders? She doesn't like math any more, doesn't like Mrs. Lishman.

Mr. Kozak, her last year's teacher, got everybody involved, she tells her parents. It's just not the same this year. Because she has never done poorly before, it must be Sue's fault, her parents think.

Leah missed some early classes for volleyball games, falling slightly behind, just enough that everything that had always made instant sense, the light bulb that had always gone on, didn't. She is actually so close to being where she has been every year before, only two or three good nights of homework, only one good chat with Sue, and all her scattered pieces would fit again. Instead, she · feels lost, stupid, tells herself that she can't do math, that Mrs. Lishman's a bad teacher.

She no longer knows how to behave in class. She's not used to being quiet, not used to asking questions about things every-one else knows, not good at things she doesn't like, that aren't fun. Everything had always been fun. Now everything feels like work. She misses feeling smart, surprising herself and others with her new behaviour. Now she sits at the back of the room, with Pat when he's here, asks whiny questions, interrupts, builds a barrier between herself and Sue, and every so often makes an unconvincing attempt at playing the "dumb kid" role.

What's wrong with Leah? Her parents want to know, she wants to know herself. Sue has talked to other teachers who know her. It was the trauma of breaking up with her boyfriend, some say; it's her new boyfriend, say others; it's the kids she hangs around with; it's Pat. But it isn't. More than she is acting like Pat, she is acting *out* Pat. Fall a little behind, feel more stupid than smart, lose the feeling of fun, and the rest follows. In the chicken-and-egg cycle of poor results and belligerent kids, the poor results come first.

Now more than her June mark is on the line. A few days ago, she found out she had been accepted for a student exchange to Germany. It begins next fall. She needs an 80 per cent average overall to keep her spot; much less than that in math and she won't make it. She has fifteen weeks to find the old Leah.

◆ ◆ ◆

Jody arrives early to Cathy Sylvester's science class, leaves, and comes back just after class begins with Jennifer and Tracy. Jennifer was away a few days last week. Cathy again asks for her note of admission from the office, just as she asked her yesterday and the day before. "Tomorrow, miss," she said then, and then again. But Cathy has decided that "tomorrow" is finally today.

Jennifer isn't impressed. She starts into her story: she had the note yesterday, she explains, but forgot she had it, now the note is in yesterday's jeans, at home. She is a little defensive at first as she searches for each next thought, then as her own story becomes clear to her she becomes unapologetic, even angry. Cathy says she will see her after class.

Cathy begins the class by reviewing last night's homework. She asks Tracy to read her answer to the first question. Tracy isn't listening.

"Tracy?" she repeats.

"Oh God," Tracy mumbles.

"She's asking you a question, Tracy," Nelson announces from the front of the room, a big smile on his face. Tracy's mouth hangs open. She's too stunned to send him back a piercing look; that will be for later.

"Did you do the homework?" Cathy asks.

"Um, um, I did the first question –" she blurts, then stops herself – *no, stupid, that's what she asked for* – "er, I tried it. But I, I –" then her confidence returns with a rush, "but I didn't understand it." She sits back on her stool, triumph on her face. The perfect answer. More perfect than any she could have come up with doing the homework itself. Then she might have been wrong, embarrassed, might have felt stupid, then Mrs. Sylvester and the others would know. This way, she didn't even have to spend time on it. What can be more sympathetic, what is more human, than someone who tries but doesn't understand? Others who try and do understand get all the rewards. She gets none, yet *still* she tries. There is something quite noble about her. If there is fault – and this is the best part – it is Cathy's. *I try, why can't you teach me properly?*

When she and Cathy are done, Jennifer pipes up,

"My parents say you give me too much homework. It gives me headaches."

Then Jody, her tag-team partner, right on her heels: "And they don't want to pay for headaches."

Even if Tracy, Jennifer, and Jody seem like a threesome, they are not. Tracy is the weakest, both as a student and a personality; she depends on the other two. Jennifer is doing poorly but hasn't yet given up. Her mind is still often in the room, her headaches perhaps a symptom of anxiety about her results. Last week, doing an experiment on conductivity and convection currents, she even raised her hand, "Miss, did you know that if you've been smoking, if you light a match in the smoke, the smoke will disappear?" Applied science Jennifer has applied many times. Then there's Jody. She never misses a day, does well on labs and tests, and, though her questions are often graceless and inappropriate, she *does* ask them, she *is* listening. She is the strong one. No matter what else is going on in that back corner, she has one eye and one ear focused on the front. She can handle disruptiveness and still do well. She has ambition; she has standards. Tracy and Jennifer may be her friends, but she will not let them get in her way.

Lately, Nelson has sometimes been in that back corner too. It began with a lab the class was working on. Jennifer and Tracy were there, but Jennifer was working with her deskmate, Jody, so Tracy couldn't move back to fill her spot. That left Tracy by herself, and at the front of the room, also by himself, Nelson. It was the opening he was looking for. Maybe Tracy could use some help, he suggested, so he brought back his lab equipment. Maybe they all could use some help. The day was a triumph. But afterwards, only Jennifer *or* Tracy would be away, or both of them, and Jody doesn't really need help, so Nelson had been stuck at the front of the room. Then one day Jody announced to Cathy that she was cold.

Cathy moved to turn up the heat. "Miss, I'm hot," Nelson said.

The room stopped. Nelson smiled, "Jody, would you like to wear my jacket?" With the class as their audience, Jody smiled, "Yes, thank you." Nelson walked to the back and draped his shiny New York Yankees' jacket over her shoulders.

"That was very chivalrous," Cathy smiled. Nelson smiled back, then looked puzzled. "What's 'chivalrous,' miss?" One of the other kids told him. Nelson beamed.

The next day, they were to do another lab. The girls' equipment wasn't working. Nelson noticed it before they did. He walked to the back with his.

"What are you doing, Nelson?" Cathy asked.

"It's chivalry, miss," and beamed again.

Last week, before he had even the chance, a voice sung out from the back of the room, "Nel-son, do you want to come back here?" It was Jennifer's siren call. He was back in a shot. And so long as they are working on a lab, focusing on something outside themselves, everything is fine. Otherwise, Nelson gets too excited, and already on an emotional precipice, he goes over. Several times lately, Cathy has had to move him back:

"Nelson, I think you'd better come back to the front."

"Why, miss?"

"I think the girls are distracting you."

"No, they're not, miss."

"I think you should still come back."

"Aw, miss." Head down, body slumped, he would trudge back to the front.

Now their routine is shorter:

"Nelson."

"Aw, miss."

◆ ◆ ◆

Maria Cheung is checking homework. She starts down the aisle nearest the side board, several kids in the rows ahead race to keep ahead of her, Sophia does not.

"Where's your homework?" Maria asks.

"I don't do it, miss."

Maria scowls and writes an "X" beside Sophia's name in her book.

Fighting her guilt, but not very hard, Sophia smiles, "Aw, miss, I do it tomorrow."

Sophia has had an up and down ride since her arrival from Belgrade four months ago. So bright, so lively, so likeable, so energetic, initially she seemed a model student. In class every day, on time, ready, and from the moment a teacher opened his mouth until his last word, she stayed with him. For Sophia, the rest of the kids seemed not to exist. In math, it was just her and Maria. Every question Maria asked seemed a question for her; as other hands went up, she answered. When Maria worked step by step through a question on the board, Sophia at her desk worked through it with her. The x's and y's of one line, played with, manipulated into a slightly different arrangement of x's and y's on the next. "Ohmygawd," Sophia would say aloud as she began to see the picture change. Still more on the next line. "Ohmygawd," she'd repeat, more of the marble chipped away. And when the image of the answer finally became clear, one more time "Ohhmyygawwdd!" No one portrayed the joy of learning better.

Sophia's experience is like that of so many immigrants. The first few weeks, everything so new, so different, so impossible to cope with – then suddenly, impossibly, you realize you *can* cope with it. The immense sense of excitement, relief, achievement. I *can* make it here. I'm going to be okay. Except when the straight-and-narrow of survival seems no longer in doubt, what then? Life becomes more than just algebra. Now Sophia sometimes comes late and doesn't do her homework. She is letting her fingernails grow. Last week, in the midst of her sickness – "I think I going to die, miss" – she arrived one day with a light blue cloth tied stylishly around her neck. Like a scarf, she thought; like a cold compress, it seemed. She has joined the drama department's production as stage manager. Cast members call her "the dragon lady." In class, she has begun to negotiate like everyone else – "Miss, miss, you can't have test today. I have drama. I get home only twelve o'clock in night. I don't study." She has a boyfriend, though he doesn't know it yet. "He's real cute," she told her drama class. Recently, she and her mother moved out of her aunt's apartment into an apartment of their own. They spent one weekend just buying furniture. "It was ghhrrreat," she told the kids.

She is getting louder and more aggressive in class. She answers every question, or tries to, putting everyone else immediately out of the game except for two or three who have become louder and more aggressive to compete. There are now mutterings around her, " 'Sorry, miss,' " the kids echo, when Maria corrects another of her too-exuberant blurts; " 'Miss, miss,' " Nelson mocks, as again Sophia clamours for Maria's attention. "If *you* ask, maybe *you* do better," Sophia snaps back. She is discovering a whole new world. Teachers who talk to kids, who smile, who act like friends. So she treats them like friends, sometimes doing what they ask her to do, sometimes not. School was never like that in Belgrade. She'd to work so hard to reach the road that led to medical school; there was so much competition, school had to be the focus of her life. Her dream hasn't changed, but her country has, and now she has discovered different roads – for brief excursions, for lifetime detours, who knows? Of all the priorities in her life, math is now near the bottom. She is able to write a whole new story for herself – what will it be?

Chapter 6

Monday, March 7, 12:45 p.m.

Dave Sands, head of the history department, walks into the euchre room shaking his head. It is lunch time.

"Hey, Sandman, what's wrong?"

He has just come from an Attendance Team meeting. "Things have really gotten bad," he mutters. "Last semester, we thought we had it under control. I don't know what's happened." The players shake their heads, their eyes never leaving the cards.

The Team has decided to try something different. Skipping classes is so prevalent that it has come to seem as if everybody's doing it all the time, but the problem rests mainly with a core of twenty to twenty-five chronic skippers, kids who have learned how to play the system and are winning. Skip a class, get a detention; skip a detention, get two; skip them, a detention with a vice-principal; skip that and a few more, a suspension. By then, much of the semester has gone and so has everyone's patience. A class moves quickly, a curriculum must be covered, the students need to be here to learn all they are supposed to learn. To learn that they can't always do what they want to do. They will have to face that reality all their lives, with other adults who *have* learned, who will be much less patient than teachers and administrators.

But some kids don't care about any of that, and the system can't seem to make them care. They don't play by the rules. They aren't embarrassed, ashamed, they don't feel the disappointment of a lower grade, the humiliation of failure. To a kid who's been hit with uppercuts all his life, here's a detention, teachers say. *Slap slap*, take that! Who are teachers kidding? And always staring back at them, a face that says *make me*.

The system's bluff has been called. Kids don't care that teachers are older than they are, that they stand at the front of the room in a suit and tie (though probably they don't). They've grown up with adults who don't want formality and distance, who want to be friends, so kids treat them like friends. They've learned to have separate lives from those of adults. Adults have learned to have lives separate from them. Kids have their own rooms, their own TVs, computers, and phones. They have part-time jobs, their own money, their own friends. They've learned to go their own way. They come to school, their teachers look like their parents: why should they treat them any differently? Why would teachers, whose own kids don't treat them differently, think that they would? These kids have never learned how to defer to authority. Like a friend, they'll spend time with you if they want to spend time with you. They'll respect you if you earn their respect, not because they're supposed to, not because you are called "adult" or "teacher." Like a friend, you have to earn that respect every day. If you do, your relationship will work fine. It will be better than it has ever been, in fact. But if you don't, if you're not trained right, or it isn't in you, or them, the result will be hell.

Today teachers need to explain their rules and values, and never having asked that of their own teachers and parents, many have never learned how. *Be in class, don't be late, do your homework*:

kids want to know *why*. If they're smart enough to pass, to do well enough to get into some college or university, *why* do they need to be here every day? If it takes them longer to graduate, so what? There are no jobs anyway. Everyone knows a guy with a PH.D. pumping gas. *Why* do I need to go to university? kids ask. *Why* do I need to come to class?

Because *I* told you so, teachers say. That's not good enough, kids reply.

"You gotta kick 'em out," Brian Fink, a math teacher, says to Dave Sands and the others. "If they don't want to be here, let 'em go. See ya next semester. Give 'em a reason to want to come back."

Dave Arthurs nods. "They need us. School is their social group."

"But you can't kick 'em out," ET snarls, and the others nod. "You can't." Most of the time the law won't let you, or the system won't. "Whether you should or shouldn't doesn't matter. You can't."

The Sandman shakes his head. "What we can't get any handle on is lates. It's hopeless, out of control." He chuckles. "I used to give my classes 'Being There' tests. When things got really bad, I'd say, 'Okay, we're gonna have a test,' just as class began. 'John A. Macdonald was Canada's first prime minister, true or false?' Five questions, just so those who *were* there got some reward. So the others paid a price."

Dave Arthurs nods. "Yeah, I thought we should've done something a couple of weeks ago during the snowstorm, for those kids who *were* here."

"You didn't buy 'em donuts, Davey?"

"I, I —" Dave stammers, "— when I start breakin' even, then I'll buy."

This time eyes look up from the cards. So many possible responses. "Davey," the Sandman laughs, "life expectancies haven't exactly hit a million."

Earlier in the year, the Scarborough Board of Education in Metro Toronto's east end implemented a "zero tolerance" policy for students who carry weapons or commit violent acts at school. Since then, two students have been expelled for life. A few days ago, the Minister of Education announced a plan of his own, requiring school boards to enact anti-violence programs within eighteen months. Violent incidents are occurring in schools; whether they are more frequent, more violent, or only more frequently reported, doesn't matter. They *seem* more common.

Kids are different today, adults say, even my own kids, plus all these other kids with different colour skin, different clothes, speaking different languages, from different cultures. We can't even pretend to know what's going on in their minds. So many are here because of wars in their own countries. What horrors have they seen, with what damage to their psyches? At the moment of showdown, embarrassment, challenge, when face is at risk, what will they do? And in a high school, face is always at risk. The whole place is a tinderbox. Fifteen hundred high-strung adolescents jammed in together. Trouble never more than one wrong look away. Outside school, put these kids together six and a half hours a day, day after day, and the fights would never stop.

Violence could happen here, kids believe that, and teachers, parents, media, and politicians believe it, too. *If he's got fists better than mine, I need a knife better than his* – and the arms-race logic gathers its momentum. Weapons real or imagined, it doesn't matter. An incident across the city or next door, it doesn't matter. The hint of violence once in the air won't be washed away. Asked if they feel safe, kids and teachers, almost all of them, say yes. Reading the government's new anti-violence policy, one teacher remarked, "Hell, the worst incident of violence I've seen in this school is Dave Arthurs at the euchre table." Yet now in a classroom, when teacher confronts student and student holds his ground, teacher doesn't push the issue as once she might have.

What's inside the kid's pockets, under his hat or turban, in his heart? She doesn't know.

Every day, as classes begin, during each lunch period, and when classes end, Principal Terry Chaffe patrols the school: "Keep moving. Don't you have some place to go?" He looks under stairwells, goes where kids – most probably intruders – might convene unseen. He wanders the parking lot, looking for kids sitting in cars, for a face that doesn't belong. About 3:30, he goes to his captain's perch, the classroom on the second floor where Sue Lishman teaches her double grade-nine math. From there, he scans the parking lot, the sidewalks, waiting, watching until only the stragglers remain. Nearly everything else that can go wrong, he can make right again. His fear, everybody's fear, is that one big incident that has never happened, but might.

Yet while the media's attention is focused on violence, the key discipline question in every school is "skips" and "lates," the petty stuff that affects the learning of every kid in every classroom every day. How do you stop it? You can't throw everybody in jail who litters or runs red lights. The bluff has been called. *Make me.*

Everyone shall have the right to, and the obligation of, education, the mind of an enlightened people says, to make better, more prosperous citizens. Everyone shall have equal opportunity, the mind of a democratic people says, so up to seven years of high school education is guaranteed to all. Everyone can learn, the mind of a scientific people says, so everyone must graduate from high school. Everyone must graduate from high school, the mind of an affluent, economic people says, so we can compete around the world. The system must be made to work, the mind of the taxpayer says, because these are my children and I have paid my share; because, the mind of the politician says, the system is in my hands and the system must work.

Then one little voice says, No, I'm not interested. I don't want to be here. I don't care if I am late. If I need more than seven years to graduate, so be it. If I don't graduate at all, so be that too. I don't care if education is my obligation as well as my right. I don't care if my country needs me to learn to compete around the world; if my parents think I should; if by dropping out I cost teachers their jobs, and politicians theirs. You have your grand scheme, but I want to do what I want to do.

But you must care, the system says. The system needs you to care. It only works if you do. If you don't, the system will have to care for itself. It won't change its democratic, scientific, economic, and political mind, so you must *seem* to change yours. A "late" leads to detentions, to detentions skipped, to meetings, to suspensions, which lead to more time lost in a short semester, to failure, to loss of self-esteem, to dropping out, to not graduating, to parental anger, to political pressure – *stop!* The system can't permit that. Then *it* has failed. So even if your crimes escalate, your punishments, after a certain point, will not and cannot. The system must only appear to clog, nothing more. The problem must appear technical. Adopt a new procedure, create an Attendance Team, and the problem is solved. But the problem isn't technical.

The Team has a new approach, Dave Sands tells everyone. There are now two tiers of offenders, the chronic and the rest. Maximum and minimum security. For the chronic, skip a detention and it's straight to the vice-principal. There isn't one person here who thinks it is the answer.

There is something so demoralizing to teachers about skips and lates. From the kids, a message that says: I don't care. From the system that tolerates them: I don't care if you learn. Yet teachers are supposed to jump in with both feet to make these kids learn. For teachers, the issue has become symbolic. You – kids, parents, administrators – have got to give me a reason to make that commitment. You try; I try. You give; I give. You care; I care. Make me? Make *me*.

The worst days for skips and lates are Mondays and Fridays; first period and last period, and right after lunch. Most kids eat in the Caf, many eat in the glut of neighbouring restaurants, where time flies by, and where, in the company of the like-minded, courage to skip comes easy. No more so than at Mickey's, a converted bowling alley just a few hundred metres from the school. Years ago, it was owned by Mickey's parents, and when Mickey got day passes from prison, he'd help out. Outside, its sign now reads, "The Arcade," but to everyone who goes there it is still Mickey's.

The building is long and narrow, dark and smoky, the front filled with video games and Foosball tables, the back with pool tables, everywhere loud with kids and music, especially during the first lunch period. Pat comes here every day he's at school. He stops first at the Italian place next door for a slice of pizza and a Diet Coke, rarely bothering to sit down, then breezes through a side door into Mickey's, greeting his buddies as he goes. It is his respite from the rest of the day. From too many people telling him how smart he is, how he could do so much better, how he is throwing away the chance he's been given. On aptitude tests, in math contests, where attendance and homework offer little advantage, where everyone starts even, he tests at the top. Truly gifted. At school, at home, he is a disappointment. Whatever good he does is what he could have done all along. The rest is head-shakes, rolled eyes, criticism.

Why don't they just get off my back? Maybe I don't want to do better, maybe I never asked for this chance, maybe I don't like being smart. You have to work to be smart. There's always something to live up to, an obligation to do something with the smartness. An obligation to somebody else. Who needs that? But at Mickey's, I don't have to be nothin' to nobody. And here, if smart counts, I'm smarter than anybody.

But the teachers won't give up on Pat. He is the perfect candidate for help. He can do the work and everybody notices him. It's just a matter of his finally seeing the light and of one of them helping him see it. What a feather in both their caps. But the teachers don't understand. At this moment in his life, Pat just wants to slide. He doesn't *want* to do well. Most of his school life he's been in Enhanced classes. Last year, he was in the full program; last semester, he dropped Enhanced history and science, this semester English. He has only math left and he tried to drop that too, but his counsellor stopped him. Doing well has become a prison, and he wants out.

It used to be easy being smart. He just had to go to school most of the time. He could be lazy, late; he could skip, do none of his work, choose his own friends, do whatever he wanted, be whatever he wanted to be, and still be smart. Smart on his terms. Now smart means staying home at nights. It takes time, takes wanting to be smart, caring about being smart, worrying, risking, the pain of failing never far away. Being smart on *their* terms. And he doesn't even know if he can pull off smart any longer. For him, the answer was always just there. He had lived enough, done enough things, had enough common sense and whatever else he was born with, he just knew. Now sometimes he doesn't. The teachers think he can still do it, but they just see a kid who has the brain to do better. Smart is more than just having a brain, it's habits, it's the attitude of learning. He doesn't have those, and he's so far from having them now he can't even imagine them. Sleeping in when he wants, going out with his friends wherever and whenever: that's him. A lot more him than the need to be smart. He'd have to change so much about himself, he'd have to be somebody else.

To live up to the burdens of doing well, he'd have to feel his life under some control, have to sense that, if he does all he can, he won't be cut off at the knees by someone else. But where would this sense of control come from? Not from home: his parents split up long ago; he used to live with his mom, until she kicked him out. Now he and his little brother, "the smart one in the family," he calls him, live with his dad, though that isn't working either. His older half-brother, who went to Kennedy off and on for years, until finally he left last semester, is still with his mom, but not for much longer. In a few days, he's going to jail, on drugs and weapons charges – fifteen months. With good behaviour, he can be out in five.

Not from inside himself either. Every school is filled with stories like Pat's, many much worse. Stories that on paper seem to lay out an irresistible destiny. Yet some teachers bleed too much for hard-luck kids like these. They come to know the details of a kid's story and imagine the rest, but not knowing the kid and never having lived a life like his, they imagine wrong. Details aren't destiny. These kids may be abused or ignored at home, but there is so much more to them. They want desperately to escape that existence for another. That's why they come to school. They don't need teachers to smother them with sympathy, satisfying their own need to wallow in another's tragedy. Help me, these kids say, really help me, give me a chance to be someone else, someone who is going to make it. If you feel too much for the abused, ignored me, you give us both a crutch, and we'll both use it. Knowing we can fail, we both will. So, many of these kids take control themselves.

Albert sits two rows over from Pat in Sue Lishman's class. He is from Hong Kong. A few years ago, he came to Canada with his father, mother, and younger sister. His father worked as a civil engineer in Hong Kong, doing soil studies mostly, but to do the same work in Canada he needed experience in Canada that no one would give him. After working for some time as an insurance salesman, he returned to Hong Kong a year ago. Albert hasn't seen him for months. Five weeks ago, Albert's mom was diagnosed with breast cancer. She has finished her first round of radiation treatments and is waiting for the next. Albert, an honours student in the Enhanced class, quiet, who still speaks heavily accented English, hasn't missed a day of school this semester.

Pauline is one of the island of newcomers who sit at the front in Noel Lim's class. Her journey to Canada began in Vietnam more than two years ago. Her parents had been planning her escape for months. Finally one night, they brought her to her uncle's and said goodbye. The children were given "sleeping drugs" to keep them from making noise; she climbed into one of the five small boats, and with thirteen others set off. They sailed through the noisy silence of the night, on and on until they came to a bigger boat. They jumped quickly aboard, some of the children awakening from their soundless sleep, and set off again, seventy-two of them. By the next afternoon, they had reached the international waters of the South China Sea, and a landless horizon. For two days, nothing changed. Then the wind started to blow; the waves rose higher and higher. With each wave, she remembers, it was like rising to the top of a mountain, then falling into a deep valley on the other side. The boat's engine stopped; then started again. With no room to lie down, Pauline just sat and tried to sleep.

In the middle of the night, the boat began to shake, so hard it seemed about to explode. Water poured over the sides. The storm continued through the third day, and the fourth. Then it stopped. That night, they saw a light, evidence of the land they hadn't seen for days. Fearful this was a "robber's land," the men formed into a circle, huddling the women inside. It turned out to be Malaysia. The next day, the police rounded up Pauline and the others and brought them to a refugee camp. Her parents, a brother, and a sister still live in Vietnam. She and two older sisters live in Mississauga with a guardian. She speaks poor English and her writing is not much better. Yet every night she works at it. She had a 76 per cent average the first semester.

Why Pauline and Albert, and why not Pat? It could be Pat. He might wake up tomorrow and say, I don't care what's gone before. I'm going to do all I seem capable of, and more. No one is going to drag me down. It could happen, but it won't, at least not now. It's hard to do, so it's too hard for most, and he is used only to easy. Going home when he wants, doing homework if he wants, meeting at the donut shop at eight with Willy, Chad, and the rest of the "group," hanging around, going to someone's house for a party, in summer to the park. Then at 11:30 or midnight, drifting home. No hassles. At home, he's surrounded by fatigue and guilt, sometimes his mother's, sometimes his father's, everywhere else people know his brother and nobody messes with him. It's not a bad life all in all, if people would only let him live it. Instead, they keep wanting him to be something *they* want him to be, and he'll have none of it. He knows about expectations. He's had some of his own about the people in his life, and they let him down. And he hurt. He's not going to let the same happen to him. Any expectations others have of him, he'll fight, smash, until they write him off, forget him, ignore him, never count on him for anything. He will put himself beneath expectation. He will be whatever others insist he isn't.

With him at Mickey's are Willy, Chad, Leah, and Donald. Willy is transformed, his classroom edginess is gone. He plays doubles Foosball with Pat and two others. Pat is pretty good, Willy much better. At every opportunity, Willy whips the handles around, ripping the ball faster than sight. He wrestles playfully with Leah. "You used to be so short," he laughs, sidling up beside her, crouching down to where she used to be beside him. She laughs too. Here no one shouts at him, ignores him, feels sorry for him. Here, he's just Willy, a good guy. Everybody needs a place. For the good students, it's the classroom. For Willy, Pat, and scores more every lunch period, it's Mickey's. At video games, Foosball, and pool, they're the ones who are in command, in control. So they come every day and stay from the beginning of lunch until the end, and leave not a minute before. Five minutes to walk back, to their lockers for books and then into class, ten minutes late; but not officially late. Except those times when Mickey's feels too good, when what faces them ahead in class seems too much, and, "screw it," they decide to stay. Terry and the vice-principals have talked of speaking with the proprietor of Mickey's, to get his cooperation in getting kids back to class on time, even joking about installing a school bell there, but they never have. They talk to other merchants, but Mickey's seems too out of bounds for them. Not one teacher has ever set foot inside Mickey's, seen Pat and Willy as they are here. Mickey's to them is what the staff room is to students. A place that belongs to someone else.

◆ ◆ ◆

The Caf looks full. At one end is a stage, at the other the kitchen and a self-serve cafeteria line. Big tables with benches attached, like portable picnic tables, lie end to end in eight rows. A quick glance, and it looks just like a roomful of kids. Look a little longer and a pattern emerges. Look longer still, and maybe something else.

For many years, the Italians sat in one corner of the room, the rest of the white kids in the other. That pattern began to change in the 1970s, now every hint of it is gone. The black kids, mostly Jamaican, take up about half the first row just inside the door at the kitchen end. James, Nelson, Marv, Rodney, Sheri, Lydia, eating, playing dominoes or cards, the most visible and audible group in the room. A few empty spaces, a scattering of kids, then the Muslim girls in their *hijab*, isolated and apart near the stage. In the next few rows, small discrete clusters of Asian kids, the Hong Kong Chinese with their books out doing homework, the Vietnamese eating or playing a card game they call "Assho." A few white kids also playing cards, some from Cathy's science class, Rob and Doug; many of the girls from the grade ten Enhanced class, Simran, Rohita; groups of Indian kids, kids from Vietnam and Hong Kong, from Guyana and Trinidad, from Africa,

Fahad and his friends among them. Everyone sitting tellingly where the unconscious puts them, where the conscious keeps them. For these kids know. This is my spot, that is theirs. The first day of semester is chaos. Hundreds of newcomers to the school, squatting where they have no right to be. But not for long.

Fahad seems entirely at home in the Caf. In another of his clean, bright, Madras plaid, short-sleeve shirts, though winter is far from over, talking, laughing, working, whatever strikes him, whatever the moment calls for. Yet he came to Canada from Kenya less than a year ago. His parents have at home records of their family tree, which dates back 1,400 years to the time of the prophet Mohammed. They lived in Arabia at the time, and as the Islamic Empire spread, the family moved with it, as far as India, near Bombay. His family, generation after generation, were farmers. Then around the beginning of this century, Bombay grew rapidly and the large farms surrounding it were broken up. The family moved away; some to Mauritius, some to South Africa, some to England, all to some part of the British Empire, which seemed their birthright. Fahad's great grandfather, on his way to join up with family members in Mauritius, took a ship from Bombay to Mombasa, Kenya, then missed his connecting ship. By the time another came along, he had already begun to settle in Kenya. There were few cities then, very little of anything in the interior except at crossroads and stops along the railway the British had built. His grandfather began what would become a family business, establishing general stores along these routes. He would travel to the coast to buy his goods, then bring them to his stores and out into the bush to sell. Years passed. Children were born who needed schooling, so mothers and children began moving from these outposts, to settle in the cities. Fahad's family chose Kenya's capital, Nairobi.

His father was an electrical contractor, working primarily on big buildings and hydroelectric dam sites, so busy he had to turn down much of the business that came to him. His mother was a travel agent. But in the 1980s, things started to change. International agencies and western governments decided to tie aid to democratization. Under pressure, Kenya began devolving from one-party rule. With a single governing party no longer a possibility, tribes came to create their own parties, scores of them. Differences became externalized, more passionate, more public. Blacks turned against Indians. Violence and corruption escalated. The university, with its own peculiar stresses, shut down. Fahad's father could no longer not see what was coming. His sons might reach university age and have no university to attend. Educated people with the wrong colour skin might have no jobs. Borders were being closed. The ties of empire were frayed, England would no longer take them in; India, a part of their distant past, was too crowded. They decided on Canada.

Fahad remembers his feelings when they first arrived. Everything so big, the buildings, the highways six lanes wide, the space! Relatives drove them north of Toronto to their place on Lake Simcoe, mile after mile of space. Yet, instead of feeling liberated by the expanse, he felt strangely constricted. The buildings so high, they took away his sky; the roads took away his ground. The houses, the malls, and the parking lots stole his beloved bush. He had only to go two or three miles from Nairobi and there wasn't a soul, no evidence that anyone had ever even walked the ground. In the midst of the African savannah, under a boundless sky, a speck in space and time, he felt in the presence of greatness. Not greatness that made him feel irrelevant, but which inspired him, made him feel big, made him want to do great deeds. To pay homage to the gift of that greatness by making it greater still. But here he feels cut off. All that greatness paved over, built up, it's so much harder to feel the presence of God. He can feel his imagination shrink.

He'll get used to it, he supposes. There is so much to like about Canada. It has given his family a chance when they had none. Here, there is a future, his father decided, so here they moved. He does like it. He will like it. But some of what he will get used to, he doesn't want to get used to.

His father is now an electrician, on his own, though here he works small projects, houses mostly, and while in Kenya everyone sought him out, he must now do the seeking. He is busy, but he can do so much more, yet no one knows that here, which upsets him at times. Fahad's mother is looking for a job, his younger brother is settled into elementary school, as Fahad is at Kennedy. What he had known about Canada had come from school and CNN. When he arrived, he was so afraid of sticking out. This Indian Muslim boy from Kenya in the land of ice and snow, he was sure he'd be the only one. The diversity of Mississauga and Toronto stunned him; Kennedy stunned him more.

The fast of Ramadan, which began nearly a month ago with the new moon, is now nearly over. Fahad and his family have been getting up at 4:30 every morning. Before sunrise, they eat chapatis, then fast through the day until sunset, when they break the fast with dates and an evening meal. Many religious activities, more time reading the Koran, have added to Fahad's already full days. On Sunday, when the nearly invisible sliver of the harvest moon is likely to appear, and Ramadan ends, there will be feasts of celebration, and far from feeling tired or hungry, "I will feel like a new man," he says.

When asked, he says he doesn't know yet what he wants to do in his life. Then a tiny smile creeps onto his lips. "I want to do great things," he says. He looks around at the land and sky and wonders why we would be put on this earth if not to do great things. To make things better. To be remembered like Einstein. Einstein is known everywhere, he says. In the middle of that African savannah, in the middle of Mississauga. Years from now, his name will still be known. Why not try to be like Einstein? he asks.

Sabesan doesn't think about Einstein, or indeed about much of anything. He is too busy. He sits where he always sits, in the far row of the Caf near the window, with a group of his Sri Lankan friends, here, as in the classroom, with the calm, composed face of someone who knows, with the bright eyes and trace of a smile of someone who is always just ahead of you. Yet in Maria Cheung's math and Cathy Sylvester's science classes, he is doing poorly. Cathy and Maria are not sure why. He speaks good English, reads well, grasps the concepts of math, there seems no reason why he can't do better. He must be lazy, they think. When Maria checks homework and again his isn't done, he gives no explanation, just a slightly bigger smile and a mumble of words she takes to mean he'll do better tomorrow. But tomorrow is rarely different. Lately, as Maria has pressed him, when she offered him a tutor, a senior student, after school, Sabesan has mentioned a job. "I can't do it, miss," he says. "I've got a job." But when tutors are mentioned, and especially when detentions are given, everybody's got a job, so she's not sure.

Sabesan and his family left Sri Lanka when the civil war began in 1983. His father, a sailor on an oil tanker, had travelled all over the world and decided Germany would be best for his family. They moved to Hamburg and lived there five years. Then five years ago, they decided Canada would be better. His father was born with one shortened leg, which now gives him trouble and prevents him from working. His mother works as a housekeeping maid at Stage West, a hotel and dinner theatre in Mississauga. Sabesan also works there, as a busboy, from 4:30 to 9:30 p.m., Monday through Thursday, and from 5:00 to 10:00 p.m. Friday; all day Saturday and Sunday from 9:00 to 6:00. Forty-three hours a week on the job doesn't leave much time or energy for homework. He doesn't quite tell his teachers how much he works, nor do they quite know, nor do they know if his parents appreciate the consequences of their decision to allow him to work these hours.

Perhaps half the kids in the Caf have part-time jobs, and many more would have them if the recession hadn't hit so hard. The part-time job may be the single biggest change in the life of teenagers since the time their teachers were young. Except for paper routes and babysitting, almost none of them had outside jobs. When public education became universal about a century ago, most kids had chores to do around the house, the farm, or in the family business. But only a handful went to school for more than a few years, so the collision of increased homework in higher grades and family responsibilities rarely happened. This century, families moved from farms to cities, household appliances cut time needed for chores, education became more important to futures, so more kids stayed in school longer. For decades, there was no conflict between studies and paid work. Any money earned outside the home was handed over to the parents for the family's shared benefit. A kid had no money of his own, and there was little for him to buy. The teenager as consumer had yet to be invented.

By the late 1940s, after years of depression and war, the North American economy was burgeoning. There was money to make, and money to spend. Families that had been put on hold were rapidly taking shape. More people got married, more kids were born, "baby boomers" as they would be called. More houses were built, suburbs grew, more cars were sold. A larger family bounty meant larger allowances for kids, finally money of their own to spend. Teenagers became a separate group with its own identity. It was money that did it. Blue jeans and white T-shirts gave teenagers a look; rock and roll music, a sound; jalopies, the residue of those millions of new cars, gave them independence. An allowance was no longer enough: the part-time job at the local supermarket or gas station was necessary to afford all the stuff manufacturers provided for teenagers to buy. But there weren't enough supermarkets or gas stations. The real revolution came with fast food restaurants, and the explosion of the service sector.

Hamburgers at 59 cents or 49 cents: with pressure on prices, there was also pressure on wages. People were exchanged for machines and process, higher-priced people exchanged for lower. And who were they? In the growing economy of the sixties and seventies, the only adults available were the long-term unemployed or new immigrants who spoke little English – both second choices for many employers. Why not hire instead the bright-eyed teenaged sons and daughters of neighbours and friends, with their "go get 'em" energy? That made sense to employers; it made sense to kids and their parents. A part-time job would give kids a dose of responsibility, an appreciation of what they have, make them learn that in this life they have to work for what they get. That's how it had been for families earlier in the century, thought their parents, memories of their own parents' era frozen and idealized in their adult minds. Those families had worked together and stayed together. Even if work today took family members into different places, it still represented an important shared experience.

A part-time job gave kids the chance to experience the discipline of work. Kids can ignore parents and finesse teachers, but this was a boss, unimpeded by affection or statute, who had no obligation to put up with them. These kids had to produce or they would be fired. It was a chance to work beside older people, to learn from them and about them; to learn some practical skills they could take with them into some future workplace. Far better than the fun and games of clubs and sports whose lessons, so indirect, seemed nearly invisible. A job was the direct route to maturity. It was also another way to keep kids busy, off increasingly mean streets. For those who might drop out, it was a few hours a week in a workplace that held no bad memories, earning money for some of the freedom and independence they craved, perhaps helping to keep them in school longer.

But if part-time jobs have achieved some of their goals, their

unintended effect has been more significant. Some work disci-
plines are learned on the job, some skills too, though many fewer
than parents would like to think. For kids, most work time is
spent not in the company of older workers, but with kids like
themselves. It is from the money that kids have taken their greatest lessons. Money that doesn't go into a family pot. *I worked for
it, it's mine*, kids today say. Though in the last fifteen years family
incomes have struggled to keep up with inflation, "designer"
tastes and expectations have taken hold among teens in part
because of this additional pocket of income. A kid wants new
Doc Martens and Birkenstocks. His parents refuse to buy them.
They're too expensive, they say; but crumbling under his relentless pressure, they agree to a bargain. We'll give you the money
it costs for the entirely adequate no-name clothes and running
shoes we always bought you, and you can buy what you want,
using your own money to pay the difference. So the kid works
and buys the coveted item, and feels the sense of achievement and
success that comes from having bought it himself. But he hasn't
really bought it himself. And now he has designer tastes, designer
standards of success and achievement to take into the future,
where soon he'll have to pay the entire price for these tastes, as
well as for his own shelter, his own food, and so on and so on.
More than anything, part-time jobs have created a false standard
of living and a false sense of independence among teens. They
have helped to generate the destructive impatience kids feel
when, out of school, unable to find immediately the job they
want at the salary they want, they complain, "There are no jobs
out there," and feel the weight of personal failure and disappointment.

Sabesan is only an exaggerated example of the effect of
student employment in schools. Teachers, administrators, the
whole education system, have become intimidated by part-time
jobs. Teachers still remember the myths, the selflessness and

discipline a kid's job used to mean. They know that in the context of a family's survival homework may seem a low priority. But what happens to school standards? If a few kids don't do their homework, the authority and confidence of the teacher, the power of the group, shame these kids back onto the straight and narrow. If a few more don't, the teacher's weapons shrink rapidly. A teacher gets tired of fighting, of nagging and criticizing, of excuse-spewing, unhappy kids, so he eases off, gives less homework, checks it less often, marks easier. He adapts. The kids get better grades, they are happier. Their parents are relieved that they don't have to hassle their kids about homework or grades.

Teachers, parents, kids: they have all made choices, but at what price?

Selva doesn't sit with Sabesan or the other Sri Lankan kids in the Caf. Usually, he doesn't eat here at all, preferring to go to Chicken Land and play Foosball with Philip and Imran, who are also in Sue Lishman's Enhanced math. But today, the three of them are here. Selva is in the midst of an adolescent's uneven growth. His body not yet taller or wider, his ears and nose already adult size, he looks like Topo Gigio.

Selva was born in Canada, in Mississauga, as were his older sister and younger brother. His father came here from Sri Lanka in 1971, went back to marry Selva's mother, then they both returned. He came many years before the civil war, when with so few of his countrymen here he could make Canadians feel about Sri Lankans what they felt about him. Now he is what *they* are and that bothers him, and it bothers Selva even more. Selva won't even read the *Toronto Star*. Every murderer is dark-skinned, every dark skin is Sri Lankan, every Sri Lankan is him. Then he shrugs his "what can you do about it" shrug.

With his smoky, deep brown, unmistakably Sri Lankan skin, Canadians see in Selva someone who doesn't look like them, and assume. They stay away from the dark unknown he represents, go the other way, or ask him where he's from. Not long ago, he realized that would never change. He has played the game as well as any Canadian could want: his parents, both working, both tax-payers, not burdens of the welfare system, he and his sister both honours students in Enhanced classes. He's in the choir at school, plays basketball on Saturdays, his greatest passion is hockey. Yet asked if he feels Canadian, he pauses and says politely, "No."

He lives about three hundred metres from the school. Ten minutes after classes end, he is home having a snack; by 3:45, stick in hand, he's out at the end of his street playing ball hockey. His street is a cul-de-sac, with a big turning circle at the end, big enough for baseball in spring and summer, hockey in the fall and winter. Several Poles are amongst his group, a Sri Lankan, a few kids who play on real hockey teams. Sometimes his street plays against other streets, a clash of styles, for Selva's group plays a little rougher than the others, but after a few complaints, they always find common ground. He plays every position but goalie. Usually, he's a small darting forward, who prefers to set up goals than to score them himself. Above all, as he puts it, he hates to lose. "Winning makes me feel better," he says.

A year and a half ago at Christmas, Selva travelled to Sri Lanka for the second time in his life. He went with his mother and sister; his father, having to work, stayed home. Selva is a Tamil, as are all but one of the twenty-five or so Sri Lankans at Kennedy. A minority of less than 20 per cent of the island's pop-ulation, Tamils have historically held a disproportionate per-centage of civil service jobs and spaces at universities. Beginning in 1956, the majority Sinhalese started to right the imbalance. The fight has been going on ever since, constitutionally at first, now in a vicious civil war.

Selva expected to find a beautiful island of sun and water, palm trees, rich forests and mountains, but one that was poor, under-developed, and unsophisticated, that had nothing to do with his existence in Mississauga. He was shocked. Sri Lanka wasn't backward at all, nor was it even that much different, he found. He liked it. When the family returned home, he asked his father if they would ever move back to Sri Lanka. His father said no.

Selva feels a closeness to Sri Lanka now. He shares some of the rebelling Tamils' passions; he admires, almost envies, their discipline, their courage, but the civil war they are fighting isn't his war, he insists. He hasn't earned that right. Yet, if his father hadn't come to Canada twenty-three years ago, he thinks he'd be a Tamil Tiger today, hiding in a rainforest somewhere or, like his uncle and cousin, dead. From the vantage point of his age and distant Mississauga, neither the violence nor the inhuman discipline their cause demands shocks him.

There are so many obvious divisions among the hundreds of kids in the Caf. The blacks, the Muslim girls, the Hong Kong Chinese, the Vietnamese, the white kids, the Tamils, the Polish girls, and lots more. Sitting separate and discrete, with very few who seem to bridge the divide. But these kids don't spend their days with the same kids in a specific class the way kids used to – what else besides race or ethnicity is there to bond them, to give them an identity? Less clear is how much of their social pattern is mere habit: for a few minutes in a long day, the comfort of speaking in your first language, to say what you really think and feel, to people who share life stories with you, to whom you can speak in short form, without need to explain, without fear of misunderstanding. And how much is a deliberate desire for separation from those who aren't "our kind"? Although these widely diverse kids may not be each other's best friends, day after day they do demonstrate towards each other at worst a benign indifference, a tolerance, maybe even an acceptance; at the best, a willingness to live together.

◆ ◆ ◆

The week feels unbearably long. Many of the kids are sick and away, many teachers are sick and trying to hang on until Friday, when March Break begins. Cathy Sylvester is going to Montreal for a few days with her husband, Maria Cheung and Rick Ray are staying home, Maria to spend some less interrupted time with her young son, Rick to be a pool rat at his daughter's swim meet. Noel Lim is going to the Bahamas, Terry Chaffe to Hilton Head for a little golf and tennis, if his left elbow holds up. He keeps aggravating it in his regular squash games, which he refuses to give up. Tendonitis is for old guys, he laughs.

A few miles south of here, kids from more affluent schools are already packing for southern beaches, but not many of Kennedy's kids. A few will visit relatives nearby, or take day-trips north to ski; most will stay home. Today, as a welcome hint of things to come, fresh flowers showed up in the staff room and office. They brought great smiles of excitement. Spring really is coming! Except noses soon started to wrinkle. *The smell's so strong. I can't take it. I'll move them a little. They're pretty, though. But so overpowering. I'm getting a headache. I'll just move them a little more. Everyone else is enjoying them – they must be enjoying them. They're beautiful. But, man, they stink. I can't get away from them. It's like Airwick pouring out of the vents.*

All day long, the flowers moved. When school ended, the staff room and office emptied into the parking lot, grateful for the smell of winter.

Chapter 7

Tuesday, March 22, 6:15 a.m.

He arrives in deep darkness every morning at 6:15. He hangs up his coat and drops his old black lunch pail on the table in the custodians' room, then goes to the furnace room to check the boiler, to make sure there is enough hot water to warm up the school. He moves from there into a semi-lighted hall, turns down another, and walks towards the front of the school. He unlocks the offices, turns on the lights, walks to the kitchen and Caf and does the same, drawing open the tall Cafetorium curtains.

He turns into the outer halls, unlocking each outside door as he comes to it. Some are mostly glass, others are metal with a checkerboard of small glass squares cut into them. Years ago, some principal decided not to keep replacing the glass as it was broken, instead to cover over each window with a metal flap screwed into the door. Not much glass now remains. He looks for signs of wear and tear in the halls, marks on walls, lights burned out. Every few steps he scrapes up gum with his putty knife from the cold terrazzo floor, making notes in his head of what he needs to do later. There isn't much vandalism in the school, in the course of a year a few broken windows, some graffiti in the bathrooms, the messages much changed in the time he's been here. In boys' bathrooms, where once were drawings of girls, with girls' names and phone numbers, now are drawings, names, and phone numbers of boys. In girls' bathrooms, drawings, names, and numbers of girls. What once were anti-Italian messages are now racial: "Niggers are Skum" (under that the reply, "But we have all white girls," under that, "Fuck you"); "White is fucken thief, was thief, will always be thief." He checks the washrooms, to see that they are clean, with toilet paper in every stall. He checks the classrooms that have outside walls to see they are warm enough. His routine never varies. He moves as if someone is watching him, in his walk a slight shuffle of age, an old man's steady, relentless rhythm, all done at a young man's pace. Every morning, he primps and fixes his school. He is the host, his guests are about to arrive.

Leo Colasante came in a second wave of Italian immigrants in the late 1950s. He is from Pescara, about 150 miles east of Rome on the Adriatic Sea. He had finished his two years of military service and, returning home, could see little opportunity for himself. He moved to Belgium, just south of Brussels, and for two years worked as a coal miner nearly a mile underground. His stomach burned, his sputum turned grey; he decided to move again, to Canada. It was 1957. For five years, he worked construction when work was available, including a few weeks paving the Kennedy parking lot. Then, on June 17, 1962, he began here, and except for a few years at another school, has remained since. On Local 25445's seniority list, which includes 823 names and hangs on the custodian room wall, he is number one in all of Peel. Most of the names near his name are Italian; most newer names are from Eastern Europe.

Today, as he does every morning at 7:30, he meets with Principal Terry Chaffe. A few days ago, he discovered a broken window in the Caf; Terry has had a chance to investigate, talking to lunch supervisors from both periods, but nobody saw or heard anything, he reports to Leo, and shakes his head. Leo, in his heavily accented English, tells him that the Caf was cold this morning when he arrived, and so too were rooms 248 and 249 in the front of the school. He will try to find the trouble. Terry reminds him to keep room 154 open during parts of each lunch period for Muslim prayers. In three minutes, their meeting is over.

In the outer office, ants have been discovered coming out of the walls. Nabbed as he leaves Terry's office, Leo takes care of them. He has a plaque to put up outside the vice-principals' offices, from the Ministry of Education commemorating Kennedy's fortieth anniversary. He leaves and returns with his tool box, drills two holes in the wall, cuts off two small pieces of wood dowling and hammers them into the holes, then hammers nails and hooks into them. The new plaque hangs beside another, which reads,

Love Leo Day
April 12, 1988
May this tree grow as we remember
all you have done for us.

The Board had decided to commemorate the work of its outstanding employees and singled him out. There was a ceremony at the Board offices and another at the school. A birch tree was also planted in Leo's name in the school's courtyard. Actually, the tree wasn't planted until a few days later, and Leo planted it himself.

At nine o'clock, after the kids are in their classes, he mops the front entrance and locks many of the doors he had unlocked two hours before. He has a coffee break at 9:30 a.m., then sweeps the corridors on the west side of the school with his wide, dry, push mop, as his assistant, Harry, does the same on the east. He walks from one end of each hall to the other and back, around and around, like a Zamboni driver on an ice rink. At 11:00 a.m., he helps set up the Caf for lunch; then cleans it and mops it when second lunch is done. Between times, he has more mopping and sweeping, locking and unlocking, changing lights, scraping up gum, doing whatever the day demands and teachers require. Making sure he does his job right the first time, he says, so teachers trust him, and ask his help again.

The building is old. Every September, in the late summer sun, under a fresh coat of paint, it has the bright, whitewashed look of a Spanish colonial city. But the veneer is thin. When eyes get accustomed to the light, and after a few months' use, a tiredness shows through. Nothing he cleans can he make look truly clean, nothing he fixes stays that way for long. Yet he never appears discouraged. Discouragement isn't an emotion that occurs to him. You do a job because it has to be done, and you do it again tomorrow. And the kids *are* good, that's what he likes best about his job. They treat him well. There aren't the fights there were seven or eight years ago, the broken bottles, blacks against whites, when blacks were new to the school and very much the minority. Now, with so many ethnic groups, everybody feels a minority.

He seems never to tire, never to stop moving. Ask any of the 1,500 kids and 100 teachers to think of Leo, and the same image pops to mind: in his custodian's pale blue shirt and dark blue pants, walking, always walking, going someplace, in his hands a mop, his push pail beside him, his arms and body swaying back and forth with the wide, sideways, figure-eight sweep of his mop heavy with water and grime. That and a smile on his face – nobody questions a smiling face. In the halls, everybody's glad to see him, yet almost never does conversation follow. He moves on; they move on.

Work was and is his means of communication. Leo is disdainful of most of his assistants, who work hard to get the kids

on their side, but drag their feet. During the summer, his neighbours get out in their yards and moan about the problems of the
world, then hour after hour solve those problems, except their
roofs still leak. He lives nearby. Every day at 3:30 p.m. he goes
home and helps his wife. They have been married thirty-eight
years. She has been sick for more than a decade. They eat at
4:00 p.m. except when their daughter, a psychologist, eats with
them. Afterwards, he putters about fixing things, cutting the
grass, shovelling the snow, doing whatever needs to be done.

If he ever had a dream, he says, it was to be a builder. Like
some of his Italian friends in the late 1950s, buy a lot, build a
house, live in the house, buy another lot, build another house,
sell it; and so on. Now he is sixty-four years old. Next December,
he will retire. Maybe then, he thinks. He doesn't worry about
retiring. It will happen. He'll have no shortage of things to do.
His only concern is his health. Active all his life, he finds no pleasure in TV or books. He needs good health to allow him to keep
doing the things that bring him satisfaction.

Leo's job is routine. In this place of youth and learning where
excitement is craved, there could be no dirtier word, but the kids
like and respect him because of the pride he takes in his work
and the respect he shows them. In his own way, Leo is also their
teacher.

◆ ◆ ◆

For Principal Terry Chaffe, it has been a routine day, except one
teacher hasn't shown up. In most jobs everybody gets delayed
sometimes, takes a day off, plays golf, has family matters to attend
to – but not teachers. Not without some explanation of sickness
or accident, not without a phone call. Yet, nothing has been heard
from this teacher. It's only ten o'clock, Terry wouldn't worry,
except in his more than eighteen years as an administrator, this
has never happened. He has his vice-principals checking, calling;

the teacher was to go on a field trip today, the buses were waiting, finally Terry had to cancel them. Between appointments and drop-ins, he slips into the outer office for updates.

A girl walks into his office as slowly as she can manage. She is doing well in every subject except computer science, and often skips the class. Now, she says, she wants to drop it. Terry wants to know why. It is her last class every second day, she explains. She has a job at a drycleaners' from 4:00 to 7:00 p.m. and has to go by bus. There's not much time; she needs the job. She lives with her sister, and they support themselves; last year they moved here from Pakistan. She doesn't need the course to graduate, she says. Terry is not very sympathetic. Why haven't you talked about this with your teacher? he asks. Why haven't the two of you done something? Nearly half the semester is gone. You may not need this course, but you signed up for it. You have a responsibility to see it through, or to deal with it in some other way. She nods. She agrees to talk with her teacher before anything else is done.

Next is a boy with a different problem looking for the same solution. He wants to drop math. His teacher has told Terry he won't pass because he doesn't want to; if he won't pass, the boy reasons, he doesn't want the failure showing up on his transcript. Terry, impressed with his logic if not with his actions, offers a deal: you're only taking two other courses, stay in math, try your hardest, and learn what you can so the next time you'll have a head start. We'll meet again in June. If I see that you've put in the effort and still want to, I'll let you drop the course. "You know I'm right, eh?" he says to the boy. "Sometimes the less you have to do, the less you do." The boy nods reluctantly.

Next is a teacher. Terry sits behind his desk, she takes a chair in front of him. The mid-morning sun has made no inroads into the room. The dark wooden walls, wooden chairs and desk make it seem like perpetual dusk. She isn't feeling well, she says. She's now on a new medication for Chronic Fatigue Syndrome, and the only doctor's appointment she could get is during today's staff meeting. She will need to miss the meeting, she says. Terry nods. Maybe this new medication will make me a new woman, the teacher says. You do seem a lot better than a year ago, Terry offers brightly. I had a complete relapse about a month ago, she tells him. They fall silent. Her illness has brought on extreme muscle soreness; she is taking painkillers, but her knees often buckle on her at unpredictable, sometimes embarrassing, times. The virus has caused lesions on the hypothalamus of her brain, she says, which affect her thyroid. Currently on a fruit and vegetable diet, she has gained twenty-two pounds. "I'm just trying to get through this," she smiles wanly. "You've really kept at the teaching," Terry says with admiration. "I do it to forget the pain," she says.

Terry is also worried about another teacher. Dynamic and talented, she is obsessive. She works and works at things to get them just the way she needs them to be, then grows bored and needs something new. She is young but she isn't strong, and now has a young son who has been sick lately. Scary sick, high fevers, vomiting blood. She brought him to the hospital for tests, he seemed a little better, they came home and he got much worse. His temperature went up to 105 degrees Fahrenheit. She brought him back; he was in the hospital nine days and just last weekend came home. He has a virus somewhere in his body, the doctors tell her. They tested for meningitis; they told her many kids die each year after displaying similar symptoms. She stayed at the hospital with him. Now the shadows normally under her eyes are deep and dark and extend down her cheeks.

A science teacher pops his head in the door. He is responsible for equipment safety at the school, and twice a year he and Terry do a safety audit. They arrange a time for next week. Two business teachers want to talk about creating partnerships with local businesses. They mention some things these companies might do for the school. But what can we do for them? Terry asks. Partnerships like this don't work for long unless there is some mutual benefit. Perhaps their employees could use the gym for sports or dances, he suggests. The teachers promise to find out. As they leave, they ask if he will write a short article about them for the teachers' union newsletter, on "innovative teachers." He says he will.

Next into his office is an adult student who is very agitated. Somebody is following her, she says, taking photographs. She has been to see Terry before with the same story; Terry has checked it out, and found nothing to it. He listens to her again, calms her, and she leaves.

Moments later a teacher walks in, closes the door, and tells Terry she's pregnant. She is due in the fall. She will need to be off on leave next semester. A boy comes in with a note from his mother. She wants him excused for Juma prayers each Friday at noon, outside the school. It means the boy would miss at least one class a week. Terry calls his mother. There are many Muslims in the school, he tells her, and very few go to these prayers. It depends on how religious you are, the mother explains. Terry, although respectful, is determined. "And it has to be between 12:30 and 1:30?" he queries. The woman is insistent. Terry tells her he will speak with her son's teacher for that period and call her back.

A man has been waiting for some time; Terry is expecting him. The man's nephew has just arrived from Somalia. Some of his records have been sent to the school. Terry says he has read them, but because the boy is nineteen, he wouldn't be assigned to this school anyway. The man says his nephew is fifteen. Terry asks for more documentation. Next, a girl who graduated last year. Terry welcomes her into his office and they sit down. He asks what she is doing. She's working, she says, to save enough money to go to university in the fall. Squirming in her seat, she avoids the point of her visit. Finally, she says that her boyfriend did a painting for her last year, which she later gave to the school. Now she wants it back, for personal reasons, she says. Terry likes the painting, which hangs outside the gym, and had assumed it would be there forever. He says she can have it, but asks for a few days to find a replacement.

He looks at the clock over his door; he wears no watch. It is almost noon. In the outer office, there is commotion. The missing teacher has arrived. On Terry's face is a look of relief, wonder, and uncertain anger. The good news is that the teacher arrived safe and sound; the bad news is the same. He had been late to bed last night, he explained, shut off his alarm this morning and had fallen back to sleep. Terry invites him into his office and closes the door.

◆ ◆ ◆

Lunch time in the euchre room. A game is going on, several players are waiting, among them Dave Arthurs.

He has started betting basketball to change his luck. He knows nothing about the game, doesn't like it, doesn't watch it. In ProLine, any basketball game won by fewer than five points is considered a tie. Of the six picks he needs to win, he selected three as ties and won them all, five out of six in total. He is ebullient.

"Almost won *seventeen* hundred bucks," he announces.

The others don't even raise their heads. "That just means you lost, Davey."

He has stopped hearing them. "They should drop it to five games."

Their eyes don't leave their cards. "So you could win four?"

"Hey, did I tell you about this friend of mine?" he continues. "She bought this Lotto 649 ticket. Had all the right numbers, just a week too early."

This time the cards drop, the players certain they heard him correctly, certain they couldn't have. "So she got all the numbers wrong," the Sandman asks.

"No, she just missed them by a week."

They look at each other and go back to their game.

"Hey, did you guys hear those teachers on CFRB during the break?" he continues. No one had, or no one lets on. "These two guys, I mean, if you're a teacher, you don't go on these shows," he says, his agitation building. "Anyway, this guy's trying to justify what we make. He compared teachers to NHL players, figured out a player works only thirty hours a year. And I'm saying, 'Get off the radio!' Geez, it was embarrassing. So you know what happens? People start calling in – 'If you guys are any indication of what teachers are like, no wonder the kids are in such bad shape.' Blah blah blah. Another lady calls up. 'Yeah,' she says, 'I live a hundred yards from a school; at 3:20 every day the teachers are in the parking lot. They beat the school buses home.' Then she says, 'I'm looking out there now and there's not a car in the lot!' She hangs up. Then the host says, 'Oh yeah, it's March Break.' I wanted to call up and say, 'Lady, if you're any indication of what parents are like, no wonder the kids are in such bad shape.'"

They all laugh.

◆ ◆ ◆

Sheri isn't here for Noel Lim's class, nor is Kelly, nor are two or three others. Nelson, James, Lydia, and Shiva are here, of course, and so are the ESL kids at the front of the room. The class is still reading *Romeo and Juliet*, the background wave of noise remains, Noel ploughs on undeterred. He spent March Break in the Bahamas, and has come back tanned and nearly rested. Just before he left, as he was waiting for his flight at Toronto's Pearson airport, he was startled by voices.

"Hi, Mr. Lim."

"Hi, Mr. Lim."

"Hi, Mr. Lim."

"Hi, Mr. Lim."

Four of his students, three boys and a girl, from his General-level class were about to leave on the same flight. As he would soon discover, they were also going to Cable Beach, staying at the same hotel, on the same floor.

Fortunately, Noel likes these kids, and now after the trip, he likes them even more. They live in all kinds of family arrangements, none of their families with much money, each kid having a part-time job to pay for the trip. Without anyone at home looking out for them, they have learned to look out for each other, creating a family of their own. A different kind of family, more pragmatic and fluid, held together by circumstance. If the group works, it stays together; if circumstance changes and it doesn't, it doesn't, and new families form.

These kids are so familiar with each other, so different from his generation, he thinks. They offer hugs and kisses instead of handshakes, they touch. To the adult eye, used to nodded hellos, they seem indiscriminately intimate, yet they are not. Their social hierarchy is not pyramidal, but flat. Lots of friends, none of them much more special than the rest. To them, pairing off as boyfriend and girlfriend seems antisocial, narrow, suffocating. They work together and play together as a group. They are buddies, girls and boys, anatomically different, but maybe that's all. Why can't I be friends with a girl without her being my girlfriend? they ask. Why does sexual tension need always to be present? Do three guys and a girl going to the Bahamas, conveniently sharing a room, need to be anything more than friends?

Within hours of their arrival in the Bahamas, they had scouted out the facilities at the hotel, made plans, drafted itineraries. They had checked out restaurants, bars, and clubs. Whenever he'd see them, it was always, "Hi, sir," "How are ya, sir?" followed by an update on what they were doing. And every night at 6:00, two pizzas arrived at their doors from Dominos. Each kid had a budget of one hundred dollars a day, just as he did. They played the dollar slot machines, he and his teacher friends played the quarter ones. The girl won six hundred dollars. When the kids left, they were making plans to come back again, with her six-hundred-dollar nest egg, when the school year is over.

Noel wonders what these kids' own families will be like. Their lives so different from his generation's, yet they know how to live without having much money or apparent success. Maybe kids in more traditional families will find it harder. Having to live with traditional expectations and standards, with an unforgiving image of success, in a time of broken families and insecure futures: how will they cope? He admires what these kids are doing. Yet do hugs and kisses for everyone also signal a lack of commitment to anyone? Is pairing off really an emotional rehearsal for later? Is it necessary practice in family-building? And if families aren't built to stay together, what happens then?

Noel enjoys immersing himself in life's complications. He likes to get under the lid of things to see them as they seem to be, and to imagine the rest. Just before his trip, he saw Mike Leigh's film *Naked* and was struck by it. Its main characters, living a grim, degraded life in Manchester, decided to move to London for something better and find the same conditions they left behind. So different from most British movies he sees – *The Remains of the Day, Room with a View* – and from the great English novels he grew up with in Guyana. Yet he enjoys those too, the lush surroundings, the sweep of tangled circumstance, yet where so much is left unfelt, unsaid. So different from American movies, which offer him a sunset to walk into. They upset him. *He* wants to walk where his imagination takes him.

And that's what he wants for his students. He will offer them a strong, sturdy platform of language, he'll circle and underline ceaselessly the flaws that hold them back, then he will wait for them to forge their own way. He will not control their minds with *his* inspiration and *his* reward. Their minds are their own – what right has he? He insists on that same freedom for himself.

In the staff room with his collegues, it may seem otherwise, but he keeps everything to himself. He knows that offering to others a blank face and unexpressed words only makes them wonder. So he laughs louder, talks louder, puns, scandalizes, the more outrageous the better, he gives everybody an American ending – to keep everything to himself.

He has the class read *Romeo and Juliet* aloud for much of the period. Nelson was first with his hand up to be Romeo, first to be Mercutio and Benvolio and Tybalt. Noel chose others instead. Without Sheri, there is little drama to the reading, the pace stutters nearly to a halt. With twenty-five minutes left in the period, the kids go back to working on essays Noel has assigned them. The background hum grows louder. Noel sits at his desk marking other papers, waiting for kids to approach him with questions. Not many do. Class ends.

✦ ✦ ✦

It started out like every other staff meeting. The teachers were in the library, sitting in their portable metal chairs, some listening, some not. Terry was standing at the front, moving the agenda crisply but patiently along. Charity Week, Education Week, a report on next year's school organization, on Transition Years, on the Hard to Serve and Social committees, another by the Ontario Secondary School Teachers Federation, the teachers' union, on the state of their now nearly year-long negotiations with the Peel Board. About 4:25, an hour into the meeting, Terry called for "other business." Two more items were brought forward; then nothing more. Teachers began rustling out of their seats; Terry cleared his throat. There will be another brief staff meeting after school tomorrow, he said, not quite casually.

Everybody stopped. A meeting for what? What has to be discussed tomorrow that can't be discussed today? This has never happened before. They began quizzing him. There's nothing more I can say, he said. On the whole, is it positive or negative? someone asked. Terry paused. "It's just something we have to get through."

They were buzzing on the way out, buzzing in the halls and staff room the next day. "He's retiring"; "We're getting a new building." "Yeah, and renaming it Bob Rae High." "It's a new zero tolerance policy." "Terry's coming out of the closet; he's admitting he wears elevator shoes."

Nobody straggles in to today's meeting. The buzz continues. Terry walks in with two people no one has seen before. "They look like health department to me," someone mutters.

"We have an active case of tuberculosis in the school," Terry announces. There is sudden silence, then a hum of conversation much louder than before. He continues; the noise abates. The infected student has been identified; the case was contagious but isn't any longer, the risk of transmission is minimal. Those closest to the student, all the student's classmates, about two hundred kids, the student's seven teachers, and his or her counsellor will be tested. The student is in no extra-curricular activities. Terry is careful not to identify the student in any way, not even by gender. "I can't tell you who the student is," he says, and the undertone of grumbling returns.

"That's ridiculous," one voice mutters loudly.

Terry stops. "That may be ridiculous," he says, his face unyielding, "but that is the law."

The student is still in school, on medication, and is no longer infectious; the case was discovered in the last few weeks. The student was probably already infected before coming to Canada. The disease is transmitted by coughing, but casual contact is usually not enough to spread it. For those who do contract TB, treatment by antibiotics is very effective.

Tomorrow morning at 9:40, Terry says, he will make a special announcement to inform the school. After that, certain kids, classmates of the infected kid, though not so identified, will be called to the office to pick up letters that explain what has happened, and their need to be tested. General testing is not necessary.

He concludes, his face serious and steady, "There is reason for concern, but no reason for panic." The meeting breaks up.

Chapter 8

Tuesday, April 5, 12:58 p.m.

It happened last Thursday, the day before Easter weekend. Sue Lishman had known what was coming and what it might mean. She had gone through the same thing most of last year. She had told herself not to think about it, there was nothing she could do. The numbers at a school change from year to year, because of total enrolment, course selection, pupil-teacher ratios negotiated with the Board, this year because of the government's Social Contract as well. The changes aren't usually significant, except to the few who are affected. Last year Sue had been at the bottom of the school's seniority table, and would have been declared excess, but Kennedy needed math teachers, so she had been able to hang on. This year, she wasn't so sure. For several weeks, Terry had been working through the numbers, and finally he knew: next September, he will lose two math teachers.

At noon, he had called Sue in and handed her a letter. She thinks he said he was sorry to lose her, she isn't sure, and the rest she can't remember. Her department head, Debbie Lang, asked if she wanted someone to take her last class of the day. "No," she said, "I'm fine." And she was, almost instantly, her tall, straight, bright-smile self. She walked briskly from Terry's office the length of the school to her classroom. Simran, Reba, and Rohita were standing by the door to the room. "Hi, miss," they said cheerfully. "What're we doing today?" Her fragile trance broke. Tears welled up, her lips quivered. "Oh, I don't know. We'll get to that," she blurted, and walked away. A few moments later, she came back and gave her lesson.

The holiday weekend was a long one for Sue. "You'll get another job," her husband reassured her, and probably he was right. But if two math teachers at Kennedy got letters, how many more got them in all of Peel? There can't be that many positions open. Last year, math had saved her. This year, if she had taught music, she'd be fine. She spent the weekend lurching from emotion to emotion: All the work I've put in – it's not fair; it's the way the system works. Once you get your permanent certificate, you are secure forever. Or until the Board investigates you, builds a case, spends hundreds of thousands of dollars and years of time to try to get rid of you, which becomes the same thing. I accepted that when I got into teaching, and I still accept it, she thought. I'll get another job. All this is no worse than a couple of weeks of uncertainty, and a few days next year getting used to a new school.

She marked tests and worked on her résumé, which got her down even more. It looked so thin. Where were all her activities, the committees she had served on? What had she been doing these last two years? All her doubts returned. No one can see inside a classroom. In a duel of résumés, would she stand a chance?

There were suddenly so many things to think about. Her husband is with a company that needs to grow to survive, to take over its competitors or be taken over itself. It might not make it. They have been living with her parents, saving money, waiting to move into a new house they've bought, at the end of the school year. Now what? They have too much money tied up in the house to walk away, yet they need both their incomes to make the financing work, or else they will have to borrow from their parents, which they will not consider. But these concerns aren't what is making her feel so unsettled. This is about teaching, what she loves to do and now perhaps what she cannot do; it's about what she felt that moment she was walking down the hall and saw Simran, Reba, and Rohita.

Back at school this week, she's trying to be up. She eats in the staff room with Doris, Theresa, and Horace, who are upset for her and tell her so often. Her brother has been at Kennedy this year helping in science classes, putting in his own time without being paid, with the hope of getting into some faculty of education next year, with the hope of getting a job the year after. Because he wants to teach. Last week, he received his acceptance into the Faculty. What can he be feeling now? She's so up and down. She finally asked her classes to bear with her. She's been having a hard few days, she said. Her Enhanced class, of course, wanted to know more. "What's wrong, miss?" She told them. "Does that mean you got fired?" Pat asked.

Today, she received the list of schools looking for math teachers and Thursday she has appointments at Cawthra and Turner–Fenton. Doris's husband is at Cawthra; he'll put in a good word. Turner–Fenton is where Sue went to school herself. It was just Turner then, a goody-goody smiles-and-dimples school, as she describes it, upper-middle class, WASP. It isn't like that now. Fenton, the tech part, has been added to it, and prosperous, rural Brampton is changing. With a stake in Turner being what Turner was, she's not sure she wants to go back. In any event, she will know her fate soon. The dehiring/hiring process happens fast. Jobs get posted, and any teacher can apply, not just those bumped from other jobs. Eight days from now, the successful applicants will be informed, and another sequence will begin. If she isn't selected, if teachers with permanent positions are hired, their old spots open up, the deck gets reshuffled, and she and others can apply again. By the end of April, she will have a job next year, or have no job. That, she says to herself, is when I'll worry.

There is another complication. Kennedy is losing two math teachers, Sue and Patti Vandrus. Careful to have supported each other through this uncertain year, now they're competing for the same jobs.

◆ ◆ ◆

Don Spence has been in Guidance – at Kennedy it's now called Counselling – nearly twenty-five years. His wife is a teacher, their daughter is a teacher. Earlier this year at a staff meeting, when someone stood up and said that the provincial car licensing bureau was issuing new licences with the letter sequence "TLK," several teachers turned in their old plates for new ones. Don was one of them. He is earnest and a little shy, yet comfortable with kids. Though much of his day is filled with kids with problems, he hasn't retreated to the safe, distant ground of irony or cynicism. His caring shows through. When Terry Chaffe, the principal, respects someone, he says he has "a lot of time for" that person. Terry has a lot of time for Don Spence.

Earlier in Don's career, he was at a school in an affluent area, and there most problems were future-centred. What is the right path for my child, the right courses to take, the right university to attend? At Kennedy, and in most schools now, the problems are ones of here and now. Kids have options they didn't have before. They can escape abusive homes, go on student welfare, drop in and out of classes. The law has moved to protect them, but sometimes Don wonders if it hasn't gone too far. A little trouble at home, a parent cramping your style, and six hundred dollars a month in student welfare payments doesn't look too bad. Especially if you get a part-time job, especially if you move in with four or five other kids all with the same deal. Go to bed when you want, see whomever you want, make a few classes to keep the cheques coming in. Not bad for parents either. One less hassle around the house, the state supporting your kid, your kid off the streets. Not bad for an employer either. He can pay minimum wage and still have kids banging down his door because the rest of a liveable income is paid by the taxpayers. Except it's no life for a kid, Don believes, a kid needs parents. Sharing an apartment with four or five others, and their friends, how much homework do you think gets done?

Last year, 127 kids at Kennedy were on student welfare, nearly one-tenth of the school, about average for Metropolitan Toronto. This year, he's sure there are more. It's too easy, he says; we're all lazy. Parents and kids should be pushed harder and longer to sort out their differences. He sees these kids every day, talks to their welfare case workers. They stay in school, the cheques keep them here, but the system isn't working. It keeps them off the streets, but mires them further in a lifestyle where the right kind of learning doesn't happen. The problem is more than with welfare kids, Don believes. Lots of others get almost no emotional support at home either. Supporting them then becomes their teachers' job, because learning won't happen without support, and helping kids learn is what teachers do. But how do you do it for all these kids? A teacher needs to be a second father or second mother, and do these kids even know how to be sons or daughters, or want to be? It's easy to say to teachers, Do better with what you've got, or with what more we give you, but some things can only be done by parents and family.

In some ways, kids are being educated now better than ever, Don believes. In social matters – sexism, racism, getting along, working in groups – in life skills and new technologies. The brightest kids are now being exposed to so much more than they were years ago, and they thrive. But what about the rest? Now there are so many different kinds of kids, with different needs, starting at such different places. How do we help *all* of them? When Don was in high school in the late 1950s, most kids didn't graduate. A few years earlier, many fewer graduated still. But they weren't doomed to marginal lives. The path to success didn't run only through university, there were plenty of "grade eleven drop-outs" who made it. Smart young men and women whose families needed another income, who wanted to get on with their lives. Work was the solid, respectable alternative. Someone could start at the bottom, at bottom-rung wages with bottom-rung expectations, needs, and lifestyle, and work/learn his way up. Now the ladder starts at the second storey. Maybe the drop-out can do the job, maybe a high school education isn't necessary, but we don't have jobs for everybody, nor the time to sort through a pile of applications to find the uncut diamond. For those who don't graduate, there is no ladder, no rungs to work up. The future for them is on the street, in a revolving door of dead-end jobs.

Some kids make appointments with Don, most just drop in. Today, the first to arrive is a real star. She is graduating this year and next fall she will attend one of the Toronto universities, so she can commute from home. Her father drives a taxi, her mother is unemployed. She has an older brother who is a construction worker, and two younger sisters. She wants to go into journalism, she has done some writing and acting at the school, but not as much, she knows, as most of her competition. She has vastly more life experience to bring to the stories she would report, but that isn't easily conveyed on an application. For some time, Don has helped her plan her path, her applications are in, now they are waiting. Today's meeting is brief: to remind the girl that someone is thinking of her; to remind Don of the rewards of his work.

Next is a boy who arrived in Canada a year ago from Vietnam. The rest of his family is either still in Vietnam or dead. He is living alone on student welfare, but two months ago, his cheques stopped and he doesn't know why. His landlord has been understanding but he senses that is about to end. Don tries to reach his welfare worker, but an answering machine tells him nobody will be in the office today. The government's Social Contract has led to cutbacks in service. He will try again tomorrow, he says, and meet with the boy when he knows more.

A pretty, vacant-faced girl walks in. She isn't on student welfare herself, but her boyfriend is, and she has left home to live with him. She was living with her mother; her father is gone but he occasionally returns, bringing disruption before he disappears again. She may have been physically abused. Now she and her boyfriend aren't getting along. She doesn't want to go home, but staying where she is isn't good either. Don agrees. He has made her a deal. He will help her get student welfare, which at her age, sixteen, isn't easy, if she improves her attendance. He knows, and knows she knows, that if he doesn't help her, she may drop out of school to get regular welfare so she can afford a place of her own, and then he will lose her entirely.

The next girl is having problems with a teacher. She and Don have talked about this before; Don has talked to her teacher. Don thinks it is mostly the teacher's fault. The girl and her family came to Canada from Poland three years ago. She likes the less rigid school structure here, and has done better. Her English is good, though she doesn't think it is, being far more aware of what she doesn't understand than what she does. But, like Sophia, her abrupt manner has brought conflict with this teacher. She also has a problem at home. A tumour has been discovered near one of her father's kidneys, and because of the pain, he has been unable to work. His next doctor's appointment is in a few days, and the family fears the worst. If the girl drops this course because of her teacher, she won't have enough credits this year for university. She must either go to community college, or wait a semester.

She seems not much bothered by either prospect; Don is more concerned. She promises to try again, and Don promises to get the teacher to do the same.

A boy sits in the outer office with his dog. Don goes out to get them. The boy is actually twenty-two, he moved this year from Vancouver, and is blind. He lives with two "visually impaired" adults. "They're only half-blind," he laughs. "They can't even get that right." His dog, named Neely, after hockey star Cam Neely, is not much more than a puppy and has only recently been trained. He seems dangerously attracted by squirrels. When they run across the road, he runs after them, his master dragging and shouting after him.

This meeting with Don is just to "keep up to date." There were problems in the fall with getting Braille math books. The school had known he was coming, but with adult students plans aren't usually made until they arrive. In the meantime, Don arranged for some kids to act as volunteer readers for him, but the Braille books were several weeks in coming. Everything has been fine since.

Another boy drops in. He had been having problems of all kinds in his classes. Don thinks he might have some attention disorder and had arranged for him to be tested. He saw the doctor this morning, the boy tells him. Don says he will speak to him again after he talks to the doctor himself.

Two more boys enter, both grade nines, their eyes directed straight ahead or to the side where the other isn't, never crossing an imaginary line between them. They haven't been getting along. One is Indian, the other black. The Indian kid is athletic with a quick tongue; the black youth is fat, slow, with a painfully high-pitched voice. Kids pick on him, no one more so than the boy beside him. A teacher sent them to Don a few weeks ago. They talked through their problems with him, promised to do better; this is the follow-up. Things are okay now, they both say, without warmth, but without fire. Their teachers have told Don the same. He looks pleased. They seem to have learned something, he says. They nod. He asks them how their marks are, if their parents will be happy with their mid-term reports.

"Oh, my parents are never happy," the Indian kid says. "They always find something. But I'm doing well. Last semester, I got honours."

The other boy, who isn't doing well, says solemnly, "My parents will be very proud."

Next a girl from Vietnam who has lived in Canada thirteen years, yet her English remains poor, and the progress of her learning seems stopped. School may not be the best place for her any more. Don has been trying to help her imagine what might come next. She mentions that her brother-in-law is in graphic arts. He asks her about that, yet she seems to know little. Still, Don thinks, it is a place to start. He suggests that she spend a work day with him sometime. The school would allow her to miss the time; she and Don could meet again afterwards and talk about it. He needs to find her something that will get her life moving.

Another Vietnamese girl whose welfare cheques have stopped; a girl who wants to drop a computer course, whose story then goes on to a mother who doesn't understand her, doesn't like her, who is going through menopause . . . A girl who was put in the wrong math course but who now, too late in the semester, can't change. A girl in grade ten who is anorexic and alcoholic, whom Don and others are just trying to nurse along until help arrives. She loves drama, but next semester can't take the drama course she should. Can she take the course one grade more advanced? Don will talk to the drama teachers.

The next boy arrives highly agitated. He starts his story in the middle and it comes out a muddle. "Like my grandfather's sick, eh," the boy blurts, "but if he calls my dad, I mean you know how my dad is. And it's really not my fault."

Don stops him and gets him to begin again. His grandfather is sick, the boy repeats. He's paralysed on one side and can't recognize anybody. "He's like a vegetable, eh?" the boy says, then laughs, not intending to, then goes on. Something about the boy then being able to get a ride with someone to see his grandfather in a hospital downtown, but having a detention, one of many, and his ride leaving early, and telling the vice-principal that. Then saying to the vice-principal to go ahead, give him a month of detentions, he doesn't care, he has to go. Then getting mad and saying some other things that were probably out of order. But he has a temper like his father's, he admits, changing direction. Then the vice-principal saying that he is going to call his dad, and him saying back, you can't do that. You just can't. "Everything's so shaky at home," he confides to Don, fear in his eyes. "I'm just trying to keep them together. You know how my dad is. He's going to find out I skipped a detention to visit my grandfather and who knows what'll happen."

Don knows some of the rest of the story; gradually he finds out more. There has been a nasty split in the family. The mother has left. The father was gone too for a while, and the boy moved north to a small town to live with his godfather. Then he found his way back here, to live with his dad, but his dad is sick. He has an enlarged liver and can't work any more. He just sits at home, the boy says, sleeping and watching TV. He has this awful temper, something just triggers him and he's gone. The grandfather in the hospital is on the mother's side. This is a war and the boy must choose. If his father finds out his plans to visit his grandfather, the boy tells Don, he could be kicked out of the house. He has to tell his father himself. He'll tell him tonight, or tomorrow for sure. He just has to find the right words. Just don't let the vice-principal call my father, he pleads.

Don says he will speak with the vice-principal, but he wants to see the boy again in two days, after he has talked with his father. The boy nods. Don changes the subject. He asks him about the year, though he already knows the answer. School has never worked for this kid. He is always in trouble, failing or almost so. Last spring, midway through the semester, he quit school and went to work at a marina. It was a nothing job, but he did pretty well at it. His boss liked him and gave him more and more responsibility. He couldn't believe how good he felt. He worked hard. He stopped checking his watch every fifteen minutes. He was actually doing something well. He could see, however, that his lack of education was holding him back, so he returned to school in the fall, this time with a more positive attitude, but it's been a disaster. One step inside the doors, and he was stupid again. No matter what he does, that's how he feels, that's how his teachers seem to feel about him. Don nods. It's time to go to work full-time, he says. You can go to school at night.

Chapter 9

Thursday, April 7, 6:45 p.m.

Parents' Night. Jackets and ties have been donned, and all day the school has felt like a newlywed's home before the in-laws arrive. Finally a chance for parents to put a face to a name, for teachers to witness once more the awesome power of genetics.

Both of Elaine's parents are here. Elaine has an older brother also at Kennedy. In the fall, her parents divided up, one went to see Elaine's teachers, the other her brother's, but they had found that frustrating. So today, they saw their son's teachers together after school, and are seeing Elaine's together tonight. The couple is older, with hard-working faces, and they are dressed respectfully for the occasion. Originally from the Philippines, they speak a heavily accented English. Their daughter has no accent.

Elaine is doing well in Enhanced math, Sue Lishman tells them. She's a good student and a pleasure to have in class. Elaine's parents smile. Sue glances at her marks sheet, "She has an 81 at the moment," she says, smiling back. Both Elaine's parents say only, "Oh." Sue stops. Every mark is relative; a parent's or kid's ambition is hard to know. Elaine is a little worried about math, they tell her. Sue nods. She has heard this often before. For a lot of kids, math is a "lightbulb" subject, she tells them. For years, they just look at a problem and "the light goes on." Then one day it doesn't, and they don't know what to do. They get frustrated, and suddenly think that they can't "do" math. She tries to tell these kids it's not like that. That for everybody at some point that light doesn't go on. The question is what you do then. Elaine's parents listen carefully. Elaine has to learn that math isn't unique, Sue says. It's just another language, written in digits and letters, but to be decoded as any language is, using reason and action. Elaine already knows this about English, she needs to learn it about math too. If she does, the lightbulb may never go on for her again, but she'll have discovered its switch. Will that happen this year? Sue shrugs and smiles. Elaine's mother laughs. "I think it will," she says. "If Elaine gets all As, she knows she'll be getting some money from us."

Sukhjit's mother comes alone to the interview. Shy, gentle, neatly dressed and groomed, wearing traditional Indian dress, she is a heavier, older version of her daughter. She has a hearing aid in her left ear. Sue says Sukhjit is doing fine, can probably do a little better, but there is no cause for concern. Her mother nods. At home, Sukhjit is a very responsible girl, she says, and gives them no problems. It does seem to her and her husband that she talks too much on the phone but, she smiles, she is a good girl. The interview goes quickly and quietly.

Not so with Leah's parents. They are older; Leah has brothers and sisters in their thirties. They arrive with something on their mind. Leah's mother sits close to Sue, and holds in her lap a folded piece of paper. Leah has a 59 average in math at the moment, the lowest mark she has ever had in any subject. Leah says she's having trouble understanding, and she's gone to you for help, her mother says, but *you* haven't helped her. *You* are hardly ever there. Sue's back is immediately up; their talk is off the rails. She is *always* there, she says, quietly, defensively, sternly, every morning by 8:15 at the latest, after school for at least ten minutes; she's learned that if nobody has shown up by then, nobody's going to show up, and she leaves. But if anybody does, she stays until four o'clock or later. Yes, Leah comes before class, but at 8:35, and other kids are already there. That's what Enhanced kids are like. They come early, put equations on the board, demand your attention. There's always competition for Sue's time and Leah isn't fighting very hard.

Sue doesn't need to continue her explanation, but she does. The class has also gone through a difficult unit based on factoring, which they did earlier in the course, she tells Leah's mother. If kids had trouble with factoring, they had a hard time with this, yet when they were doing factoring, Leah never asked for help. It's only these last few days that she has interrupted – "I don't understand, miss." But Sue can't stop mid-lesson and go back through material that only Leah doesn't understand. That review has to follow the lesson, come after school or before, and Leah never turns up.

Sue isn't finished. She leafs through her binder as she talks, looking for more support for what she is saying. She depends on kids to exercise their own responsibility, she says. It's up to them to ask if they have a problem, up to them to call a buddy to get homework and do that homework if they are away. They're old enough. Learning habits like these are crucial. Sue catches her breath, waiting for something else to come to her. Nothing does.

Sue may be right in all she says, but her real message, unintentionally conveyed by her tone, says that it's *Leah's* fault that she's falling behind, not mine. Leah's parents sit attentively; the mood turns almost friendly. Her father seems almost won over, but not her mother. He arrived thinking that whatever problem existed was probably Leah's fault. The wrong friends, boys, volleyball, the phone: things he's been complaining about for weeks. Leah's mother arrived thinking that it was the teacher's fault and, Sue's explanations notwithstanding, she will go away with the deep-down feeling she was right.

Leah is so close to doing well in math. The real problem is that this is the first time she has had a real problem and she doesn't know what to do. Neither do her parents. Leah has always breezed along, done well, never felt the dummy. Worked hard, but always with the certain reward of getting things right at the end. Leah will learn math when she learns what to do when things go wrong. But the one real opportunity her parents and Sue had for some mutual understanding started badly and now the answer seems murky. With a finger pointed at her, Sue pointed back. She has left Leah's parents and Leah with a crutch. Because Leah has an excuse to do less well, she likely will.

✦ ✦ ✦

Rick Ray has his classroom more or less organized, or at least more neatly piled. Charlene walks in with her mother, a pretty, tastefully dressed, well-groomed, middle-aged woman. Kennedy encourages kids to attend with their parents, but they rarely do. Charlene's mother speaks very good English, with the slight lilt of the Islands. They are from Trinidad. She and her minister husband, Charlene and her brother, also a student at Kennedy, have been in Canada less than a year, though they have relatives here and have visited many times before. Rick tells her mother how well Charlene is doing. Disciplined, responsible, hard-working, her homework always done, she is a quiet leader, he says, someone who has all the attitudes and habits of success. Charlene watches, listens, and smiles a slight smile. Charlene's mother says that yes, Charlene is like that, and they are very proud of her.

Fahad's mother and father are next. They have the same quiet presence as their son. Rick smiles and shakes his head, and says he doesn't know where to begin, that Fahad is an excellent student and a wonderful boy. His parents have heard this many times before, and they hear it again with a shy, embarrassed smile, with pride and determination. He *is* a special kid, we love him and want him to be all that he was born to be, his father says. It isn't so easy for them at their age to find a way in this country, but perhaps it can be different for Fahad. He says that he has been thinking of taking Fahad on a trip across Canada, stopping at historical sights, taking in all that is his new country, helping him understand. He thinks Fahad is old enough now; maybe this summer. Rick nods enthusiastically. "That's a great idea," he says.

Fahad's parents leave, Rick follows them into the hall to greet the next parent on his list. Willy is there with his mother. She doesn't have an appointment, she says, Willy forgot to bring home his appointment slip. She wonders if they might talk with him. She is a small, round, friendly-faced woman, and she knows what she is about to hear. Rick motions them into the classroom; the three of them look as if they are being led to slaughter. They sit down, glance at each other and glance away. There is an audible, sympathetic silence as they try to find just the right words.

"It's been hard," Rick begins, just to get some words out of his mouth, "but I'm not really sure that bad news is in order," he says, gaining confidence as he goes. "I wouldn't have said that the first few weeks of school." Willy was rarely there, and late when he was. "But recently things have started to change." Not expecting any positive words, Willy and his mother begin to brighten. "He's in class, contributing. When he and Patrick and Chad do that, they make the whole class better." Rick tilts his face towards them as he does when he gets serious, his bald head bobbing at every word. A class is like a team, he says. It has to work together.

Willy and his mother nod back. He has played hockey for years, until this year, and she has often been the manager of his teams. "He has to learn that," she says. "It's very important. I know that from my work." Rick nods. Willy listens intently.

For Rick, it's time to change the tone slightly. Willy is too inconsistent, he says. Then turning to him, "You've got to be in class more often, on time, and with your homework done." Willy nods, looks at his mother, and shakes his head. "Just like when I was a goalie," he says. "Good one game, bad the next." His mother nods, but won't leave it at that. "Not really," she says. "And not in the playoffs. You were always at your best when it counted."

All those years she has heard it and seen it: "Poor Willy," roll-your-eyes, take-a-deep-breath, shake-your-head Willy. She knew what they were all thinking: what kind of mother must she be? And with the finger pointed directly at her so long and so hard, she would point it back in the only direction it could go – at Willy. *It's his fault, don't look at me. I tell him to go to school, do his homework, study, but he just doesn't listen. What can I do?*

But that's not what has happened. Willy's mother isn't pointing fingers. She is here tonight, even though she knows the bad news she will hear. She sits comfortably in this room with Willy beside her, and he seems equally at ease with her. She loves him. He is her son. She wishes he'd do better. He's got to do better, she says. Last weekend, he turned sixteen; he has to start thinking about his future. Willy nods with the same concern. Every year the school tells her he should go to vocational school, and she fights back. He's not going there, she says. You just want to get rid of him. To her, vocational is a gulag, pure and simple, and she's not going to accept that for Willy.

But now what? None of them has an answer. Willy's not getting what he needs at Kennedy, but even if the school decided to ignore everyone else, bring in specialists at whatever the price, make Willy everyone's full-time project – would it work, could he make it even then?

"I don't know how it got to be this way," his mother says, shaking her head. "In grade one and two, he was doing so well. His teachers used to say how smart he was. It was that year with Mrs. Pinkney, and you had whooping cough," she says, turning to Willy. "She ruined you."

Their time is long past up, but Rick isn't finished. Risking the good feeling of the moment, he bears in on Willy. "Just remember how it's been the last few weeks," he says, and Willy nods intently. "Go home now and make sure you're ready for that test tomorrow."

"Test tomorrow?" Willy's eyes widen.

"Yeah," Rick says, "on all the stuff we've taken so far."

"What's that?" his mother asks.

Willy has a hard time saying, "Oh, uh, on the black stuff and South Africa, and, uh, Canada, and Laurelle. Yeah, yeah."

When Willy and his mother leave, it is with a tiny jolt of encouragement, something they haven't had much of since that year with Mrs. Pinkney. And why shouldn't they, Rick says afterwards. "They've heard the rest so many times. What good would it do to hear it again? And Willy *is* doing better. Not well enough, not nearly. But to be in class, on time, to contribute, to be here tonight, for him that's a great achievement. He should hear that."

✦ ✦ ✦

Noel has had a steady stream of parents, but not many from his grade ten class. A young girl walks into the room. She introduces herself as Pauline's sister. Pauline escaped from Vietnam by boat and has been here less than a year. Two of her older sisters came later, their parents remain behind. She isn't much older than Pauline and seems not to speak or understand English as well. She is late for her appointment and keeps looking at her interview sheet as if she is still not sure she's in the right place. Noel asks her how Pauline thinks she is doing in the course. "Very well," she says, smiling. Noel, less certain, responds that Pauline's average is 55. It's a difficult course, he says. It's not just grammar and spelling, things that can be learned by rote; it's literature. It has to do with the way you express yourself, with style and facility with language. Pauline needs lots of practice, he says. It's a big jump from ESL to grade ten Advanced English. Even if she passes, she might be better off doing the course again. Or taking it at summer school, or at night school.

Pauline's sister smiles, looks at her interview sheet, and leaves.

A few years ago, Noel had two Andrews in his class, one a "genius," the other not. The genius's father was a minister. It was Parent's Night, Noel had finished one interview, and, looking down his list, saw that Andrew was next. "You must be Andrew's father," he said to the man waiting in the hall. "Yes," the man nodded. Noel motioned him into the room and they sat down. Noel went on and on about what a good student Andrew was, what a pleasure he was to have in class. The man smiled. He said something about not having heard many comments like that before, but Noel didn't notice. The interview ended. Noel walked him to the door, and looked into the hall. Standing there was another man, in a clerical collar.

A week later, Noel called the first Andrew's father. He explained, apologized, and began talking about the other Andrew. There was silence on the other end of the phone. "Yes," the man said finally, "*that* is my son."

◆ ◆ ◆

For her interviews, Maria Cheung is sharing the double math room with Sue Lishman. It is late in the evening. Sabesan's father

is next on her list. She has had a number of exchanges with
Sabesan the last few weeks. "Why haven't you done your homework?" she has asked again and again. Again and again she has
heard, "I couldn't, miss. I had to work."

"Why don't you see me after school?"

"I have to work."

"What about in the morning?"

"I'll try, miss."

Then Sabesan wouldn't show up. He told her finally about his
forty-three hours of work a week, about how he can't even
begin his homework until midnight, and if he stays awake long
enough to do it, he's too tired to come early in the morning to
see her. She has gone over her marking sheets. He is failing, but
not by much. He seems to have some ability in math and could
pass. The other day, when she asked him if he really wanted to
do better, he said yes. She asked if he really wanted to continue
in school. Again, he said yes. Tonight she has resolved to ask his
father if it's really necessary for Sabesan to spend so many hours
at his job.

He is a big, handsome, smiling man, whose once pitch-black
hair has turned a deep smoky grey. She explains to him what she
has talked about with Sabesan. He nods. Yes, Sabesan has been
working all these hours, he says. I was the one who made him
get the job, and now I'm sorry, his father admits. I was wrong.
He needs to get his schooling. Last night, I talked to him. For the
rest of the semester, he's going to work only on weekends. Maria
is pleased.

A few minutes later, Sophia sweeps in with her entourage.
Rather, she bounces in with a big grin, her mother walks timidly
in behind, and out in front of both, Sophia's cousin, whom she
calls her sister, tall, blonde, full-figured, in her early twenties, and
dressed in black leather. Before the three of them even reach their
seats, the cousin blares:

"How can it be! This girl passed her exams for medical school, and she has no credits. No credits!"

Maria doesn't know what hit her. "Excuse me?"

"No credits. She writes these tests, she passes them. She should be in a higher grade. They put her here and give her no credits. How can it be? They're just holding her back."

Maria says that she doesn't know anything about that. It's something to discuss with Sophia's counsellor.

"I know. I know," the cousin says, a smile now on her face. "It's not your fault." She has Maria on her heels; that is enough for now.

Sophia's mother seems not to speak English, but to understand at least a little. Sophia's cousin has been in Canada seven years and works as a bartender at Club Energy, the baddest hangout in the area. She speaks good, lightly accented English.

Talk turns to Sophia and her behaviour in class. She is doing well, Maria says, an 84 average, but she's concerned about Sophia's demeanour. She is so aggressive and loud, she doesn't give the other kids a chance, and they're beginning to resent her. She needs to learn to get along. Sophia moans.

"It's the same," the cousin smiles. "All her teachers say the same. It's true. She can't get along with other kids. They don't like her. Even at home she has to have her way. Watch *her* TV shows . . ." Sophia moans again.

She looks to Maria for support. "But, miss, nobody in class says nothing. They just sit there. In Yugoslavia you must get 85 per cent just to pass. It's so hard to get into medical school. You must answer every question. Teachers, they must notice you. Math was my weakest subject. I hate it in Yugoslavia." She smiles suddenly, "But I like it here, miss," then her face clouds over. She begins to cry. "They hate me, miss. I know they hate me."

Teachers talk often of the need for kids to "get along." They even set aside marks for social skills on their final report. But, like Maria, they never explain why to the kids or their parents. Most of what kids will learn in their lives will have nothing to do with books or computers or TV. It will come from other people. Not getting along means cutting yourself off from much of life's learning, but for now that message is lost on Sophia.

✦ ✦ ✦

Cathy Sylvester has one more parent to see: Tracy's mother. The woman who gave birth to that sullen weight of attitude who sits in the back corner in period two. When she walks in and sits down, she doesn't look at all the way Cathy expected: a little soft and pudgy, like a mother from a 1950s sitcom, as emotionally frail and flighty as her daughter is hard. As Cathy begins to set out Tracy's problems in class, her mother rolls her eyes and laughs a nervous laugh. She knows the story well. It has been going on a long time, she says. Tracy is so stubborn. She gets something in her mind and there's no changing her. She's tried, tried in all the ways anyone can. Nicely, angrily, with humour, as a mother, as a friend. Nothing. "She just knows how to push my buttons," she says.

And Tracy has that one big button to push. Her parents' divorce. Back her into a corner and she will lay waste: "You're the one who caused this mess."

She is fifteen, her mother over forty, yet in their house Tracy is in command. She was bred into a life of turmoil and knows how to live it. Her mother doesn't. She has friends, Jennifer, Jody, and lots more, not necessarily ones that her mother would choose for her but friends who look after each other. They create a life of their own. Her mother can't do that. Too busy making a home, working, she is without the time or circumstance to have a network of friends for support. Tracy can leave any time, she has some other place to go; her mother cannot. She needs Tracy far more than Tracy needs her, and Tracy knows it.

Yet in her mother's stories about Tracy, Cathy sees something that hasn't been obvious in science class, yet has been there all along. The stubbornness, the will. When Tracy sets her mind to something, her mother says, she can't be shaken. No matter how high the mountain, she will climb it. What she has set her mind to now, however, is a social life, and the mountain in her way is school. What can Cathy, what can anyone, do to turn her the other way? Tracy is a seasoned fighter; if only she had some constructive direction in which to fight, some goal, Cathy thinks.

What about Co-op, she says to Tracy's mother. Working a job part-time, yet keeping her courses and her friends at school, it would expose Tracy to new challenges, give her the chance to see where she might go. Tracy's mother says that Tracy has talked about Co-op, but says nothing more. Cathy tries again. Finally, she says, "What if *I* say something to her?" This is what Tracy's mother has been looking for. "That would be a good idea," she says. "I'm not sure anything I suggest would go very far."

✦ ✦ ✦

It was a good turnout. The parents, guardians, or other family members of about three hundred kids came to meet their teachers. Most teachers had their interview sheets largely filled, nineteen appointment spots from beginning to end. Yet even if they had all been filled, they would be seeing fewer than one-third of the total number of kids they teach. What about the other parents? Who are they and why weren't they here?

Pat's parents, Chad's, Rodney's, Jamie's, Monika's, Sheri's, Quentin's, Kelly's, Jennifer's. Nelson had signed up his father, but he didn't show up. Why not? Parents are busy, maybe they had other commitments, or were working, or had other kids at home who needed their attention. Maybe the appointment sheet never reached them. But more likely they didn't come because they never come. Somewhere along the line, they have learned in their lives that doing something, getting involved, makes no difference.

I don't know who my son's teachers are. I don't know their names. I'm not even sure what he's taking. It's hard to keep up, and kids his age don't want to talk about anything, especially with their parents, especially about school. Besides, I can't help him any more. I never took what he's taking, or was never any good at it, or I've forgotten, or surely I must have. If I do try, I feel stupid, or he doesn't understand what I'm saying, he thinks it's me, I think it's him, and another battle we don't need begins. What would I ask his teachers anyway? What could they tell me that would make sense, that I could pass on? That would help? And I don't want to hear what I know they're going to say.

It's nearly always the parents of kids who are doing well who show up. More than half the Enhanced class parents came; from the other classes, fewer than one-quarter. And why wouldn't they be here? How onerous is it to hear four times a night from four different teachers what a wonderful daughter or son you have; by extension, what a wonderful parent you must be. The parents who spend time around their kids, who feel that kids and family are first priority: they came. The parents who have discovered that, if they are around, their kids *will* talk to them; and who, in talking with their kids, have discovered just how interesting these kids are, how much they like them and want to help them: they came. The parents who have felt the energy and excitement of their kids, their hopefulness and optimism, curiosity, joy in discovery, appetite for life; who through parenting have felt their own youthful spirit rekindled; who have learned that more important than quality time are the accidents of quantity time: they came.

The rest are not bad people. It's easy as a teacher, standing at the front of a classroom, to think they are. Who would allow a child to arrive day after day, late, homework undone? Yet really these are parents not much different from the teachers themselves: worried about their kids, confused, often weak, sometimes in over their heads. Bad parents perhaps, yet most of them care in their own fashion. It's easy too for a parent at home to think the worst of teachers whose students arrive day after day, late, homework undone. Yet most of these teachers care too. Why don't they both do better? Surely a parent knows how to parent; surely a teacher knows how to teach. Maybe they have just lost track. Maybe they have forgotten just how important they are in kids' lives. Maybe if they knew they'd do better.

Chapter 10

Tuesday, April 12, 11:15 a.m.

Sophia was very quiet the day after Parents' Night, and still seems subdued. Sabesan had his homework done, Willy was in class Friday and yesterday, but isn't here today. He's in the counselling offices. It's been decided to test him again. Even Tracy seems more "positive." Leah had a talk with Sue, and yesterday in her test she got a 72, not what she wanted, but "better, at least."

Sue is still haunted by the interview with Leah's parents. She had known it would be trouble when she saw Leah's mother. Her mouth was so tight. Still, she hadn't been expecting the vehemence of her reaction. Leah's problem certainly isn't ability, so she should have assumed her parents would be concerned, but she didn't. Sue isn't good at confrontation. She's had so little of it in her life that, when it comes, she doesn't know what to do. When Leah's mother offered her the bait, she rose to it. She had done the same this fall with parents of another student, only worse, and they had been so upset they'd complained to the principal. Not yet a parent herself, Sue seems not to understand parents' passions, or to appreciate that their hostility might really be a plea for help in dealing with their child.

In the few days since, Sue has kept replaying the interview in her mind. She has resolved that the next time, instead of counter-attacking, she will try to sketch out for parents her view of the child, so that it is that view, not the child itself, or her, or the parents, that will focus the conversation. Perhaps then the mood will be less threatening.

She did promise Leah's parents to move Leah closer to the front, but decided to wait until yesterday. She didn't want the change of seating to seem connected to Parent's Night. Yesterday, she asked Leah and Pat a question and, when she couldn't hear their answers very well, suggested, "I think you two should sit up here."

Nelson's father wasn't at Parents' Night because Nelson forgot to tell him. But Nelson has had some good days lately. Yesterday in science, Cathy divided the class into six groups. The textbook presented a problem: Oil has been discovered offshore. Each of the groups is to be a commission of inquiry examining various related questions to decide whether to allow drilling. Nelson got his chance to work with Jennifer, Tracy, and Jody. All the groups were to prepare yesterday and present their case today. But Jennifer, who was here yesterday, isn't here today, and Tracy, who *is* here, wasn't yesterday, so neither can take part. It's down to Nelson and Jody.

They walk together to the front of the room, Jody deter-mined, Nelson confident and proud. Jody begins, Nelson draping an arm around her shoulder for the nanosecond it takes her to throw it off. Her talk is straightforward. Drilling means a better economy and more jobs, not just for oil workers, but for fishermen and others as well. Any potential problems, especially oil spills, can be handled. There's no reason not to go ahead, Jody opines.

Now it's Nelson's turn. He begins cockily, but more or less repeats Jody's position. The class isn't impressed. "That's just what she said!" someone yells. Nelson carries on, unimpressed with them. He starts into an elaborate defence of Jody's environmental safety plans. He seems only to have the vaguest idea of where he is going, the last word of each thought triggering whatever comes next. He's getting himself in deeper. "And if we ever had an oil spill," he says, "we'd build a dam around it to keep the oil in." Eyebrows rise, including Jody's.

"What sort of dam, Nelson?" Cathy asks. He raises his hands, opens them, and holds them apart in the shape of an oval. He looks down at them and, dissatisfied, walks to the board, picks up some chalk and starts to draw. Jody walks with him. He makes a wavy line for water. He's getting his confidence back. "But how deep is the water?" someone asks. "And how can you build a dam so deep?" His eyes squint nearly shut; these kids are starting to get on his nerves. He draws two lines perpendicular to the water line; then it hits him. He turns from the board and faces them, suddenly cool and knowing – but he gets too excited. "And, and," he stutters, "oil is less dense than water, *of course*." A grin covers his face; he slows himself down, but just barely. "So oil, *of course*, will float on top of the water." He's got them. He stops for what seems to him a good half minute, actually about three or four seconds, to allow his words to sink in. Even Jody looks impressed, and Jody doesn't impress. He starts up again. "It'll work," he shrieks. "And it won't cost much." Then he forgets himself and draws his dam lines much deeper than he needs to, nearly to the bottom. He's in trouble again.

"But how much will it cost?"

"What'll it be made of?"

He pauses. His head steady, in left profile to the class, his eyes madly scanning the wall in front of him. "Ah, it's high tech," he says. "It's, it's –" he spots something, "– poolar. Yes, it's made out of 'poolar.' A poolar screen."

The kids are beside themselves. "And how much would this 'poolar' cost?" they ask.

"Not much."

"How much?"

"Not much."

"It'd cost too much."

"No, it wouldn't."

"Yes, it would."

Getting nowhere, he finally writes on the board, "200$." They laugh. He adds another zero.

"And if the oil well went dry?"

"We'd just move the dam."

Uh oh.

Jody has heard enough and walks back to her seat. "Jody! Jody!" he calls out to her. She doesn't even turn around. Like Lucy to Charlie Brown: "You're on your own," she snaps.

"So how would you move this poolar dam?"

He draws a hook on the front of the dam, then a tiny boat – the laughter increases – then a huge motor behind the boat, far bigger than the boat itself.

"And how would the workers get to the dam?"

He draws a helicopter, then a ladder and door. Then another helicopter.

"And how would you clean up the spill?"

"With a giant sponge," someone yells. They all laugh.

"But what if there's a hurricane?"

Without pause, he draws a roof over the dam. "Like the SkyDome," he grins.

Cathy thanks him for his "very creative presentation." He walks to the back corner and sits down beside Jody, who turns away. Cathy goes on to something else. A voice suddenly interrupts her. "Oh, did I tell you," Nelson chirps. "It's also got a day care for the kids."

As the next presentation begins, Nelson starts fiddling with a box of candies. For days Noel had been trying to sell boxes of chocolate-covered almonds to raise money for the prom. He had the boxes stacked in a carton, which he sat on his desk and carried from classroom to staff room and back. It seemed always with him and always full. Nelson asked if he could help, and he's had the carton with him ever since. To those who claim to be broke, "I'll spot you," he says, "you can pay me tomorrow." He has offered to open a box and sell the almonds individually, almond by almond, five cents a piece. Yesterday in science, first to arrive as usual, he stood guard in the doorway. "Nobody gets into this room without buying a box," he snarled at everyone who pushed by. He accosted two science teachers who were merely going into the back room for supplies. Each bought a box. Then he pitched Henry, who can hardly speak English. He described the crispy texture of the almond, the explosion of flavour at first bite, then, on entering the stomach, how it "disperses all around, and fills you up. Actually, you wouldn't have to eat lunch. You'd save money!" he enthused.

Overhearing, Cathy laughed. "You're sure a great salesman, Nelson."

"If I'm such a great salesman," he said, "why don't *you* buy a box from me?"

"I'm not an easy sell."

The class over, again he filled the doorway. "Nobody leaves this room without buying a box."

In math class this morning, he took the boxes from the carton and arranged them on his desk in a store-window display. He even sold one to Quentin. Sheri growled at him from across the room. "All you do is harass us. We buy one just so we don't have to see your face again."

He has sold more than fifty boxes.

✦ ✦ ✦

Like Tracy, Quentin wasn't in Cathy's science class yesterday so he has nothing to present today. He just sits alone at his desk, sometimes watching through his squinted eyes. His story is getting curiouser. The first two weeks of the semester, he didn't miss a day, the last three weeks he's been hardly here a day. His good start is long gone; he is now so far behind and disconnected that even when he is here, nothing makes sense to him. He doesn't listen, doesn't learn; he survives one day to stay away the next, and the day after and the day after until he's embarrassed enough to put in another pointless appearance in class. And his eyes. That squint. There's got to be something wrong. Every few days, Cathy contacts his guidance counsellor. What about Quentin's eyes? What's being done? He has an appointment with an ophthalmologist, she's told, or he's had one and has another soon. Weeks pass and as they close in on an answer, his absences pile up and his semester dies.

So many people know pieces of Quentin's story, so few have had the time or energy or need or desire to stay with it to the end. Those who know him best seem haunted by him. He symbolizes so much. He was born in Jamaica, the youngest of four brothers of three different fathers. His next-older brother was kicked out of Kennedy last year for poor attendance. Quentin will be eighteen in two weeks. His is a common Jamaican–Canadian pattern: man and woman marry, have children, father leaves, mother goes to Canada, children stay behind with grandmother. Mother saves, brings kids to Canada years later. Kids older, mother semi-Canadian, now don't know each other very well. Mother, new man in her life who isn't their father, boys, a history of bad experiences with male adults – father gone, grandfather gone – move in with stepfather who doesn't want them.

Quentin joined his mother in Canada when he was twelve. He was placed in grade seven, appropriate to his age, at the Valleys, a nearby elementary school. He spent two years there. It had no special programs for newcomers to Canada; he was put into a regular class and got passed along despite his obvious difficulties. In Jamaica, he had had little education, had developed few of the habits of learning; he lacked the instinct and training that make someone stay with a problem, work through its steps, grapple with difficulty and frustration. He was fine when he knew the answer; he had no skills, no strategies for figuring it out when he didn't. After his two years at the Valleys, he arrived at Kennedy two years further behind, feeling two years stupider.

At Kennedy he was given special help. He spent a year and a half in ESL classes. His problem with male authority figures continued. In classes with male teachers, he would shut down, go quiet, sullen, become impertinent. At the sight of one male teacher, he fell over in his chair as if in a dead faint, and just lay on the floor. Then he was put in Dan Henderson's electronics class.

The good thing about a tech course, Dan Henderson says, is that, the first day of the semester, the kids arrive excited, fresh, without any history in it or in anything like it. Right away, they get to *do* things. They *see* things happen. The academic subjects require such a leap of faith. Little of what they offer seems relevant or important; trust me, teachers say, eventually you'll see. In electronics or auto mechanics, you see right away. By the time you see the science or math of it, the stuff you can't do, you're doing it; by the time you realize book learning is required, you're already hooked.

Quentin was good at electronics. He was an adept radio operator and worked hard towards his licence. It may have been the only thing he had done well in years. His performance in his other classes improved as well. When good feelings weren't enough to get him to school, Dan was on the phone. "Haul your ass out of that bed!" he'd yell. The next day, Quentin would be there.

But Quentin had more corners ahead. Dan remembers now that he was squinting a little by the end of last year. He didn't take electronics this fall, though Dan had hoped he would. He was doing better, and he probably thought he could handle the subjects he needed to make up. By the start of this semester, Quentin's squint was more pronounced. His counsellor, and a vice-principal, and his former ESL teacher, Carolyn Quinton, decided to get to the bottom of things, now that there seemed a bottom to get to. An optometrist told them that Quentin has a conical cornea that distorts his vision. Glasses, which he wears occasionally, or soft contact lenses can improve his sight slightly; hard lenses reshape the cornea and would work much better. A corneal transplant, now common and relatively simple, would be more effective still, but it's usually done only on adults. A conical cornea often appears in combination with severe allergies, which Quentin has, in tall kids with long, thin arms and fingers like his, and often in families with a history of eye problems, which his family has. The teachers and counsellors seemed finally to be getting somewhere.

Next Quentin would need to see an ophthalmologist to confirm the diagnosis, and set the next steps in motion. An appointment was made, but Quentin lost his government health card. It would take a few weeks to replace it, and the semester was moving on. Down the line was a bigger obstacle. He was going to need hard lenses, and who was going to pay for them? He had no money, his mother had no money. Is she on welfare? his counsellor asked. If so, he might qualify for help under some support program. Quentin didn't know. Does she go out of the house every day? the counsellor asked. Sometimes she does, sometimes she doesn't. They arranged his health card, his appointment, his prescription, certain that he'd qualify under a welfare program. To keep things moving, Carolyn Quinton went with him to the optometrist and paid the fifty-dollar deposit on his hard lenses herself. A few days later, unbeknownst to everyone, Quentin returned to the optometrist and got back the deposit.

The staff's patience, which had worn transparently thin, now shattered. All the time that had been put in, all the people in his corner: he had let them down. It's not easy for a teacher to decide to get involved with a kid, especially one like Quentin. So much about a kid in need is beyond a teacher's control, so much can be easily undone, rarely does anything really change. But this time, several teachers *had* gotten involved. With Quentin it seemed as if a single trigger could be pulled and everything would be different. These teachers imagined vividly how the world would suddenly appear clear to Quentin, the frosted glass of his impaired vision gone. His posture straightening, his head rising; all the things he couldn't do all these years because, he thought, he was stupid or inept, he would be able to do. A lost life suddenly found. Then he collected that deposit.

The next day, Carolyn Quinton asked him why: Because I don't have the money to pay off the rest, he said. Why lose the deposit too? I wanted to get it back for you.

Now the teachers are trying again. Quentin still needs his appointment and his card. He will get his hard lenses, welfare will pick up the cost. But the lenses won't be easy to get used to. Quentin must take them out every night and clean them or his eyes will become sore and infected. Will he do that? Or, as he has done all his life, will he do it this week and not the next?

♦ ♦ ♦

Doug sits one desk over and one desk back of Quentin. He is one of the first to class on the days he is here, and one of the last to leave. When others ask questions of Cathy, he hovers nearby. Not likely to have done the homework himself, or the reading, or the lab, he has no questions himself to ask, but he wants to be around. When everyone else leaves, he will come out with something, funny he thinks, interesting he hopes, awkward and abrupt to be sure. Always with a big, sudden smile, a smile that *wants* to be seen, acknowledged, embraced. Doug is lonely, and doesn't know how to make himself unlonely.

His parents split up five months after he was born. They had married right out of school, high school sweethearts; he was their only child. They were still very young, with lots of time to create new family arrangements, and new complications for Doug. His father remarried and moved ninety kilometres north to Barrie; he and his second wife have a five-year-old son, Doug's half-brother. After the divorce, Doug lived with his mother, who married a man with two sons of his own, now twelve and ten, who are Doug's stepbrothers. Then his mother and step-father split; his stepfather and stepbrothers now live in a small town in British Columbia. When the marriage was breaking up, Doug moved to Barrie to live with his dad. It was grade eight and he stayed a year. Last year, he moved back with his mother. With all the disruption, his mother's biggest hope is for them to have a place of their own. To save money, she has moved in with her sister and husband in Newmarket, a commuter suburb north-east of Metro Toronto, and Doug has moved in with his grand-mother, his mother's mother, in Port Credit, not far from the school. Doug's mother is manager of the fish section at a nearby Mississauga supermarket. She must commute every day, almost an hour in unbusy times.

Doug spends some of his weekends with his father and half-brother in Barrie. Twice last summer, he entered fishing derbies with his dad. Occasionally, he stays home with his grandmother. Most other weekends he is in Newmarket with his mom, not staying with her in her apartment over the garage, but in the main part of his uncle and aunt's big house. His uncle is an accoun-tant and has several businesses. Now in his early forties, he is semi-retired, and his aunt has stopped work entirely. They have their house in Newmarket and a place on Marathon Key in Florida; Doug has twice gone scuba diving with them there. This semester his uncle arranged for a condominium in

Whistler, B.C., through a client, and Doug took a week off school to ski with them. They have no children; they treat Doug almost like their own.

Last weekend, after Doug had received his mid-term report, the family all had a little talk. You can do better, his mother and aunt told him, but you're doing fine; you're not, his uncle said. Sixty-seven in science, 77 in phys ed, 78 in computers, 51 in English: those marks won't get you anywhere. Maybe into a community college, but certainly not university. You've got to do better. Doug respects his uncle, and will do better, he thinks, especially next year, and the year after, and certainly in his last year of high school, when marks really count. He could do well, he knows, and his teachers know it too.

Doug has had a busy semester. He has on-road driving lessons on Mondays from 4:00 to 5:00 p.m. Tuesdays and Thursdays he has in-class driving lessons from 6:00 to 9:00. He works with his mother in the fish department at the supermarket on Wednesdays from 4:00 to 9:30, often on Friday nights and Saturdays as well. He plays house league hockey every Saturday during the winter; his coach asked him if he wanted to play one level higher next year, which would mean another game and practice a week. Now he has tryouts for the school baseball team. His grandmother is old and needs help around the apartment. She does the cooking, he vacuums and washes the floors, they do the dishes together. Tuesday, Wednesday, and Thursday nights he isn't home before 10:30; that's when he does his homework, about half an hour a night.

That was enough to get him by last year, even this fall, depending on which subjects he was taking. But science, with labs to write up, demands the grind of daily homework; English requires reading, and reading takes time. He *needs* to get his driver's licence if he is to have any social life at all; he *needs* to take driving lessons to get his licence; he *needs* his job to pay for the lessons. He *needs* to play sports, his uncle tells him, to learn discipline and teamwork. He *needs* time for his mother and father, uncle and aunt, on weekends and special trips. His grandmother *needs* help at home. He has no vacuums of time in his life to fit in the semester's increased demands; there are no easy things for him to give up. His sixteen-year-old life is too complicated. Doing well requires the opportunity to lose track of time, to try something until you can master it. Making and keeping a friend takes the same kind of time, but Doug has never had the chance. He's never learned how. Just as he has never learned to sit in one place for two hours a night, let alone to think, concentrate, or work at something until he has command of it. It takes more than will. Skills that he should have learned years earlier, when learning was easier, he now struggles to learn for the first time, with all the complications of life tugging at his sleeve.

Who will help him? Not his mother. You need to feel your own life in some kind of order before you can help order someone else's. Not his father. His life has been too separate, too distant, for too long. Nor his grandmother, she is too old; nor even his uncle, the one person in the family who understands the connection between the right habits of life and success. He's only an uncle by marriage, and it's not his place to take on Doug's problems.

What about Cathy? We've all seen the movie: dedicated teacher befriends lonely, misunderstood kid; kid defies all expectations, makes good. It makes a better story than any about a dedicated mother or father, even an unselfish uncle or grandmother, because the teacher isn't family and has no obligation outside the classroom. She saves the kid out of the best of human motives, because he or she needs help. An entirely credible and inspiring story, one that has happened and will happen again.

It's the bottom of the ninth inning, the kid is down 3−0. He's had his chances, fifteen runners have reached base, yet each time he's about to get back in the game, he strikes out, or his parents do, or his brothers or sisters, or his friends. Now three more runners fill the bases, two outs, a pinch-hitter is sent to the plate. The kid's teacher. A home run wins the game; anything short of that leads to defeat. In baseball and in life, ninth-inning grand-slam home runs almost never happen. The teacher has little chance of saving the game; others may have had far better chances earlier on. It may be unfair to expect, even to think, that a teacher can make this kind of difference, yet none of that matters. *She* is the hope.

Several years ago, Cathy had in her class a truly gifted kid who wouldn't learn. Gifted kids are usually obsessive, she says, and his obsessions had been turned 180 degrees the wrong way. He wouldn't take a note; no matter what anyone did, he simply refused to learn. Only two things in his life seemed to matter to him: doing bicycle tricks, and Tae Kwon Do. Later, she learned there was a third. His mother had divorced his father and remarried, and there was a new baby in the family. His third passion was to punish his mother, his stepfather, his new sibling, everyone who had changed his life into what he didn't want it to be. Retribution became his one true goal. Not long ago, Cathy saw him again. He had dropped out of school and was drifting from job to job; several years later, he was still working hard at punishing his family.

About the same time he was in her class, Cathy's own kids were reaching an independent, imperfect age. She wasn't ready for the problems they posed. She had grown up in her perfect little suburb of Port Credit, the only child of her perfect parents. She was a good student, member of the right school clubs, reasonable and responsible; she wanted what they wanted, thought what they thought, and together they moved through her perfect childhood. It would be the same with her children, she was sure. Able to control so many of the variables, the amount of TV they watched, the kids they played with, she could control the outcome. Except her first child was slightly hyperactive. Once he said to her something that Nelson might have said, "Sometimes I get so excited, I can feel my head blow off." She would ask him to cut the grass, he wouldn't; pick up his clothes, he wouldn't; do his homework, he wouldn't. That was it. No explanation, no superior reasoning, nothing to justify his actions, just *no*. She doesn't know why he was that way, but she was immensely relieved when later he found a goal for himself, attending university, and everything began to change. Then nothing could stop him. He finally saw that, although cutting the grass and picking up his clothes wouldn't bring him any closer to university, the discipline and habit of doing these chores would.

"Motivation comes from within," Cathy likes to say. It isn't what she wants to say or believe. She is a scientist and a parent, she wants problems to be reduced to clear, identifiable steps, which if taken will produce the result she wants. But that's not how it is. "I'm not sure you really can motivate someone," she continues. Then not quite liking the sound of her own words, she amends them, "at least over the long run." Most of her Enhanced kids have that motivation, as do many of the kids in her upper-grade classes, even those who aren't especially gifted. The good student has a goal that will see him or her through the slog of hard work to where achievement and reward lie. But why that student and why not others?

Certainly it has something to do with the home, with parents who set the right expectations, offer the right assumptions, who help their kids write the right stories for themselves. But there's more to it, she knows. Some kids will simply have none of it. Same family, same circumstances, same air to breathe, two different blobs of *being*, one writes one story, the other another. She used to think she knew why, but teaching and parenting can make anyone humble. Now she knows only that kids who succeed work hard, have a goal, and are self-motivated, but in this recipe for success which ingredient comes first, and in what amounts, is anyone's guess.

She is a professional. She knows her subject, comes to work every day prepared. She is upbeat and pleasant to show the kids that she likes being here, with them, and loves what she teaches. She wants the classroom to be a "happy place, so they'll want to come and keep coming." Her goal each day is to give them "a good hour" in every way. She tries to embody all of the homilies she likes to sow among them: "You've got to work hard in this life"; "Life is choices"; "You've got to have a goal"; "Motivation comes from within." She doesn't just stand at the front of the room behind her big desk, the traditional "sage from the stage," but goes out among them. Encouraging questions before and after class; during class, especially during labs, walking up and down the rows of desks, looking at their work, hearing their voices. Over a grasshopper being dissected, talk comes easy about lots of things, including those that matter most in a kid's life that day – a fight with a friend, a part-time job, a mother in the hospital – giving her a glimpse behind the adolescent veil. The talk is never for long, there's always another voice, "Miss, miss," to keep her moving.

She tries to say "positive" things – "Good question, Nelson!" – because, she knows, this may be the only good news these kids hear from an adult all day. She refuses to get upset. A "calm and relaxed" room allows endorphins to be released, so learning comes easier. She can't remember the last time she "blew up" in class. If I do, I'll say something I shouldn't, she says, and kids remember. One unfortunate phrase – "You're so stupid" – can define and last a lifetime.

For Doug, Cathy's involvement has meant someone to talk to, it has pushed him to spend a little more time doing labs, preparing for tests, with slightly better results. Will that change his life, generate better habits, lead him to university instead of community college? No. But it will lead him into the next grade, where one year older, one year closer to the crunch of university applications, he might find his own motivation to work at the level of his ability. "There's only one of me," Cathy says. "I can't take seventy kids home, even if I wanted to." But really, she asks, why should she want to? If the kids and their parents don't do their share, why should she do more than hers? "Doug's dad is in Barrie, his mom's in Newmarket, he's dying for love," she says. "Crying for it. He hangs around my desk, acts out here and there, just to get my attention."

How much of what she says is true, how much does she really believe, how much is her own fatigue and rationalization, how much is to allow her to get on more easily with her own life? If changing someone else's life requires getting involved in such a way as to jeopardize your own, how many of us will do it?

Halfway through a semester, kids and teachers get tired, worn down by the build-up to mid-term reports, the tests that have to be set, studied for, marked, and results entered. By this time, it seems to kids, a teacher likes you or doesn't, a course is boring or not, you will do well or won't. Hope remains, but reality has replaced fantasy, and energy needs motivation. In the early weeks, teachers spend a lot of time establishing routines, setting standards, bringing strays back into the fold, inciting, encouraging, with the hope that by mid-term the stragglers will be able to take over more of their own load. Doug isn't doing that, and Cathy's patience is turning to annoyance. He seems so capable, yet so lazy. He half-does his homework, half-does his labs; half-does everything. Hovering at Cathy's desk, he tries to be playfully contrary. Cathy doesn't get his humour; he doesn't get her impatience. His smile is too anxious, too needy. As ususal, the more he is looking for from others, the less he gets.

✦ ✦ ✦

A few weeks ago, Cathy was doing a lesson on electrical circuits. Some circuits are in parallel, she explains, so if one light goes out, or is turned off, the rest are unaffected. Some others are in series, where if one goes out, they all go out.

"Why?" she asks.

"It's like Christmas lights," Doug says, just back from his ski trip.

"Right," Cathy says excitedly. "But why?"

"One goes out, they all go out," he mutters; he remembers.

"Yes, yes, but why?"

"Murphy's Law."

Chapter 11

Wednesday, April 13, 8:32 a.m.

Posters had begun appearing around the school weeks ago – "The *Kronicle* is Coming." Last week, a tag was added to each one, "April 11." Then a few days later, the second "1" in all the "11"s was changed by hand to a "3." Today, the *Kronicle* came. There are newspapers at every classroom door and bins of them in the front foyer near the office. The *Kronicle* staff are everywhere, proud in their brand new *Kronicle* baseball shirts, the open-mouthed, growling Kennedy Kougar on the front, a big "94" on the back. For the first time since the mid 1970s, Kennedy has a school newspaper.

Eight tabloid-sized pages long, one page each for "Literature," "Classified," "Sports," "Culture," "Social," and "Entertainment," the first two pages for "Current Issues." Beneath the masthead, its first front-page headline screams out in big black letters, "Is Our School Racist?" A mixture of seriousness, provocation, and timeliness, the story offers the perfect subject, the perfect tone, for a school newspaper.

"T. L. Kennedy has a bad reputation," the story's opening line accuses. "If one were to enter the hallways of TLK on any given school day, he would witness one of the most multicultural places of education in the province. Naturally, given the growing nationalism of regions over the globe, he would expect problems to arise between certain ethnic groups of students. Problems driven by racism." The writer, a respected senior student, is white. "This quick assumption would, perhaps, be correct in some schools. However, at TLK, racism is not as evident." Groups of kids from similar cultures do hang around together, he acknowledges, racial slurs are whispered or written on bathroom walls, but there is no warfare between groups. The majority of kids and teachers simply would not put up with it. "Our school is representative of the 1990s' mood," the writer concludes, "equality and tolerance among diversity." Canada is a multicultural country, Mississauga a multicultural city, he continues. If the story of the Balkans and the former Soviet Union is that different cultures fight, here the story is that they do not. There may be some violence and racism in the streets and arcades nearby, sometimes between students, but that is there, and this is here. The story is illustrated by a photograph of four Kennedy students, one white, one Oriental, one South Asian, one black; the black kid, with a bandanna on his head, is Nelson.

It wasn't easy for Principal Terry Chaffe to give his approval to the newspaper. On the one hand, the prospect of a school paper was tremendously exciting. He had been thinking for some time that the school needed a kick of sorts. Kids come and kids go, sometimes semester to semester, before roots can be put down. A school should hold a special place in their lives, he thinks. That's how it had been for him, and when he sees kids rushing out the door at 3:10 to their part-time jobs, to Mom's place on weekdays, to Dad's on weekends, he worries that they are missing something, a connection that makes life feel a little more worthwhile, that makes you want to hang around school a little longer, do just a little more and better. A school newspaper, Terry thought, is a chance to get kids thinking and talking about the school.

On the other hand, he knows, it is risky. After all the thinking and talking, who knows what the kids will say. The excitement he's looking for will come only if the paper is written with a student voice, expressing how the students think about the things that matter to them. A heavy staff hand will kill it. But he also has powerful adults to deal with – parents, taxpayers, education officials – who may feel it isn't appropriate that students write about sex, or drugs, or racism, or abortion. The question is: Who has final authority over what goes in that paper? As principal, it has to be him, even the kids accept that. But how will he exercise that authority, and how will the kids respond? They will surely push at the limits, as kids must; he will surely feel his limits pushed. The kids will cry "censorship," he will cry "responsibility," and after the second or third issue, they will either give up on each other in an explosion of frustration, or realize that tension is part of putting out a newspaper. For what is the real learning experience here, for the other students as well as for *Kronicle* staff? Is it the direct experience or the indirect one? Is it in learning enough about homosexuality or abortion to write an article, or is it in the research, the writing and rewriting, the give-and-take with editors, the meeting of deadlines, the debate inside the paper's offices and outside amongst students over propriety, acceptability, and community standards? In the end, the real question for all of them: Will Terry and the kids be able to accept the messiness of putting out a newspaper and the public debate that follows as the essential learning experiences?

The layout of the paper is good, Terry thinks, and so too the range of subjects covered. Besides the racism story, "Current Issues" includes articles on Ontario's new graduated licensing system for young drivers and on Scarborough's "zero tolerance" policy on school violence, and an essay on the environment entitled "It's Our Earth – Let's Help!" There are three poems and a short story in the "Poetry Corner," notices for "Education Week" and the school's formal dance in June; an article about the girls' junior volleyball team, and about the curling team on its way to the provincial championships; a "Kultural Kalendar" for May, listing not just the traditional holidays, Mother's Day and Victoria Day, but "Boy's Day in Japan," "Id-ul-adha," a Muslim celebration marking "the success of Prophet Abraham in the test taken by Allah," and the "Ascension of Baha'ullah," commemorating for the Bahai "the passing of Baha'ullah after 40 years as a prisoner."

There is a tribute to the Person of the Month – "some-big-shot-who-hasn't-really-done-anything-but-gets-it-just-because-they-are-an-in-the-limelight person, right??" the article reads. "WRONG!!!" Rather, it's Harry Hilts, one of the custodians and "everyone's pal." A horoscope column, adapted slightly to the school setting. Message to Cancer: "If you shake [the vice-principal's] hand you will have good luck for a whole month." To Leo: "Stay at least ten feet away from any science teacher." An advice column, "Dear Anonymous": "My parents do not care. [They] never seem interested in anything I do. They always have excuses for not spending time with me. . . . I don't know how to let them know how much this hurts me." Signed, "Hurt." The student "Dear Abby" suggests that talking to parents directly may lead to more fighting, so to write a letter instead. "I know this hurts a lot, but some parents are incapable of giving the love that all children deserve. Therefore, the best solution is to look elsewhere for emotional support." There is a review of the drama department's play in a local school festival, the one for which Sophia was stage manager; a review of *Miss Saigon,* which many drama and music students attended on a field trip to

Toronto, the *Kronicle* Kritic awarding it "4 out of 5 Kougars." A "Krossword" puzzle; the Music Charts, the top ten for "R&B," "Pop Canadian," "Rock American," and "Metal"; two comic strips, and an article by Rohita on the Black History Club, started by students "who wanted to know more about their culture." "NO, YOU DON'T HAVE TO BE BLACK TO BE INVOLVED," she writes.

As the day goes on, a consensus among kids and teachers develops: a good, solid first issue with too many typos and spelling errors, which particularly aggravate Terry. There will be one more issue before school ends.

✦ ✦ ✦

The Black History Club has lobbied unsuccessfully for some time for a Black History course at the school. Its request, delivered politically to politically sensitive ears, has muddied the easily muddied waters. Are the club's motives in pressing this issue academic or political? Are the school's motives in denying or ignoring it academic or political? Would teaching such a course be an admission of past wrongs, a gesture, a capitulation, a trendy move? As a school are we teaching black kids, white kids, and Asian kids, or *kids*? If there is a Black History course, why not a South Asian History course, a Chinese History course? Shouldn't we be teaching instead to the new realities of these kids? They are living in Canada. Canada is their new country. They need to know about life here, our history, our literature, our ways. Already they start so many years behind; scarce resources of time and money should be spent helping them catch up. Maybe so, critics say, but to teach them our ways, don't we need to learn some of theirs, if only to make them know we care?

The Black History Club meets every week. Lately, however, Lawrence Dillard, the club's driving force, a former Kennedy student now at York University, has been busy with a part-time job, and hasn't always been able to make it. Without him, meetings have become sporadic. Last week, he couldn't attend and a student speaker was arranged to talk about the Somalian experience in Canada. Just eight kids gathered in their meeting room, and teacher Ed Wugalter, the club's staff advisor. The speaker didn't show up. Ed had a video ready just in case on the black history of British Columbia, and a handout from a news story about Khalid Muhammed, assistant to Louis Farrakhan of the U.S.-based Nation of Islam, who had been refused entry to Canada to give a speech, on the basis of the country's "hate crime" laws. Khalid Muhammed, among other things, had referred to whites and Jews as "bloodsuckers." Ed asked the kids if they thought he should have been barred: is freedom of speech an absolute right, or a relative one that can be overridden in certain circumstances?

Indirectly at first, then directly, they began to talk about what it feels like to be black in Canada. What they really want, they said, is to be judged not as "blacks," or as members of the "black community," but as their own selves. Whites aren't "oppressors," Jews aren't "bloodsuckers," but some whites and Jews are, just as some blacks are "criminals," but most blacks aren't. One girl in the group is twenty years old with a twenty-month-old son. She talked about newspaper stories, stories on TV, a murder, a suspect, a photo – a black. She knows that at home the viewers, who are mostly white, see that photo, see a black, not a person; they see her and her life is affected. Curtis, who in Lawrence's absence seems the leader of the group, talked about going into a store, any store, any time. He can't help it, he said. He looks around, he sees every eye on him, he senses in every mind the apprehension: "He's going to steal something." It's never *not* that way, he said. The others nodded. It may be the same for every spike-haired punk and metal head, except *their* visibility is by choice.

They can go home, remove their metal and cut off their spikes. Curtis can't wash off his black skin.

Do you know how that makes me feel? he asked. How do you feel? Ed Wugalter asked him back. What do you do? They shrugged; what *can* you do? A few weeks earlier, a white woman had been murdered while eating in an upscale Toronto café called Just Desserts. The killing was on the front pages, leading off the news, day after day for a week. People get killed every day, Curtis said, black people, Chinese people – tiny news stories, unnoticed deaths. Here a white victim, an upper-middle-class neighbourhood, four blacks accused, and it's everywhere. And each of those accused is him. Why can't they see me as me? he asked. But you can't just hate others for hating you, they all decided. Hate hurts too much, takes over your life, turns you into something you're not. That's what is so terrible about these stories. It is having someone who isn't me and doesn't know me *define me*. A white, seeing a white murderer's face in the paper, doesn't see himself. Why should I have to see me?

Matthew is the only black born in Africa among the group. He talked about this black perception problem, quietly, eloquently. "I know what I am," he said. "They may see me a certain way, but that isn't me. I know it isn't me, and it never will be me. I know who I am, what I want to be, and I will be it. Nothing will stand in my way. Not you. Not me." How can he sound so sure? Maybe he hasn't been in Canada as long as the others, maybe he's had different experiences, or the same experiences but has seen them a different way. Maybe his story will always be different; maybe it won't.

Offering a Black History course may or may not be a political act, a gesture, an admission, a capitulation, it may or may not be academically valuable, but it would give black kids a story that is theirs, a reason to see themselves as they feel themselves to be, a *them* that isn't what others say it is. Another reference point, something to hold onto when the images all around them, the experiences of their lives, make them wonder.

✦ ✦ ✦

A few days ago, Noel was discussing the persistent use of the adjective "black" in *Romeo and Juliet*. What does "black" symbolize, he asked.

"Evil," said Ryan.

"Power," said Nelson.

✦ ✦ ✦

Claudine Blake began working at Kennedy last November. She was hired through a program created out of the recommendations of a provincial government task force on racism. Visible minority kids, especially black kids, face special problems in this society and so need special help, the report concluded. She is here two days a week, at another high school two other days; the fifth day she spends at the Board offices. She is twenty-six years old, black, without much experience in special education and teaching, with much more in basketball. Tough and determined, she is trained in the intimacy of sports. She likes to get close to people and to know them well.

She and the counselling department identified twenty-two kids, Sheri and Quentin among them, with the intelligence and strength of personality to succeed, but who weren't doing well. She spent much of her first few weeks with them conducting group sessions on managing and coping within the school, on writing résumés, on job search skills, on conflict resolution. She learned quickly, however, that her real job was one on one. She had to get to know each kid, know his or her story well enough to uncover the root causes of the failure, to know each of them well enough to care. To explain them to teachers, and teachers to them.

One of the kids she counsels arrives to class almost every day in his baseball hat. Wearing hats in school is against school policy. To his white teacher, one such slip is ignorance, two is accident, three and he wonders: is this kid trying to show me up? It may be that the kid is just forgetful, wears his hat from the moment he wakes to the moment he falls asleep, and doesn't know it's there. Which is it? Unless you talk to him, you'll never find out, Claudine knows.

Another of her kids, Miranda, is doing better, except in science. She had a 28 on her last test. Claudine called her into her tiny cubicle-office. What happened? she asks. Miranda shrugs. Have you talked with your teacher? *No.* Why? *He's weird.* You've got to talk with him. Go and see him, today. *Ah, miss, I'll go next week.* Today. *Next week.* Look, I'll go with you, Claudine says. We'll go today. *Okay.* No, Claudine thinks again, you talk over your test with him today, and we'll see him together next week. *Ah, miss.* Claudine may act like their teammate and partner, but she knows when someone is letting the side down. They strike a deal. Miranda will go to her science class now, talk to her teacher, and she and Claudine will see him after school. After science class, Miranda returns to Claudine's office, a smile on her face. The teacher isn't at school today. They will see him together next week.

Claudine will stay with these kids the rest of the year, see them periodically through the summer; already she's trying to help them find summer jobs. Next year, she doesn't know if the program will continue, meetings about that are going on right now. She has helped some kids, she thinks, their average grades are slightly higher, their attendance is up, but there have been no dramatic turnabouts and these are turnabout kids. She finds herself so frustrated at times. A few weeks ago, from an upstairs window, she noticed some of her kids fighting in the parking lot. One fell against her car and dented it. She thought of going down to break up the fight, but decided to watch instead. She was nearly in tears. After all she had gone through with them, the managing and coping skills, the conflict-resolution techniques, and still "they had no way of working out things without fighting."

Earlier in the semester, Claudine held a "Change Your Future" conference for the kids from the two schools she serves. They spent much of the day listening to young black speakers – a lawyer, a teacher, an accountant, a businessman – talk about themselves. Their childhoods, what they liked to do when they were the age of the kids in their audience. Their intended message was "If I can make it, so can you." They spoke one after another of their hard work, discipline, and dedication, the Saturday nights at home preparing for tests or exams while their friends were out partying. They painted a rather grim picture, in fact, though they didn't intend to. Their attitude was a natural outcome of pride in their own achievement, young self-made men and women eager to recall the struggle while forgetting the satisfactions that drove them on, welcoming the kids before them into the fold of success even as they shut the door on them. Still, the symbolism of their achievement did help to get the message across. As Sheri said afterwards, she saw this lawyer, this teacher, this accountant, this businessman, and they were no smarter than she is. Ten years from now, *she* could be standing there, hushing the room with her story of being shot in the neck, her dramatic turnabout, her accomplishments as a lawyer.

Now five months into her work, Claudine is beginning to sense how wide the divide is between those achievers and her students. She didn't feel it that day, just as the kids didn't. But back in her office, as the same kids come in with the same old problems, her frustration has risen. Getting to know kids may be the first critical step, earning their trust, motivating them, learning the habits that have to be reversed, but the real slog begins when she tries to reform those habits. Change doesn't come from a pep talk at half-time of a forty-minute game, or in the midst of a season or a semester. Change comes from good habits that form and reform over a lifetime and that kind of change takes time that few kids or teachers may have the patience for. She is learning that dramatic turnabouts, if they come at all, come slowly, like the Hollywood overnight success that is really ten years in the making.

She may share the black skin of her students, which earns her an easier ear, but she is an achiever and they are not, and she doesn't know what it's like not to be one. Like other achievers, like the black speakers at the conference, like most teachers in this and any school, she doesn't really know how she got to where she is. Teachers are much better at teaching good students; the rest are often a frustrating, annoying mystery. Why don't they listen, why don't they come to school every day, do their homework, see me if they have a problem? *I* did. *I* would. Until she can delve into her own story more deeply than to the easy maxims of "worked hard," "never gave up," to the *whys*, her black skin and her love for kids won't be enough.

✦ ✦ ✦

It is an extraordinary sight. Drama class: sixteen kids of all colours, their shoes off, in a ragged circle on the floor, some sitting cross-legged, others lying on their stomachs, heads propped on their hands, almost touching, touching, two "couples" leaning against each other, an Indian girl and a black boy, an Indian boy and a Portuguese girl. Undistracted by each other, the others undistracted by them, the class going on.

Sophia, Julie, and Leeza from Maria's class are here, so is Rob, the tall, skinny kid who sits beside Doug in Cathy's class. In drama they are asked to break down their inhibitions, to express what they truly feel and think, what matters to them. Sitting on the floor with their shoes off helps, so does being this close, so does having someone who wants to hear what they say. To do well in drama, you have to trust, teacher Sandi Katz often tells them, and learn that you can. To take chances, push wider and farther at what you can do, look foolish to others and to yourself, fail, try again, and still feel that it's okay. But trust is slow to feel and easy to lose.

Two weeks ago, in one of the drama classes, a wallet disappeared, taken from a girl's purse. According to the owner, in the wallet was $105(U.S.) in cash, $50 in Canadian, and a cheque for $5,000. The cheque was dated three months before; the girl had been showing it off to everyone since, saying it was from a modelling agency. The signature at the bottom of it was her father's. The vice-principals were brought in. They asked the kids in the class if they would let them search their belongings. No one objected. They checked some lockers and found nothing. It was a bad moment for the vice-principals, and especially for the drama teachers. They felt so "cheap," as vice-principal Jan Coomber put it. The teacher-student relationship is based on trust. It is in a teacher's training, his instinct, his way of doing things. Now they had to say to these kids, "I can't trust you."

Later that day, the wallet was found in a boys' washroom, with the cheque, without the cash. One boy in the class had been excused earlier in the period and became the prime suspect. Then also the boy who found it. He told Jan that he had gone for a pee and found the wallet in a stall. How could that be? The police were called in; there is no resolution yet. The drama teachers were left to pick up the pieces, to reinstil and re-earn the trust they had been building since the start of the semester. They agonized; the kids shrugged. This has nothing to do with breaking trust, the kids said; this is just smart. I'd check our belongings if something disappeared too.

Every Monday, every drama class plays "Pass the Cane." Whoever has the cane has the floor, to talk about his or her weekend and where they "are" – how they feel – today. It's a technique to make the kids comfortable talking in front of a group. Often, their comments are nothing more than, "I didn't do anything Friday night, hung around with my friends at the mall Saturday, watched TV yesterday." Just as often, the talk is passionate. Breaking up with a boyfriend or girlfriend, trouble in the family. Last Monday, one girl talked about a fight she had with her father. Sandi mentioned to them how actors have to draw on what they know, and asked if any others have had family problems. One boy talked about his cousin, another about his aunt and uncle. One girl said that she had never met her real father, then talked about how her stepfather had such control over her mother. He runs her life, she said. The girl said she looks around at her family, at her mother's sisters and their marriages and sees the same thing. The same control, same abuse, and she wonders, is that the way it is with females in my family? Is there something in us that makes this happen? Is there something in me?

Another girl talked about going out with a guy Saturday after breaking up with her boyfriend Thursday, having a good time, but not wanting too good a time, not looking for a boyfriend at least for a while. There were nods around the circle. One boy, then two more, talked about a party they went to on that Friday night. The girl's parents were away, a golf club was put through a TV set, a CD player was stolen, one kid passed out on the lawn with a drug overdose and had to be taken to the hospital. Some kids broke beer bottles and smashed their broken ends into a wall. One boy said he met a girl there who wore a lip ring. Before the night was out, he had given her his earring to wear in her lip, she had given him her lip ring to wear in his ear.

One boy spoke of skipping his Greek Heritage language classes on Saturday. He and his friend do it every week, he said; their parents don't know. He explained that his friend, who is old enough to drive, takes his mother's van and parks it at the school so his mother can see it when she shops at a nearby store, then he leaves. This past weekend, the two of them then went home, got dressed in their best clothes, one of them put on a gold bracelet, the other wadded his money into a ball, a hundred-dollar bill on the outside, and they went to test-drive cars. First an Acura, then a Ferrari. The boy with the money talked up the salesman, at just the right moment bringing out his wad, while the other kid flashed his bracelet. "I sat in a Ferrari, miss," he shrieked. "You wouldn't believe it. I came *this* close to getting it on the road."

One girl talked about playing basketball and Ping-Pong with friends. Many talked of going to their cousins' or other relatives' for dinner, many about going to church. Two guys and a girl said they went to Square One, the big local mall, on Saturday, for a fight they heard was brewing, which disappointingly never happened. One boy mentioned how he went over to his girlfriend's, helped her and her family strip the walls, "then spent the night." He always manages to drop that in, as if it means nothing to him, knowing precisely what it means to the others.

Informal, unself-conscious, verbal, familiar, active, profane, authentic: drama class is made for today's kid. Here, Sophia is different. She doesn't push so hard or run over everyone's words. She laughs more. Others laugh with and at her. Julie, so sullen in math, is so expressive here: playful, engaged, worldly and girlish at the same time. Even Rob sometimes forgets his awkward adolescent shyness. Leeza, blank and dead in math when she is there at all, who hasn't asked one question or given one answer since semester began, is engrossed here. On Friday, with a few others in the class, she had been at a drama workshop. When "Pass the Cane" was over, she told them all about it. The exercise they did in physical touching, the trust that that requires, the maturity. She stood up and demonstrated, with an earnest pleasure she has never shown before.

In drama, kids get to know kids, kids and teachers get to know each other. They talk and listen, and because talking and listening is part of the course's curriculum, there is time for both. In phys-ed classes, it is the same. You have no time in a game to wonder what you look like and sound like, you just *do*, every action exposing you as quitter, cheater, solo artist, or good team guy, revealing you more utterly than any number of months in a classroom. Phys-ed teachers come to know kids, they have something to talk about with them, and the opportunity to do it. When they talk about their subject, phys-ed teachers and drama teachers sound uncommonly passionate, phys-ed and drama students sound uncommonly the same: the connection seems obvious.

Chapter 12

Thursday, April 28, 2:23 p.m.

Next week is "Education Week" in Ontario. Today, the Toronto Star *reports that a coalition of teachers' unions, public school boards, and supervisors has launched an advertising campaign to promote the public school system and to counter teacher-bashing. The cost: $104,000. The campaign's slogan: "Public education – feel good about it."*

This morning was "the draft" and Principal Terry Chaffe is feeling quite content about how Kennedy fared. The names of all the teachers declared "excess to school" were paraded before those principals who had declared certain needs for the fall. There were not a lot of willing takers. The teachers ranged from "young and excellent" to, more often, "old and still kicking around." When the list appeared a few days ago, Terry started checking with other principals to see who was who. Some names he knew from other drafts, some from the education grapevine – which is eight lanes wide and always informative: "stay away from" names, "trouble" names – undesirable teachers whom principals learn to hide from. When the names of such teachers come up on draft day, a principal tries hard to show that they wouldn't be a good fit for his or her school. Not that she isn't qualified, of course, or that he wouldn't do a fine job, it's just that the principal is looking for someone who can teach both electronics *and* family studies, or some such other unlikely combination.

In the end, a principal may get stuck with a mediocre teacher, or worse. Terry has more than one hundred teachers on his staff: not every one is a prize, not every one is ever going to be. One or two more so-so performers is hardly the end of the world. Teaching is no rare jewel of a profession, for which millions hear the call but only an élite corps of the best and brightest is chosen. There are more than 6,500 teachers in Peel alone. They aren't paid like lawyers and businessmen, rock stars and athletes; not everyone wants to be one. Education is a mass system, for masses of kids and masses of teachers. Some are going to be good, some are not, and no matter what this generation of vision statements might say, "excellence" is not around the corner in our schools, any more than it is in our corporate boardrooms or government offices. Besides, a few inadequate teachers on a staff, for the kid who can afford the luxury, can be important practice in independent learning. That said, Terry is grateful he emerged from the draft unscathed, without needing to take anyone.

Most young teachers on the "excess to school" list are there because of lack of seniority; for the older ones, the story is more complicated. They too have graduated from high school and university, and a faculty of education. They were hired on a probationary contract of two years; each semester, twice a year, four times in all, their work was evaluated by the principal or vice-principal of their schools. Each evaluation begins with a "pre-observation discussion," where a lesson's content and objectives are laid out, then an in-class observation, then a post-class conversation where findings are shared and suggestions made. A few weeks later, after enough time has passed for improvements, principal and teacher do it again, with a report then written by the principal to be discussed with the teacher. If the teacher hasn't improved enough, the principal visits more often. If the problem persists, a superintendent is involved, a "buff report" prepared, named for the colour of paper it's written on, and the teacher's contract is terminated. But that is rare. "Due process" takes time and is costly; teacher improvement is usually promising enough, proximity to minimum standards close enough, personal consequences grave enough, possibility of misjudgement high enough, that the teacher, with three years of his or her life already committed to the profession, is given a permanent teaching contract.

Once a teacher has a permanent contract, he or she is usually evaluated only once every five years. The procedure is much the same. Any problems result in suggestions, further visits and further suggestions, but little else can be done. If your school has a position for an English teacher and you're an English teacher with a permanent contract, you've got a job, period. If your school loses that position, because of lower enrolment perhaps, you will lose that job only if someone else has more seniority. If the Board cuts back and teaching positions are eliminated, the positions remaining are matched with teachers able to fill them, on a seniority basis. Competence is *never* an issue, nor is incompetence. If an inadequate teacher is identified, the principal will work with that teacher to improve; if these efforts fail, the principal will try to get the teacher out of his school, but he cannot fire her. It's up to the teacher to leave of her own accord. Hassled with visits and suggestions, passed over for plum assignments, disrespected, some teachers will move to what seems the greener grass of a new school, but few will leave teaching. By the time it's clear that the profession isn't for them, they are usually in their mid-thirties, with a family and lifestyle expectations to meet. What else are they going to do?

Back in the late 1980s, teachers seemed like such suckers – all their university friends, no smarter than they, making fortunes as stockbrokers or real-estate flippers, wheeling and dealing at the centre of a new and dynamic world. Today, in the 1990s, teaching doesn't seem like such a bad job. New teachers, age twenty-three or twenty-four, with a four-year university degree, begin at $36,326 a year in Peel; after eleven years, still only in their mid-thirties, they hit the top of the salary scale, $66,776, with more for assistant department heads and heads, vice-principals, principals, and superintendents. For the rest of their teaching career, they remain at the top, able to retire at full pension under the "Ninety Factor" – age plus years of teaching totalling ninety – at fifty-seven or fifty-eight. Most teachers aren't at school until 8:00 a.m., until kids and spouses are fed and out the door; most can be home most days by 4:00 p.m., in time to greet their kids when they arrive from school. Both spouses able to work, the family benefitting from two incomes, preparation and marking for the next day able to be done at home – no staying at the office until 8:00 p.m. – all that and summers off too! Not many teachers leave willingly; fewer still are forced to go.

For the inadequate teacher, sometimes both the problem and the solution lie within the dynamic of a school. Last week, Kennedy's science department held its monthly meeting. It has a new head this year, John Kanas, a lively, curious-minded man in his early forties, who even after two decades of teaching has kept his love for and fascination with his subject. Last semester, in a routine moment, he was demonstrating to a class the effect of burning magnesium in oxygen. When the bottle exploded into a brilliant white glow, one usually lifeless kid enthused, "That's amazing, sir!" and John enthused back, "I know! That's why I teach the stuff!" His predecessor as department head had held the position nearly twenty years, until retiring last June. The department has ten teachers, one of whom has been at Kennedy since the 1960s, three more, Cathy Sylvester included, since the 1970s.

In the meeting, they talked long and with great care about whether a small amount of money available to the department should go for overhead projectors or computers. They talked about what they talk about every meeting, housekeeping items: cleaning up after experiments, the equipment, its care, return and storage after use, safety. Yet it was housekeeping with an uncommon passion, housekeeping words and phrases as code for things more fundamental. Should teachers have rooms and the equipment move, or the equipment have rooms and teachers move? Tradition says equipment moves (why shouldn't teachers?); tradition says that he who uses it, cleans, returns, and fixes it if it breaks (why can't traditions be broken too?). What about safety? What about the *key*? Science in a school has to be first and foremost about safety. Dangerous chemicals are often involved, which must be labelled, accounted for, and put under the lock and key of those trained in safety. Only John and three senior teachers have keys. The chemicals must reside in their rooms; the younger teachers must go to those rooms, and ask for them. To these younger teachers, this is so demeaning in front of students. Why can't they have their own keys? Don't be so childish, they are told; this is about safety, not control. Don't treat us like children, they say back; everything is about control when you don't have it.

During the meeting, civil words are passed back and forth in uncivil tones. The older teachers on one side, the younger ones on the other, the rest lost in the middle. The conflict is symptomatic of what happens when there is no movement at the top. Beyond administrative ambition, comfortable in what they know and where they are, the older ones stay in place; the better, younger ones leave to find promotions elsewhere; the lesser ones stay, not good enough to be lured away, their ambitions, if any, now in other aspects of their lives, weak and tired after being put upon so long by the stronger ones at the top.

With the right mix, the dynamics of a department work well for everyone. The younger ones need the older ones, who have seen so much and tried so many ways, because tomorrow for them is always another day. The older ones need the younger ones for their naïvety, impatience, and joy, to remind them of why they got into teaching in the first place, and, this late in the race, to give them the kick that will see them through to the end. The older ones and younger ones need those in the middle, connected to those both above and below them, who are able to explain one to the other and get things done. Every group, every organization, even the most unbeatable championship team, needs that movement in and out, even if on paper what it had before was better than what it has now. With the right mix, one and one can equal three. Terry hated to lose Sue Lishman and Patti Vandrus, although the teachers who will replace them will be more senior: he knows that the math department will miss their youth.

For the science department now, one and one makes decidedly less than two. The atmosphere is poisonous. The older teachers make the younger ones feel inept and resentful, the younger ones make the older ones wonder what the world is coming to. Together, they make each other worse than they are. John has two assistant department heads, soon both positions will be open through retirements. He is trying to nurture two of his younger teachers towards these positions, to kindle in them some ambition. You have a chance now that was never there before, go with it, he tells them. Yet when John intervened in the meeting to give these younger teachers their chance to take the floor, they seemed not to know what to do with it. They have had so little practice, have learned so few of the habits of power. One young teacher, with energy and spark, offered snide responses at every opportunity. So long without power to have things his way, he knows only how to be right.

A few weeks ago, without intending to, Terry found himself rating the teachers on his staff. He thought he would find a few at the top, a few at the bottom, and most in the middle. Instead when he looked at his list, of the 106 of them, he rated 43 as "top," 49 as "okay," and 14 as those he'd like to "get rid of." He was surprised, pleased. Just 14 at the bottom, yet, he thought to himself, what a difference they make; like those "bad news" kids in a classroom, what a difference if they weren't here. But why shouldn't they, why shouldn't all teachers, be able to teach at least adequately? Most know their subject matter well enough. Most got into teaching for the right reasons. They like kids, find pleasure in learning, enjoy the feeling of making things better for others. They know how to learn, they have been learners all their lives. If they have a problem as teachers, their advocates say, it's because the system that prepared and sustains them has failed them. Fix the system and you'll fix them. Offer them guidance, give them a course, and everything will be fine. And to ensure that the system meets its obligations, the teachers' unions have negotiated job protections into teacher contracts.

But no amount of guidance or professional upgrading is going to work for certain teachers. About a year ago, three Peel principals, three superintendents, and some others were talking about teaching. One mentioned to a superintendent a TV show on education he had seen. There was an image, the man said, that struck him every time it came on the screen: the eyes of the students. The look of sheer excitement, literally a light, when they understood. A look vacant and dead when they didn't. The superintendent shook his head. He had been in a classroom recently, he said, evaluating a teacher who never looked his kids in the eyes. He'd look to one side, down, over their heads, always away. The superintendent pointed this out afterwards, then came back a few weeks later, but nothing had changed. It's only when you look into their eyes, the superintendent said, that you really *know*.

Teaching, he said, is fundamentally a personal relationship, a special kind of intimacy. It isn't enough to be smart, to look just into the eyes of the subject you teach, for it alone to be the source of your passion, nor is it enough to look deep into yourself to stoke that passion. A subject over time may get boring, new eyes never do. It's a lot easier, he said, never to look into the eyes of things, to avoid engagement, commitment, to escape whatever you might find. But it doesn't work. You have to look into kids' eyes too, he said, because that's where *your* rewards are.

What got in that teacher's way? What kept him at a distance from his students? Not technique. He was told what was wrong, but he didn't do anything about it. Because he didn't want to, didn't try? Because he had other things on his mind? Because he knew he didn't have to, that his job was secure regardless of his performance? Or because he couldn't? Because he has never been able to look anyone in the eye? Because he sees himself as needing distance from people? Because the superintendent pointed out his flaw, but didn't understand that looking into someone's eyes is more than a mechanical act? Because, once a good classroom teacher himself, that superintendent didn't know how to deal with someone who isn't?

In many ways, the reasons don't matter. The simple fact is that not every Joanne can teach, just as not every Johnny can read. Studies may show that they can, but in the real world of mass public education, where the changes required are complicated, the cost is high, the teachers and kids are resistant – where people are people – not everyone does. Just as there will always be Willys, Kellys, and Quentins who do not really learn, there will always also be teachers who do not really teach. But the Willys, Kellys, and Quentins move on after a few years; the poor teachers do not.

The idea of a lifetime job emerged in North America during the booming economic growth which followed World War II. The idea is now gone or going for most workers. Employees of private companies felt this shift first. Public employees, who had hitherto accepted the trade-off of lower wages for greater job security, now find private wages falling to meet theirs. Taxpayers have started asking: Why should public employees like teachers earn as much as we do *and* enjoy better job security? Why shouldn't they be subject to firing like everyone else? A showdown between the public and the teachers' unions is not far off.

◆ ◆ ◆

Not long ago, some teachers were talking about kids.

"They're so different today," one teacher said, exasperation in his voice. "And that's not just me remembering me as I never was," he laughed. "Something's happened."

"It's as if now *I* have to prove things to *them*," another teacher said, picking up the thread. The rest nodded. "Kids used to accept – what I said, who I am." An embarrassed, sad look crossed her face. "I used to feel special. I don't feel that way now." More nods. "And it's not just these kids. My own kids are the same."

"What I can't get over," a third teacher added, "is how they stand up to me. I would never have imagined doing that with a teacher."

"And it's not just the 'in-your-face' stuff," interrupted another. "That's just a game, and everyone knows it. It's when they have that look they have on their face, like *'why wouldn't I stand up to you?'* – that's what gets me."

"It's as if we're no better than they are," another teacher said. "I don't mean better," she said, correcting herself, "but being older should count for something." She laughed and shook her head. "I just don't know what happened."

Maybe it began with television bringing the camera up close, giving us an intimate view of people and institutions that had always been beyond question. Maybe we discovered that the people on the screen were no smarter than we are. But however it began, somewhere, some time, someone asked the bluff-caller's question: *why?* Why should this person have power over me?

Our society has become more democratic. We may have grown up believing it already was, but a residue of assumptions from more feudal times still remained. Hierarchies that were based on age, gender, status, colour, money, and education all conveyed certain assumptions, both to those who had these advantages on their side and to those who didn't, and it was by virtue of those assumptions that social order was largely maintained. But, the bluff-caller asked, why should any of these privileges matter? Why should somebody be able to tell me to do something, and I do it, just because he said so? I don't care if he's smarter, older, has more money, drives a nicer car. What counts, the *only* thing that counts, is that he is a human being and I am one too. And I will not defer to any other human being.

We are equals, plain and simple. Now, between teachers and kids, everything must be earned. Everything is negotiation. You talk to me, I'll listen; I talk to you, you listen. A real conversation. But you've never learned how to converse, these kids say. What you said to me always had some "take it or leave it" power behind it, but you don't have that power any more. To get me to do something, you have to make me think like you, and that's not going to come from you lecturing, or making yourself into an expert so much smarter than me that I wouldn't dare do anything but follow. I won't follow unless following makes sense for *me*. You talk with me, really talk, and maybe I'll do it *with* you.

Teachers are now struggling in the classroom with this monumental social change in the same way males, WASPs, the native-born, the educated, and the monied are struggling with it in the wider world. They all once had the tools of power and now they don't know what to do without them. Getting close to kids *is* harder now; getting close to them has never been more necessary; having adequate teachers has never been more crucial.

✦ ✦ ✦

Yesterday, Sue Lishman got the good news: she has a job next year. She will be teaching math at Cawthra Park, a magnet school, specializing in the performing arts, also in Mississauga.

Chapter 13

Wednesday, May 11, 11:22 a.m.

No Willy, no Chad, no Pat, no Marv, no Calvin. History class begins. Rick Ray writes on the board: "The Countdown to War: June 28, 1914 to August 4, 1914." Calvin arrives, then Marv, then Pat, then twenty minutes into the class, Willy. Rick stops.

"Sit down, William, and get this down."

"Sir, I don't have my books. Chad has them and I don't think he's here today." Sandee hands him a sheet of paper and a pen; he begins writing. Less than a minute later, he stops; less than a minute after that, he starts again.

Rodney looks lost. He had been doing so well; something has happened to him this week. He had started the semester cautiously, waiting to see which way the class would go for him. Not too loud or too late or too absent, not a troublemaker or a trouble-seeker, he'd always back off the fooling around just before Rick's limit was reached. Then gradually he seemed to get interested in the course itself.

Rodney likes the games, choosing teams, feeling himself on one side against another, strutting right answers, a little "two thumbs up," a little "in your face," depending on how the mood strikes. Needling Calvin, flirting with Monika, he is a lively, harmless presence in the class. But today, Rodney wants nothing to do with anybody. He sits slumped in his seat, his binder open, his eyes closed. What's wrong? Rick asks finally. "I'm sick, sir," he says with conviction. After he is certain Rodney is not too sick, Rick lets him be.

But Calvin doesn't. Every few seconds, he yammers a burst of words at Rodney who, without opening his eyes, as if swishing away a bothersome pest, twists his head, contorts his face, and yammers back some words of his own. This distracts Ahmed, who sits in front of Rodney, across from Calvin. Ahmed is a good student who has had a disappointing semester. At the beginning, Rick thought he would be one of his strong students, a rival to Fahad, but Ahmed has other priorities. He does adequately, but he has come to enjoy the social life of the class more than the work. He starts out today facing ahead in his seat, interested, intending to be involved, but slowly his head turns. He finds Rodney and Calvin irresistible. Marv sits in front of Calvin and would ordinarily join whatever fray was available, but today he seems so out of it that nothing gets his attention. Not so Monika, who sits in front of Ahmed. Every so often, Calvin says something to Rodney just loud enough for Monika to hear, and she swirls around flashing an exasperated, affectionate smile towards him. But Monika is strong enough to decide for herself which way the pull of the room will take her, and she faces the front most of the time attending to the business of the class.

Rick can see what's going on, of course. He offers a few quiet, stern words at first, then lets things go as he gets absorbed in his own lesson. He holds either side of his lectern, his head tilted forward, his face and voice hitting the highs and lows of his message. He acts out the build-up to World War I, playing to one side of the room, then the other. He talks, writes on the board, then searches for answers among the students. He ignores

Fahad's hand as often as he can, saving the harder questions for him, saving for him those moments when the class bogs down. When the kids are trying to puzzle through to an answer and can afford some temporary misdirection, he calls on Jamie. He asks Calvin, to give him something to do, Monika and Charlene because, capable but quiet, they need to be pushed. He asks Sandee and Karen, who never offer an answer on their own, because he will forget they are here if he doesn't.

He drops the class into Austria-Hungary, into Serbia, into Germany and Russia. He describes each nation's state of mind, the nature of European geopolitics at the time. He describes the escalating arms race. Germany has built up its navy; what does England do? Archduke Franz Ferdinand is assassinated, the Austro-Hungarians march into Serbia, Russia mobilizes; what about Germany? What about England and France? He talks of the psychology of war: " 'If you fail to prepare,' " he thunders, as if both houses of parliament were before him, " 'you are preparing to fail.' " He stops himself and changes character. "Some of you might want to keep that in mind with exams coming up," he smiles. The change comes too fast for Willy. "What was that, sir?" he asks. Rick repeats himself. Willy flops back into his chair, "Ah, that's beautiful, man." He remains back in his chair a few moments longer, then raises his hand.

"Yes, William, you have a question?"

"Can I be excused, sir?"

It is twelve noon. Each day Willy is here, he asks the same question at the same time. Sometimes Rick lets him go, sometimes not. He knows Willy can't give more than forty or fifty good minutes a class; ask him for more and he would probably get less. Today, Rick says yes. Ten minutes later, Willy returns. Though Rick doesn't know it for sure, he could guess: Willy was in the Caf, earphones in his ears, Walkman turned up, a small tub of French fries in his hands, dancing up and down the aisles, greeting his buddies. He returns as Rick finds himself tuning in more to Rodney, Calvin, and Ahmed than to what he is saying himself.

"Calvin! Ahmed!" Rick explodes, "I've had enough with you two. Face the front!"

The room goes quiet, Rodney goes back to sleep, Calvin and Ahmed turn their bodies more or less to face the front.

At the end of class, Rick tells Calvin that tomorrow he's going to move him closer to the front, away from Rodney.

"I won't be here tomorrow, sir," he says.

"You won't be here? Where will you be?"

"I don't know, sir."

"What do you mean, you don't know?"

"I won't be here."

"You won't be here, but you don't know why?"

"It's my birthday."

◆ ◆ ◆

Maria Cheung is checking math homework. Thirteen kids have done it, seven more than when she checked yesterday; five haven't, Sheri did half, eight aren't here. Sophia, who once always did her homework, didn't do any for the second straight day. Neither did Dwayne; he had to work, he said. Helen, who arrived last week from Hong Kong, and is only auditing the course until the end of the year, did the homework. Quentin didn't, but at least he is here, though since the beginning of the period, he's had his head down on his desk, his eyes closed. Two days ago, he was also here but, as one of the "Change Your Future" kids, he spent most of the day with Claudine Blake. Yesterday, he was at the ophthalmologist. Tomorrow, Maria will give them a test, and she knows Quentin won't come. His term average is about 10 per cent. He is in school now only because he has been getting pressure from the office: "Look, a lot of people are doing a lot of things for you.

The least you can do is show up." But they can't expect him to be here every day, so tomorrow is the day he will miss.

Peter is also lying on his desk. He says he's tired; he works nights at McDonald's. About once every two weeks, he pretends to sleep through class. His need seems more psychological than physiological. Yesterday, he didn't do the homework, nor today, but he did finish the homework due yesterday, he says. Maria discovers he didn't.

Priya writes equations from the board on a scrap of paper, grows tired of that, and begins leafing through a car guide. She was supposed to get a car two years ago when she turned sixteen, but her father thought she would spend too much time running around in it, skipping even more of her classes. Apparently he has given up, or changed his mind, and soon she will get her car, a Firebird or Mustang. In front of her, she has written on her desk:

Priya
❤s
Rishi
❤s
Priya
4 Ever
&
Ever

Sheri hobbled into class today; she sprained her left ankle playing soccer. She, too, writes down the equations from the board on a loose sheet of paper; she has no binder with her. Her textbook is open. Also open on her desk, turned over, is a paperback book, on its cover a drawing of a black man and woman, the man bare to the waist, his right arm bent at the elbow to display his swelling biceps, the woman, her head thrown back to expose her plunging neckline: *Borrowed Moments*, by Yolande

Bertrand, from the Heartline Romances series. Last week, she had on her desk *Snowfire: A Woman's Yearning*, by Kimberly Norton, from the same series.

Earlier this week, a memo was sent by vice-principal Jan Coomber to Sheri's teachers. A custodian had come to Jan and said that some kids were refusing to clear the Caf after lunch. Jan stormed into the Caf to find the kids playing cards; when they saw her, they all rushed for the doors. Except Sheri. As Jan puts it, "Sheri doesn't rush." This set off Jan even more. Sheri had already skipped Noel Lim's English class and was in the midst of skipping French. She claimed she didn't know when her last class began. Jan went over the class times with her and told her if she missed or was late for any more classes, she would be withdrawn from that course. And, as Jan's memo read, "if she is removed from more than two courses she will be withdrawn [from school] altogether." Despite Sheri's profession a few weeks ago that this time she will buckle down, she appears not to know how. There are eighty-three teaching days this semester. Jan caught her in the Caf on Day 53. In those fifty-three days, she had been officially late for math seventeen times, absent nineteen. Fewer than one-third of the days has she been properly in class.

Two days ago, Pat came to see Jan. He had been away most of the previous week, falling even further behind. He told her that he wanted to drop math. There was still more than a month to go in the semester, in theory anything could happen, he might turn everything around, but Pat knows better. Others hope when hope is gone; he stares reality in the eyes. He knows he will fail, so why keep on? But staring at reality is one thing, feeling it is another. Jan didn't like the idea of him dropping the course. There is something important about living with the consequences of your own acts, not being allowed the easy way out, she said. If he was capable of feeling any regret or remorse about school and math, she was going to make him feel it until the bitter end. She called his father. He agreed. "I don't want him to

drop math either," he told her. "He can do math, and he doesn't
need another spare" – especially one which is first period one day
(more sleep), and last period the next (with lunch the period
before, a double Mickey's). Yesterday, Pat was in math class, but
with his head down. Today, he seemed attentive most of the
period, sitting with Leah, then he laid his head down at the end.

In Noel Lim's English class, Kelly has been absent more often
than not. After her meeting with Kelly's mother, Jan had been
watching Kelly closely. For a while, she had almost perfect attendance, then started missing a little, then more. Jan called home
and talked to Kelly. She'd be in tomorrow, she promised, but she
wasn't. The pattern was repeated several times. The last time,
Kelly told Jan she wasn't in class because her best friend had died.
Jan was taken aback, but she accepted what Kelly said. More days
passed. Still Kelly wasn't in school, so Jan sought out her brother,
whose attendance isn't much better. She asked about Kelly, how
she was coping with her tragedy. The brother looked briefly
puzzled. "Oh yeah," he said finally, "her cat died."

More calls to Kelly, messages left, calls unreturned. Finally, Jan
decided to talk again with Kelly's mom. "There doesn't seem
much point now," she said, and her mother didn't disagree.
Yesterday, Kelly was withdrawn from school. If she shows up
again in September, Jan will recommend that she try something
else – night school, community college.

Doug did better after the talk with his uncle, but again the
effect wore off quickly; old habits run deep. Yesterday, Cathy
Sylvester was taking up the science homework, and asked Doug
a question. He couldn't answer it. He told her he hadn't done
the homework; he had lost his textbook. Jennifer hadn't done the
homework either. Before the period was over, Jennifer was called
to the office. She returned with a piece of paper, got Cathy's
signature, and, with a smirk for Jody and Tracy, she was gone –
transferred to a General-level class. Nelson hadn't done any of the
homework either. He is in the midst of another bad stretch. He

is always in class and on time, but his mood varies widely. Just a few days ago, he was doing so well, his "poolar" dam presentation, his chocolate-covered almonds. In math class, Maria had given them a test. When she returned it, Nelson went over his paper and found what he thought was a mistake. He deserved one more mark. Maria agreed. Julie thought she deserved another mark too. Early in the semester, she had sat behind Nelson until his excitement got too much for him, and Maria moved him across the room. Maria and Julie looked over her test and decided there was no error. "Miss," Nelson chirped from across the room, "you can give her my mark."

Yesterday, Noel kicked Nelson out of English class. They had finished watching a movie of *Romeo and Juliet*, and Nelson wouldn't sit still. He wanted to go to the library to work on his project, he said. There would be nobody there to supervise him, so Noel said no. Nelson wanted to sit somewhere else, Noel said he could work in the back room. That was fine for a few minutes, then Nelson reappeared and said he wanted to go somewhere else. Noel got angry. Go somewhere else, he said, in fact anywhere else, and kicked him out. Nelson protested all the way out the door; he hadn't wanted to push things that far. He went to the Caf and worked on his project.

Sabesan remains a puzzle. With most kids, one look at them and you can tell whether they are good students or not. From the first day, Sabesan looked like a good student. Any poor grade on a test was surely an anomaly, his teachers thought, until his poor grades piled up. His problem seemed solved when he cut back on his part-time job. Now he had all those additional hours a night, and even if he spent only a few of them on homework, he would do fine. Yesterday, he didn't do his homework for Cathy, nor the last two days for Maria. His grades have not improved.

Sabesan has no instinct to do schoolwork, just as Willy doesn't, just as Pat and Quentin and Doug and Sheri don't. Sabesan's instinct is to watch TV, go to the mall, do nothing. Having created some extra time, he has no idea what to do with it, no inclination to do his schoolwork. Perhaps for many kids part-time jobs are really as much symptom as cause. Their choice isn't between homework or job, it's between job or nothing. Home-work isn't even in the running.

In every classroom, whether it's in Philadelphia, Kyoto, Berlin, or Mississauga, a few kids "get" it, and most don't. It may be a good school or bad, good system or bad, rich or poor, ethnically diverse or WASPishly white, only the percentages differ. What is it about these kids, what has happened in their lives for things to be this way? What needs to happen for that to change?

Watch Fahad, watch Simran and Rohita. They sit in their seats so on top of things. Alert and alive, they take in a teacher's words and before those words spit out the end of their pen into their notebooks, they seem to rattle around inside them, connect on to other things the kids already know, creating something new that is theirs, that feels like theirs, that they know is theirs, with all the excitement and satisfaction that that engenders. For them, learning is absolute pleasure. They are in school every day, on time, with their homework done, because why wouldn't they be?

Watch Doug, watch Sandee and Karen, not just Willy and Pat and Quentin, watch most of the kids in any class. They aren't on top of things. They aren't necessarily behind, but they are barely keeping up. For them, a teacher's words enter their ears and spit right out their pens, no rattling around, no connecting onto any-thing they already know, no creating of something new that feels like theirs. It's hard enough for them to keep up, to make enough sense of the teacher's words to get them down. They experience no conscious learning, no excitement, no satisfaction. Only before tests or exams, and only if they take the time, as they go back through their notes, do the pieces take shape. *Oh, so that's why this, and that's why that!* For many, nothing ever takes shape;

others are years out of school before an event triggers a shard of memory and the light goes on. *That's what she meant!* Too late for the feeling about learning that makes you crave to learn more. These kids are not in school every day, on time, with their home-work done, because why would they be?

Being on top of things, in control, unrushed, able to create, feeling the jolt of pleasure that keeps you going the way a test result, a university acceptance, or a shining future, all too distant, cannot: how does a student arrive at that state? It has something to do with the habits of learning. Do your homework, be on time, pay attention: they are all so crucial, yet so empty of meaning for most kids. Said too often, heard too often, they are finally ignored. They are like a punchline that has lost its story. *Why* should I do my homework? the student wonders. Because *you* said so, because it's work independent of you which shows if I understand? Because it is practice in what I'm being taught? Sure, it's all those things, the teacher says, but something else that may matter more. Put in that half hour of homework in my subject tonight and tomorrow that seventy-six-minute class will be pleasure. You'll understand! You'll be on top of things, ahead of things, in control. What a feeling, not just for you about science or math, but about *you*. All for thirty minutes' work — not a bad deal.

"Be in class, be on time," because you said so, the student con-tinues, because it disrupts you and others if I'm not? Sure. But it's more than that, the teacher says. What happens when you sit down with friends in the Caf, when they got there before you did and someone is in the midst of a story? Maybe she will stop that story and start again, but not very often. How does it feel sitting there? What do you do? You try to get into that story, take what you hear and attempt to recreate what came before. But it's hard. Others laugh before you do, and laugh harder. Not quite sure you understand, the story not so compelling to you, often you give up on it, drift off in your own mind and wait for the story to end. Well, it's the same with school. Every course you take is a story that begins Day 1 and ends Day 83. Every class is a story that begins five minutes later than it should and ends seventy-one minutes after that. Miss a day and every next day of the story is harder to understand; miss a minute and every next minute is less compelling, easier to give up on. That's why I take attendance and tell you to be here. It's not a power trip, a test of you and me, a chance for me to break your will. When I say "pay attention," it's not to put you down. Being in class means to be here with the full resources of your mind. Nelson is here every day, but not all of Nelson is here all of every day. He has places in his mind to visit. Some kids skip out to Mickey's; some skip out in class.

So how about it, Nelson? How about it, Doug and Quentin and Pat and Willy? How about it, Sheri? You like fun. You're masters of fun. Sheri, remember the days in English when it was your turn to read from *Romeo and Juliet*, how you silenced the room, drew every ear to you; in math, when a new unit was beginning and you were there, how smart you felt, how special? I know you think school isn't supposed to be fun, but that was fun, wasn't it? If you had been here for those nineteen days you missed, imagine how much more rewarding the other thirty-four days would have felt; how the next thirty might feel. I want you here because I want you to have fun, and that's how you have real fun in school. The rest happens anyway.

The numerous daily interruptions for kids – to go to the counselling office, to see Claudine Blake – make it even harder for poor learners to learn, likewise when field trips and school games eat up classroom hours as they do each spring. This week baseball (twice), soccer (twice), track and field, and badminton all required early dismissals for the players; the ESL kids had one day at the zoo, another in Toronto; the Outers Club has been away all week. Tomorrow Calvin will take the day off to celebrate his birthday, Doug took a week earlier in the semester and went west to ski, Quentin had all those eye appointments: these kids can't afford to miss those days because they can't afford to lose the story. Then it's too hard to recapture it; too easy for them to give up.

A few days ago, Sue Lishman, recording marks from her latest test, worked out Pat's grade for the semester. Even if he got 100 per cent on each remaining test, she discovered, and on the final exam, he couldn't pass. Yet how could she fail him if he did? A perfect mark on the final would show that at the end of the course he knew the course perfectly. Whatever he didn't know in the second week or any week thereafter, was surely irrelevant. Except that he is learning math to learn work habits as well. What good in the rest of his life is perfect knowledge of Euclidean geometry? Where will that take him? He must learn he has to work from the beginning to the end. He must do well in April, not just to do well in June, but because April matters. That's why Sue has resolved to fail him even if he does pull it off at the end.

If every class is a story that begins at the beginning, every life is the same. What happens when years of a parent's time are spent away from his or her children? Others can be hired to keep a child safe and busy, but who will have the time, who will care enough, to help that child write his own best story? Science department head John Kanas talks of growing up in his Greek family in a suburb of Toronto. Whenever he came home from school, his mother was there. "How was your day?" she'd ask.

"Fine."

"What did you do?"

"Nothing."

"Nothing? You must've done something. What did you do?"

She wouldn't let the easy answer go. He had just spent most of his waking hours in a place supposed to be important to his life. If it was important to his, it was important to hers. Tell me, she insisted. I don't care if the next few moments are filled with uncomfortable silence, a mother and son discovering they have nothing to say to each other, because something will break that silence. It doesn't matter what it is, because the real message from me to you is that what you are doing matters, that doing well is important, that I care.

Who delivers that message now? It might happen over the dinner table, but with both parents tired at the end of a working day, "Fine" and "Nothing" are more likely to suffice. Today few mothers are able to greet their kids at the end of the school day. Women wanted their independence. In a world that rewards possession and achievement, they wanted money and status of their own. In a time when "till death do you part" has come to mean "for the foreseeable future," women have had to protect themselves with marketable skills. But what about the kids? They are gone most of the hours of a day; what does it matter, a parent asks, where I spend mine? After school, the kids have things to do, a school team to play on, a club, their friends, a part-time job. Everyone is home for dinner, at least some of the time. We can catch up then; there is the whole evening. The difference in time spent with the kids may be only a few hours a day, or less. But it doesn't take much to drift out of touch with your kids. You don't know them quite so well, and they don't know you. You don't feel quite on top of things. You lose confidence, don't feel as central in their lives. You're not sure you should push things, even if something bothers you, even if you think that what they are doing is wrong. You sense things aren't as they should be; maybe you still believe in the ideal of the nuclear family with the stay-at-home mom that you grew up with; maybe you feel a twinge of guilt. You know a choice has been made.

At times this semester, Rick has assumed certain basic knowledge in his students, and discovered it wasn't there. The names of provinces, capital cities, the prime minister: they know Bill Clinton's name better than Jean Chrétien's, because Clinton's name comes up on the TV shows they watch. Given a test on common knowledge subjects like these, many would fail. A few times each year, under outraged headlines, newspapers report dismal results on similar tests. How could today's kids not know? Commentators and adult readers are certain that as kids *they* knew. They remember the minutes spent each day reading the paper, getting news from radio or TV, from a current-events lesson at school. It may be that, as diarist Richard Crossman once put it, memory is "a great improver." But if they did know, maybe more than anywhere else they learned these names at the dinner table. Names come up, a story emerges, when a family has the occasion to talk.

Parents need teachers and teachers need parents. The Peel vice-principals met a few weeks ago at Niagara-on-the-Lake. One of several presentations had to do with strategies for getting parents more involved in the school. The superintendent giving the talk spoke passionately of studies which show a direct cor- relation between parents who join school organizations and attend school functions and a child's academic results. We must get parents more involved in the school, he said. Except the cor- relation is really between a parent's interest in a child and his or her results. Parental involvement in school activities is just one expression of that interest, and a minor one. The far greater chal- lenge lies in the school helping parents to become more involved in parenting at home. As it is for kids, the problem for parents is skips and lates and homework undone. The answer is putting in those few extra minutes a night that allow fun to happen.

Chapter 14

Monday, May 16, 11:30 a.m.

On Friday, Rick Ray's history class finished watching *All Quiet on the Western Front*. The film provided an overall context to the First World War; now Rick wants to return to the Canadian side of the story. He writes on the board, "Conscription in Canada in 1917," and beneath it, "Canada and WWI – how did it happen?" He draws a graph. The beginning point is August, 1914; he runs a horizontal line across two blackboards, then puts tick marks on it, one for each month, until the last one, November, 1918. Beside a vertical line with other tick marks, he writes numbers from 5,000 to 40,000, the "Number of Voluntary Enlistments in C.E.F.," the Canadian Expeditionary Force.

The war breaks out in August, he says; 23,000 Canadians enlist. He draws a nearly vertical line up his graph. In September, the number was 10,000, in October 6,000; his line moves sharply downwards. Month by month, he takes the kids forward into the war. At the top of the board, he writes "Context of the time," and beneath it, opposite the path of the line, he writes first "P. M. Borden's words: 'Canada has *no quarrel* with Germany.'"

Why would Borden say that? he asks. He gets several shouted answers back; they are with him so far, all but Calvin, Rodney, and Ahmed. "That's right," he says, "with Canadians of so many origins, Germans, Austro-Hungarians" – thundering almost like Borden himself, then reverting to his own voice – "he wanted the mood to cool."

He writes "Belgian Atrocity," as the Germans overrun defenceless Belgium, and his line moves upwards, to 14,000 in November. It moves down, then for the next several months it moves almost horizontally, with fewer than 10,000 enlistees a month. Then the gas attack at Ypres in April 1915, the sinking of the *Lusitania* in May – "innocent passengers are drowned," he says, imploringly – and what was once "no quarrel" is beginning to change. Enlistment climbs the next several months, then falls during harvest season, then rises steadily the rest of the year, reaching 30,000 in December, the month that *Punch* published John McCrae's poem, "In Flanders Fields." " 'Take up *our* quarrel with the foe,' " Rick recites. In January, 35,000 Canadians enlisted.

February went down a little; in March, more than 40,000 enlisted. Then the Battle of Verdun, "over one million casualties," he implores again. "What happens in Canada now? How do people react?" There is a fresh burst of outrage in the class, but on the board, Rick's line turns downwards, month after month, almost in freefall. In August 1915 the Battle of the Somme begins, "One million more casualties," but only 5,000 enlistees. The kids nod. The war has gone, as Rick puts it, from Borden's perception, to McCrae's perception, to the public's perception that this is a "slaughterhouse."

In February 1917, Rick tells them, Borden decides to visit Canadian forces in Europe and meet with Allied commanders. It has become a war of attrition, on both sides a life for a life, but now the number of casualties each month is exceeding the number of enlistees "almost two to one." Canada is asked to contribute more men. Borden returns home. He cannot increase the number of volunteers, conscription is the only answer. But without a referendum in support, Opposition Leader Wilfrid Laurier says he will oppose conscription. In March, only 5,000 enlist; in April, 4,800. In March, civil war breaks out in Russia, and the Russians begin withdrawing from the war. Germany moves troops from the east to the Western Front where the Allies are already in trouble. French soldiers are mutinying, the British Empire isn't responding; the Germans turn up the heat. Unrestricted submarine warfare. Any ships going into Britain, even those of neutral powers, will be sunk, the Germans avow. Food and armaments go to the bottom, so, too, thousands of civilians. The war seems up for grabs. As the class is about to end, Rick writes at the bottom of one board, "1917 Critical Year." That is for tomorrow.

Some years ago, he had been looking through the census, searching for patterns of numbers that might offer stories he had never heard, and there it was: the story of conscription's *why*. He decided he would show *All Quiet on the Western Front* first, to offer the human story, then deliver the political punchline this way. Today, he isn't entirely successful, he can never quite draw Calvin, Rodney, and Ahmed, "the three Generals," as he calls them, into his story. "Like fighting a war on two fronts," he laughs. After class, he takes Rodney aside and says he expects him to be quiet tomorrow, and to not keep asking to go to the bathroom. "But sir, I'm a casualty too," Rodney explains. Tomorrow, Rick promises, he will move him up to the front and put him in the trench opposite his own.

Why doesn't Rick throw up his hands, become outraged, give these kids hell? Because he likes them, because it's his job to do what he can with what he's got, to teach these kids history. Anything else is a cop-out. He likes to show them movies. *The Triangle Factory Fire*, to make them understand immigrant life in North American cities in the early 1900s; *Cry Freedom*, to show the black reality of South Africa under apartheid; *Glory* and *All*

Quiet on the Western Front, to show what war feels like outside the history books, to those who fight it. The idealism, the heroic game of going into battle, the carnage. But really he shows these films because they are all about good, decent people. Immigrants, Jews, blacks, whites, people like his students and not like them, so that they can see themselves, and others, as they seldom see them. All you pink-skinned native-born Canadians, he challenges, here's what it's like to go to a place you've never been, be surrounded by a language you don't understand, feel stupid, be treated as dirt and worse. It's not easy, is it? Well, that's what the person beside you is going through. What do you think now? He may smell and dress differently, he may say little except to others like him in the Caf, you may never see him from dusk until dawn, from Friday until Monday, from July to September, when he retreats into his other world, but he's not a bad person. And that black kid sitting beside you, just for a moment I want you to see him inside the skin of Steven Biko or Trent, the Denzel Washington character from *Glory*. This is what it's like to be him. It happened; it's true. Is that how any man should be treated? How do you feel when you see that? Whom do you identify with, who is most like you? The oppressor who looks like you, or the other guy?

Every way he can, Rick tells them: Like yourself, like the guy next to you, we're all in on this together. Sure, I want you to be scholars, be like Fahad, be able to read and explore and know enough of the names and events of history to construct its story. But not everybody is Fahad, and whoever and whatever you are has value too. I will see you as what you are. I'll accept you that way. I won't make you miserable for not being what I want you to be. You have dignity; you are to be respected. I will push you to learn what I think you should learn, but if you can't do that or won't, I'll find something else for you, a movie, a game, a seventy-six-minute performance of history as if from its very stage. I can't make you smart, but I will do what I can to make you feel as worthy as the kid who is.

Most of these kids know almost nothing of the names and events of Canadian history. Lacking English skills, many don't yet have the means to learn them. But history's lessons are universal, so Rick teaches to what they *do* know, not to what they don't. A focus on names and events would only make Canada seem more alien and impenetrable. What you have learned in your life, he wants them to know, what made you smart somewhere else, makes you smart here. I want you to feel the spirit of that history and carry it into the future.

Rick knows he can be too easy sometimes. At mid-term, he gave Pat 70 per cent, not because Pat earned it, but because Rick thought an encouraging mark might motivate him to do better. Rick gives as few tests as he can, and those he gives he is painfully slow to mark and return, as if he doesn't want to know how the kids did, or have the kids know either. A few days ago, he had them reading a difficult section from an old textbook. He wouldn't even ask Jamie, Marv, or Chandra to try. Instead he chose kids who can express themselves well, yet even they read the passage as if it were in a foreign language, hesitantly, sounding out words, their voices conveying no meaning. Within a few paragraphs, nearly everyone was lost. This isn't the way it should be, he thought to himself. No matter how much he believes in how he teaches, this lack of basic literacy eats at him.

✦ ✦ ✦

The day is over, most of the kids have left the school. Dave Arthurs stumbles slightly as he pushes open the office door. He has his glasses in his hands; they are broken. He appears shaken. It has been a tough semester for him. Early on his gout came back, his right big toe became too swollen and sore for a shoe, so day after day, in a bright blue sock, he made the long, slow walk from the staff room to his classroom, as students, with lockers to get to before class and no time to spare, anxiously pooled up behind him. Then it was his back, aggravated perhaps by the concessions of posture he had made for his gout. He put up with the pain for weeks, hoped March Break would heal him, and, when it didn't, was forced to stay home. I'll return soon, he told everybody again and again, but a back takes its own time. He was off four weeks. Now this.

The office staff gather around him. What happened? It takes a while for him to get the story out, even longer for those who hear it to understand. It's after school, he was in the parking lot. He was standing on the curb when this car drove up, its window open, and out of it flew something that struck him in the face. Then the car raced off. Stunned, his glasses on the ground, his face hurting, he quickly gathered himself and tried to catch the car's licence number.

The office staff are very upset. All the attacks going on in schools, it's frightening. It could happen any time to any of them. They are angry, and afraid. Who did it? He doesn't know. It must be one of his students, he thinks, who else? But why? He is a good teacher; he treats kids well. The kids know him around the school. Known as "Mr. Charity Week," he just finished heading the school's fund-raising campaign, which earned more than $3,500.

What did he get hit with? someone asks.

"A squash," he answers matter-of-factly.

It takes a while. "A squash?"

"Yes, a squash," he repeats tersely.

"A squash?"

He is starting to get annoyed.

The staff are beside themselves. Outwardly, they fight to maintain expressions appropriate to the look on Dave's face. On the inside, all hell is breaking loose. *A squash! He got hit by a squash.*

Images flood their heads: John Cleese arming would-be attack-ers with a squash. Headlines in the paper, "Teacher injured in drive-by squashing." This is embarrassing; this is supposed to be a tough school. "Metal detectors obsolete; no lunch bag safe." My God, what next – *zucchini*?

One of the staff says she has called the police. The others look at her, look away, grin, and more images flood their heads.

"Could you describe the weapon," the police officer might ask.

"Yellow, lumpy; you know, *like a squash!*"

"And you got the number?"

"Of the car?"

"No, the grocery code. Yeah, the car."

Very little is said. No one dares; no one can wait to spread the story.

Thank God it wasn't a pumpkin.

Chapter 15

Monday, June 6, 8:45 a.m.

"Six days left!!"

Sue Lishman's Enhanced math students see the message on the board as they arrive this beautiful Monday morning. Overnight, it seems, the colours have turned so vivid and bright, the blue of the sky, the greens of leaves and grass, the reds of the brick of the school and the Canadian flag rippling from its pole, even the whites of the clouds that fleck the sky. Mere days from summer freedom, the world looks different.

This weekend was the last fling before exams, and the white kids come in reddened or tanned. Leah and Selva are first to arrive, twenty minutes before class, Leah having put in several hard hours around her pool, Selva playing 3-on-3 basketball in the cul-de-sac near his house. Then Amanda, who never did make it to Canada's Wonderland, the amusement park north of the city, for her boyfriend's birthday yesterday. He was too busy, he said. Then Donald, who never gets here this early except when the drumbeat of exams finally stirs him. A few days ago he even stayed after class.

Donald is smart. Not grade-on-an-exam smart, where he scores only a little above average. Not brilliant-essay smart either; he finds writing too slow, rewriting tedious, he doesn't read enough to have imprinted on his mind the image of well-constructed, well-thought-out sentences. Nor is he street-smart. He has lived too precarious a life. Sickly as a child, his sister far more so, his father alcoholic and absent, he has had a sheltered, protected upbringing. His smartness is deep in the bone, the kind of sheer intellectual power that cuts through problems to an answer, that puts on a canvas figures and shapes that are uniquely his.

It is an isolating smartness, its explorations meandering and private, its expression mostly internal. On the outside, to teachers and kids, those he needs and wants as allies and friends, he offers a blank look, an inattention, an apparent disinterest. That look is all anyone knows for sure. Except, by now, the kids in this class, most of whom have known him since elementary school, have experienced his occasional thunderbolts of brilliance. They know he's smart, but they don't pretend to understand him.

Donald is doing much better this year than last, according to his teachers and to the kids. So much less pushy and obnoxious, rarely out of control. Many of his problems last year they attribute to his sister's illness. Eighteen months ago, eleven days after Donald's first day in high school, his sister, Jane, died. She was seventeen. At seven, she had developed Wilson's Disease: both her mother and father carried its recessive gene. The disease afflicts about one in 500,000, statistically only one in a city the size of Mississauga. In the course of the disease, copper gradually accumulates in the liver until it reaches toxic levels. Each victim suffers two "episodes" of the disease, one chronic, the next fatal. Jane's chronic episode was at seven, the other began three months before her death.

Donald and his mother moved into the hospital to be with her. Jane received a liver transplant, but her body rejected the new

organ. Donald offered a portion of his own liver, but the technology for the procedure wasn't yet available, and wouldn't be
until a few months too late. After Jane was taken off life support,
she held on until her father could get to the hospital. Together,
they formed a "family circle" around her, as Donald puts it,
making it easier for her "to go in peace." He tells the story with
a child's quiet bravado, but the hurt shows in his eyes.

Donald lives now as he always did, in fits and starts. He can't
quite find the level ground on which he can cruise day after day
with little pain or effort. His life bumps along, not so much a
struggle as a bruising. He started with a 79 in math on his first
test, then a 91, then 69, then 41. When the research plan for his
math project was due, Donald told Sue he had done his, but it
was on the computer in the computer room and he needed to
be excused to print it up. He came back thirty minutes later with
a plan that looked as if it had taken thirty minutes to do. Yet a
few days earlier, Sue had given them questions from a math
contest, no preparation required or possible, learning habits not
a factor, and Donald was first to the answer.

He has in his head the idea that to be smart is to know,
without effort or sweat. Anybody can grind out an answer, leave
that to Rohita or Simran. But to know, and to be able to let others
know before they know themselves, that is the best. That's how
he can distinguish himself from all the other smart kids in
Enhanced math. But at fifteen years old, he is just now running
up against his limitations. He's like a fastball pitcher who wants
always to throw the ball past the hitters, but no longer can. For
the rest of his life, he's going to have to work at being smart to
feel as smart as he wants to feel. He doesn't yet know how.

Today, Sue gives them a test, the last one before the exams.
Donald is the first finished, the first to Sue's desk afterwards for
a talk. He got 100 on his last test, this one, he's sure, went well.

"Miss, can I still get a 75 on the course?" he asks. Sue looks
at her grade book.

"Possibly," she says.

He interrupts excitedly, "I mean, with a hundred on my last test, my mark rose 2 per cent. If I get a hundred on this one, will it go up 2 more?"

Not a good sign, Sue thinks to herself. "No, Donald, your last test mark would've been averaged over eight tests, this one over nine."

"Oh yeah," he says, his optimism undampened. He has it all figured out: if he gets 93 on his final exam, he'll get his 75 per cent. Sue knows he might do it; he is sure he will.

Before the class ends, Sue's head begins to ache.

✦ ✦ ✦

Sue walks to her next classroom just a few metres away. It's her double grade-nine class, and she is now beyond dread. The class had started as an experiment, two classes of the same course, sharing the same room with only a divider to separate them: why not put them together? Classrooms in Japan have many more than forty-eight kids in them, without the individual attention this two-teacher arrangement would allow. But these are not Japanese kids, she knew then and knows much better now. The most basic habits of learning that should have been ingrained in elementary school – attendance, attention, courtesy – are absent in so many of them. Even this late in the semester, often her work is just crowd control. Keeping them quiet, checking homework, setting and marking tests. She had wanted them to put the date at the top of each day's notes, so each day she wrote the date on the board. Now if she forgets, they don't write it down. They are still so unsure of themselves; they have to know everything before they try anything. Every problem: "Miss! Miss!" And most who don't ask don't know either, so she has to ask them. In her own ears, she has come to sound like a bitch.

One of the kids is in grade-nine math for the fourth time. She needs two math credits to graduate so she keeps coming back. Her mind is frozen. Either someday she will quit, or some teacher will move her on; she will never really pass. But she is far from the biggest problem. *"This is too hard, miss"; "I'm bored, miss."* Voices that now seem to come from everywhere and sound like everybody. The class is too big. All it took was a few trouble-makers strong enough and loud enough to set the tone and the rest didn't resist. She wasn't able to isolate them to bring them into line; she had no place to put them.

Sue is beginning to think now that a teacher needs to be like a doctor or nurse. You care and give and do your best, but for the sake of your own sanity you don't get too close. Stay above the emotional fray. Don't take things too personally. These kids have failed before and will fail again, yet ultimately most will be okay. So don't take one bad class so hard. They don't. But when she thinks this way, she feels even worse. She *needs* to take them personally.

Today, forty-five of the kids are here. She and her co-teacher Pam Sawyer give them a short quiz, then review it on the board. Pam begins writing out the solutions; Sue stands at one side of the room. When Pam turns her back to write, the noise picks up.

"I'm waiting for quiet," she says.

"You can wait all you want," comes a voice from the back. It is Ray, a big, tough, dumb-looking kid. His buddy Darryl laughs.

Sue tries to make a point, but to beat the noise and the dis-tance she has to project her voice, which rises, thins, weakens, and dies. Tall and straight-postured, in a regular classroom Sue is a presence, here she looks so small. It's too many kids, too much noise, too much distance from front to back, too many heads to see over. A group too big to be anything but a mob. No indi-vidual existence, no individual consequences, everyone able to hide. No matter how much noise, someone else started it. It's someone else's fault.

The noise at the back starts again. Ray and Darryl are arguing. Toronto has a new NBA franchise called the Raptors. Raptors hats have begun appearing in the school. "They cost seventy bucks apiece," says Ray. "They've raised two billion dollars already and they still don't have a team." Others turn to listen; Pam goes on without them.

Last week Sue experienced her first classroom fight with these kids. She had been busy at the front and all of a sudden there was a crashing noise from the back. She looked up and saw two figures each in each other's headlock. Worse, the rest of the class was moving to gather around them. She rushed back to break them up, calling as calmly and urgently as she could to Pam, who was out of the room. One rumpled, harmless, and slightly naïve kid had been messing around with correction fluid. The other kid, smart and slightly mean, had snuck in behind him and shoved his face down into it. By the time Sue arrived, all she could see of the victim was a contorted, hate-filled face, with a Bozo the Clown white nose. She had a hard time not laughing.

It is hard for a teacher to come to the end of a semester when there's nothing more that can be done. Last year, Sue would have doubted herself – *It's my fault; I just can't teach* – but now she knows she can. As she talks about this class, she is almost in tears. If only she could have spent more time with Ray, she says regretfully. She has such a soft spot for him. Big, awkward, and obnoxious, but not if you really know him – the kid who no one really wants to know. Ten minutes a day, that's all she needed, but she didn't have it. Maybe you never have it, but certainly not the way the class was arranged. She needed to get him away from Darryl. Separate them; work with Ray. With Melina, who is so quiet. And with poor Desi, the kid everybody picks on. Short, fat, with a quivery, childish voice. She thinks now the only one she made a difference with was Joe. The drama department was putting on its play, and one of the main actors didn't work out. At the last minute Joe had to fill in. For three weeks, every second day Sue let him miss her class to rehearse. He had to have his homework done; that was the deal. When the play was done, he came to her and said, "Miss, when I win an Academy Award, I'll dedicate it to you."

This morning, the second issue of the *Kronicle* came out and in it are stories about the teachers who are leaving, Sue among them. At the end of class, some of the kids come up to her, including Ray.

"You leaving, miss?" one of the kids asks. "Miss, you can't leave. We like you," another pleads.

Ray knows why she's going. "You don't want to teach a bunch of knobs like us," he says.

"Oh no," Sue says, "I love teaching."

"She doesn't want to teach because she can do so many other things." It is Ray again. Darryl nods. Inside, Sue is glowing.

✦ ✦ ✦

Sheri had been away, missing both Noel's and Maria's classes, then she was away a few more days, but nothing unusual for Sheri. Then she remained away. Her teachers began wondering, and so too Jan Coomber, the vice-principal. She hadn't left Sheri much room with her memo; perhaps Sheri had finally dropped out. The semester-long frustration of teachers and staff turned quickly to sadness and regret. Sheri had so much ability, and was on the verge of finally using it. Her counsellor called her home. Sheri answered in a raspy, broken voice. She has bronchitis, she said. The counsellor rushed to Jan's office with the good news. It's *only* bronchitis.

Priya, who always breezed into Maria's room late with the slam of a door, then spent most of her remaining minutes examining her fingernails, writing love notes to her boyfriend, looking at car catalogues, or talking with Sabesan, has not only dropped math but dropped out of school. Her counsellor told Maria that Priya's parents didn't approve of her boyfriend, who is also a student here. They thought the best way to break up the relationship was to remove Priya from school.

Sabesan has been frequently absent too. About a week ago, the last time he was here, he asked Maria if he could still pass. His average is about 40 per cent; she told him he would need a 70 on the final. Apparently discouraged, he has stopped coming. Yet Dwayne, whose chances of passing are even slimmer, is still here. Maria really admires him for that. Nelson has had more bad days, and his marks are falling. A month ago, looking at a confusing array of numbers and letters on the blackboard, he asked Maria, "Miss, are we ever going to need this in the business world?" A week later: "Miss, I think we only learn math to give teachers a job." Lately, his twinkling spirit has turned dark. He's become argumentative and sullen. Maria checks homework, his isn't done, she makes some comment, he lashes back, "I've done it. I always do it." A few days ago, she took him aside. I'm not worried about you passing, she told him. You'll pass, but your marks are sinking and they don't need to sink. Why are you doing this? You can do so much better. Since then, he's been fine. Lively, involved, he did well on his last test and now he won't stop bugging her, "What's my mark, miss? What's my mark?"

On Friday Maria gave them their last test before the exams. When class was over, Nelson, Julie, and another girl hung around. When the others were finally gone, they approached Maria. Julie broke the silence. "Miss," she said, "we have a complaint."

"You have a complaint, Julie?" Maria asked, surprised.

"All of us do, miss."

The test was too long or too hard, that's all Maria can imagine, but they wouldn't have waited this long to tell her.

"These three girls were cheating," Julie said, pointing to the

seats where moments ago the girls were sitting. She points not
to avoid accusing them by name, but because after four months
sitting just a row from them, she still doesn't know their names.
The three girls are Indian. Maria has noticed their behaviour
during other tests. One girl, the strongest math student among
them, every so often raises her paper from her desk. But the look
on her face when she does it, that's what Maria noticed first, as
if she were trying to hide something. She had talked to the girls
about her suspicions, warned them that she would give them
zero if it happened again. They insisted they hadn't been cheating. Maria isn't sure. She has heard other teachers talk about
Indian girls and what appears to them to be a pattern of lying. The
teachers don't know if they are right, but they have a theory.
The gap between the traditional Indian lives their parents expect
the girls to live at home and the contemporary Western lives their
friends expect them to live at school is so great that they need to
become almost two personalities, each a lie to the other.
Conditioned to living this way, lying comes easier. Perhaps a
North American-born girl who does what she wants at home
and at school has less need to lie.

There have been other instances of cheating in this and other
classes, but none where kids have exposed other kids. Kids don't
tell on other kids because the fundamental conflict in any school
is kids against teachers, us against them. But these are three
Indian girls who dress differently and keep to themselves. They
don't seem like us, their classmates think, so it's us and them,
against *them*.

The semester is almost done, but Maria will watch these girls
more carefully. On the final exam, if she sees anything, she says,
"It's a zero."

✦ ✦ ✦

More inspirational signs have begun appearing on classroom
bulletin boards:

Chance favours the prepared.

Destiny is not a matter of chance, it is a matter of choice!

If you don't know where you're going, you may end up
somewhere else.

"Just Read It" signs also appeared for several days around the
school, until the second issue of the *Kronicle* finally arrived.
Bigger, now sixteen pages, with three new subject headings,
"Automotive," "Feature," which offered the "final farewells" to
teachers and others who were leaving or retiring, and "Summer
Spectacular." It has more sports, which respondents to the *Kronicle*
poll in the first issue said they wanted, more and shorter articles,
but no "Sunshine Girl" like the daily pin-up on page three of a
local Toronto newspaper. "If you want one so desperately," the
Kronicle admonished its poll respondents, "they do have certain
magazines devoted to such trash."

The lead article was about school spirit, or, as its headline put
it, "Whoomp! there it ain't!" Lots of views were expressed, but
most had to do with the school's cultural mix. "This school is
too multicultural," one student told the paper, "so there are
things that one group of people might want to do but others
might not. There's no school spirit because there aren't any activities that involve the whole school." Suggested remedies included
movies, lip-synch contests, and games like "Family Feud" at
lunch; music during announcements and lunch; an International
Night, offering varied activities for students so different groups
can socialize. One victim of school apathy was highlighted in
another article. The school's year-end "Formal" is likely to be

cancelled. It's not with much regret, as the article states; with its "ruffles, dates, tuxedos and corsages," a Formal seems out of another time, another place. Next year, the article suggests, a new kind of prom should take its place, less stuffy, less expensive, "more nineties style."

There was an article on the TB scare. No media or public panic resulted from the outbreak, several students and one teacher tested "positive," but no new "actives" have appeared and the incident has largely passed. There was an article on the school's fashion show, whose models included Leah and Sheri, and on students repeating courses to get higher grades. High school transcripts are sent to universities offering no evidence of multiple tries. That isn't fair, the article says: "Life is full of mistakes which we can never correct, but only learn from." An article on interracial dating: "Headache or Happiness?" Couples see such dating, the article says, "as a way to experience different cultures and to see different views. These couples don't expect each other to change their culture, they just expect their culture to be respected. Interracial couples don't care what other people think. They just care about each other." This issue's horoscope also included for each sign, an "LlD," Lucky lottery Day, "LLD," Lucky Love Day, and "GED," Good Exam Day. One poem in the Poetry Corner, submitted anonymously, was entitled "Teenage Dreams":

It's not enough to have a dream
    unless I'm willing to pursue it –
It's not enough to know what's
    right unless I'm strong enough to do it –
It's not enough to join the crowd,
    to be acknowledged and
    accepted – I must be true to
    my ideals, even if I'm left out
    and rejected –

It's not enough to learn the truth
    unless I also learn to live it –
It's not enough to reach for love
    unless I care enough to give it.

The Awards Assembly on Friday lasted more than two hours, but few of the kids who attended seemed bored. One who didn't attend but who was in the school for the first time in days was Quentin. He stood in the front foyer as the assembly went on, waiting for his friends. He wore his new contact lenses, which he had gotten the day before. Gone were his squint, his hunched posture and averted gaze. He was smiling; he looked great. Next year he'll be back, he promised.

The Assembly was an appropriate high to finish the year, Terry Chaffe thought. Presentations were made to the teachers who were retiring or leaving; the ceremony was moving. One teacher had been here twenty-nine years, his entire working career. One young teacher received her award in a wheelchair. A few years ago, she had had an accident, had come back to teach in her chair, but found it too difficult. She has been on leave of absence ever since, but her health now deteriorating, she has decided to retire. The biggest applause of the day went to Leo, the custodian, who received a special award as the student council's "Best Friend," and a standing ovation.

From Sue Lishman's class, Simran won an award for Spanish; Amanda, for art. Monika in Rick's class won a special "spotlight" award for "best hair," a concoction of ringlets and curls that she calls "my pineapple," which sticks straight up from the top of her head, every day always perfect. Selva, also from Sue's class, joined several students and teachers in a choir dressed as nuns, serene, beatific, who suddenly let loose as 1950s rockers. One of the nuns was Sister Noella: Noel Lim. They brought down the house.

A few weeks ago, there was a notice on the back of the staff room door. Noel's father had died. He was nearly eighty years old, had been riding a bike on the side of a road and was hit by a car. It was a Friday. On Saturday, he was operated on, on Sunday morning he seemed fine; Sunday night he died. Noel moved in with his mother for the week until the funeral. The kids in his classes weren't told what had happened. They knew only that for a few more days they had a substitute teacher, with all the opportunity for trouble that offered. It wasn't what James, Nelson, Sheri, and Wesley needed.

This past week, Noel's English class has been making final oral presentations on *Forbidden City*, a novel about present-day China. A young Chinese-Canadian man returns to his native country and gets caught up in the Tiananmen Square uprising. James chose to do his project on the square itself. He is first. He begins with his considerable charm, a big smile, and a piece of bristol board in his hands on which he has drawn a map of the square. He starts into its history. He gains confidence and begins to strut about the room with the map to give everyone a look. He passes in front of Wesley. Wesley clenches his teeth and mutters, "Flip it." James seems not to hear. "Flip it," Wesley says again. James looks down, "Oh," and turns the map right-side up. At the end, he just stops. "That's it," he says. He has to say it again. There is applause.

Pauline, the girl who escaped by boat from Vietnam, does her presentation on Chinese food. She has a heavy accent, but speaks loudly and clearly and gives a spirited performance. Sheri is next. Her subject is Beijing. She starts well and is in command. She holds her rumpled papers in her hands, but speaks from memory, the only one who does, bringing her listeners into a story she creates. They are with her. But what she knows runs out before her story does. She slows down, circles, stumbles, shows a few pictures about which she knows little, loses her audience, and fizzles.

During Sheri's and Pauline's presentations, Nelson was sometimes listening, sometimes shuffling papers and talking to Lydia.

Noel kept glancing his way, then decided to put the evil eye on him until he noticed and to keep it on him until Nelson became unnerved. Noel also decided that when Nelson made his presentation, he would talk all the way through it. He never got his chance. Nelson arrived late that day and Noel refused to let him in. He told Nelson to go the office and get a late slip, if they would give him one. He stormed to the office and came face to face with Patti Herrmann, who handles the front desk and has heard every excuse and story that imagination and circumstance can contrive. She listens as kids squirm through their lies, then tells them to cut the crap, laughs with them, and sets things straight. A few weeks earlier, Nelson had been in to see her, selling his "mouth-watering" chocolate almonds, and had gone out the door with several sales. Patti and Nelson are buddies.

"Gimme a late slip," he snarled.

"Excuse me," Patti said, barely raising her head.

"A late slip. Gimme a late slip."

"You can't have a late slip."

"I need a late slip."

"Well, you can't have one."

Patti was getting angry, Nelson angrier; this was going nowhere.

"I need one!"

"Well, you're not getting one! Whatever problem you've got, work it out with Mr. Lim."

Nelson stormed out, or tried to, but the door, mounted on a hydraulic arm, pulled back as hard as he pulled on it. Finally out the door, he turned and stormed back through the other office door, and started into the same pitch with another secretary.

"Gimme a late slip."

Patti cut him off. Nelson stormed out again.

The next day, Patti saw him in the hall. Nelson bounded over, "Hi, miss. How are ya, miss?"

Patti dug in. "Don't you ever talk to me like that again."

"Whaddaya mean, miss?"

"You know what I mean. You have no right to talk to me that way, and don't ever do it again."

"I didn't do anything," Nelson whined, looking hurt, puzzled, and embarrassed.

"You owe me an apology. You owe everyone in the office an apology."

Nelson still looked puzzled.

"Look," Patti said, trying another tack, "there was a second Nelson in here yesterday who was very rude, and if that Nelson doesn't apologize to me and everyone else . . ."

The next day, Nelson strolled into the office. "Ladies," he announced, "I understand there was another Nelson in here the other day. Well, I just want to apologize for him." He grinned and walked out.

◆ ◆ ◆

Tuesday, June 14, 10:58 a.m.

It is the last day of school and blistering hot. Most of the kids and many of the teachers are in shorts as they have been for days. The school has no air-conditioning and lots of windows. Teachers with classrooms on the second floor every so often come down to the first, their faces red and glistening, just for a break. Perhaps only one-third of the students are here, in Cathy Sylvester's science class only eight, and she isn't surprised at which ones. It's the good students who come at the end of semester, the ones who feel on top of things, who are afraid they might miss something, who know what they don't know and come looking for answers. The others don't know what they don't know, questions only betray their ignorance and embarrass them, so they stay home. They need all the time studying they can get. They also stay home because on these last days they have licence to stay home. No punishments can follow them from school, and to their parents, a son or daughter hard at the books is demonstrating a rare application that they don't want to discourage. Also at class today are a lot of immigrant kids, South Asian girls especially, and they will be at school until the lights are turned out. They hang around the halls before Christmas, in June they come when they don't need to and sit on the curb by the parking lot as others race off to holiday freedom. Raised in strict homes, school is *their* freedom. In September, no one returns to school with more enthusiasm than they do.

The kids stand around Cathy's desk listening, hoping for that *Eureka!* moment that will turn four months of *stuff* into a vibrant whole. Quickly, a few kids come to monopolize, the others drift back to their seats and talk amongst themselves. Jody and Nelson sit together. In a few weeks, Nelson is going to summer school, he says, either here or in Burlington where his mother and girlfriend live. His father, with whom he is currently living, is travelling to Australia. Nelson thinks he will take English during the summer and maybe another subject. He has failed English before and is sure he will again with Noel. He also must find a job.

Jody is going to do some aerobics at the Y, hopes to go to New York City for a weekend, to a cottage north of the city for a week or so. But mostly she wants to spend time with her boyfriend. They have been going together for two and a half years. Two and a half years, she repeats, and shakes her head: My life is passing me by. But he's a good guy. All her girlfriends tell her how lucky she is, how he doesn't cheat on her. She smiles. He wouldn't dare. She'll see Jennifer and Tracy occasionally. Jennifer is getting 65s now in her General level science class, at least according to Jennifer, and she doesn't even have to work for her marks. Jennifer's parents tell her that a pass is fine, Jody says, so she passes. Her own parents tell her to do well, so she must. Tracy has packed in the course, Jody reports. She has only six credits in all and needs thirty-two to graduate, she'll get only one this semester, and even

Tracy's not sure in what. She wants to be a lawyer, Jody says, and rolls her eyes.

Jody likes sitting at the back of class, she says. She can't hear the teacher quite as well, but she likes to take in everything, know what everyone is saying and doing, and that's difficult except at the back. She doesn't work as hard as she can, she says, but next year she will. Her courses will be harder, and it's beginning next year that universities are looking for results. She wants to be a veterinarian; she has a dog that is almost like a brother to her, she says. She's just not sure she can deal with animals in pain. She has studied hard for the science exam, all last weekend, all last night, she has never studied so hard before, she says. But on exams, she "clutches." Then her tone of effort vanishes, her familiar tone of threat returns. *"I'd better do well,"* she snarls.

In Rick Ray's history class only four kids are present. Rick is feeling better than he did yesterday. He had arrived tired and bothered; he hadn't slept very much. The night before, he had been at his son's soccer game at a park near their house. The game was going well, when suddenly, at one end of the field, kids on foot and bikes came out of nowhere towards the goalposts. The intruders were twelve or thirteen years old, his son's age; they began twirling around the goalposts, climbing on them. The referee tried to stop them, then one of the coaches, then Rick and another of the parents. All they heard back was "f-this" and "f-that." The other parent started yelling at the kids; they swore back, taunting him. The man rushed at his worst tormentor, stopping just short of him, his finger stabbing the air close to the kid's face. The kid didn't flinch. "Go ahead," he snarled, "you want to punch me? Punch me." The other kids swarmed around.

Is that what things are coming to? Rick wondered. Is this the next wave of grade nines coming in his door? The social balance is so precarious. I'm older, richer, stronger, wiser, but how powerless I really am. These kids know how to get angry, to taunt, swarm, fight, bleed, lose, and fight some more. As adults, we don't know how any more. We're out of practice. And once we acknowledge their provocation and confront these kids, we can't let it go. We can't let wrong win. But then what? What will happen a few days from now when the next game is played? Will the same gang be back, looking for more trouble? Should they cancel the game, call the cops? That's not good enough, Rick knows. All that night as he lay in bed, yesterday, this morning, he has been thinking and wondering: what he teaches his students — not events and dates, but dignity, respect, tolerance, the real lessons of history, of people living together — has he got it all wrong?

Jamie isn't here today. For weeks and months, he never missed a day. He would come before eight o'clock and hang around Rick's room to talk, to be there. Now, with the semester almost over, he is gone. He had worked so hard for so little; Rick decided weeks ago that he was going to pass him regardless of his final results. Jamie had demonstrated all the habits of learning — discipline, concentration, and desire — just not the learning itself. But that is for reasons he cannot control, Rick has realized.

Jamie's girlfriend has been having some problems, he told Rick the last time he was in class. She's in a custody fight with her ex-husband over their two children. The ex "set her up" on something, Jamie said, now he's using that against her. She's in court, Jamie is taking care of her kids, and he's so worried and so tired from worrying that on days she isn't in court he just stays home and can't concentrate on anything else. He assured Rick that it would soon be over. He hasn't been back at school since.

During this last class, Rick tries to pull together the events and themes of the course. He draws on the board a giant heart; the heart is humanity. He takes the kids back to the early weeks of the course, to the story of the Triangle Factory Fire, of immigration, sweatshops, and crowded ghettos. What do they tell us about us? he asked them. About human behaviour? Fahad describes the exploitation and mistreatment of the workers. Rick

nods; and what about the other side, he asks, what about the
workers themselves? They wanted fairness, Charlene says, they
wanted liberty and opportunity. Inside the heart, Rick writes
"Liberty," "Opportunity," and "Fair Treatment"; outside, on
either side of an arrow that jabs at the heart, he writes
"Exploitation" and "Mistreatment." He moves the kids to the
Boer War, to *Glory* and *Cry Freedom*. He writes "Racism" and
"Prejudice" along another arrow; "Justice," "Equality,"
"Tolerance," and "Respect" inside the heart. To World War I and
All Quiet on the Western Front, "Dishonesty" and "Propaganda"
he writes on one side, "Honesty," "Truth," "Law," and "Trust"
on the other. To World War II, inside the heart is "Freedom,"
"Diversity," and "Acceptance"; jabbing at it from the outside,
"Authoritarianism" and "Totalitarianism." He turns and faces
the kids. All those things that jab at the heart, he says, they are
history as we study it. But history is also all those things inside
the heart that resist those jabs. The heart is you and me. The story
must be told; as John McCrae wrote in his poem, "the torch"
must be passed. We must never let history say, "They only stood
and watched."

The four kids leave; a few minutes later, Jamie arrives. He
looks bewildered. More of his story emerges. His girlfriend has
been accused of drug trafficking. She was set up by her former
husband, who is the father of only two of her three kids. Because
of the charge, the ex has won custody of all of them. He also put
up her two-thousand-dollars' bail, using *her* furniture as collat-
eral. Jamie has been home all week, he says, not doing anything,
a little studying, hoping that his head will clear. He says that he
saw Terry Chaffe as he came in, who said to him, "I was afraid
we might have lost you." Another teacher said the same to him.
Jamie was surprised and touched. He gives Rick a big smile.
"After all I've put up with," he promises, "I'm not giving up."

Chapter 16

Wednesday, June 22, 8:54 a.m.

Both gyms are filled with desks on this last sweltering day of exams, but not many more than half the desks have students at them. Last week when it was even hotter every desk was filled, 160 in the small gym, 352 in the big one. The doors were opened to the outside, and huge fans placed in the openings to give the leaden air a goose. Kids had water bottles with them, as they do today; one had a bottle of ice. Only six have presented medical certificates to excuse themselves from exams, one a girl who is pregnant. "She's only a month!" office staffer Patti Herrmann complained when she heard. Another was from a boy whose brother had died a year ago. He had discovered his brother's body and occasionally still suffers from depression. But no one has fainted with the heat, no one has complained to the office that a blown exam was the result of an act of God or the school's lack of air-conditioning.

Amanda, Elaine, and Veronica from Sue Lishman's Enhanced math have arranged themselves in their regular class seating order, so too Rohita and Sonya, Reba and Simran, Selva, Imran and Philip, Donald and Leah. Arriving early, they took seats at the front until Sue suggested they move back, closer to the open doors and fans. They have their pens and calculators set out in front of them; the exam begins. Pat isn't here.

Sue walks to the office and makes a call. Pat's mother answers.

"Did you know that Pat has an exam this morning?" Sue asks.

"I thought it was this afternoon!" his mother gasps.

"No, it isn't," Sue says stonily.

There is silence on the line. "Paa-trick!!" she shouts, then some muffled sounds, then Pat.

"H-hello," he mumbles sleepily.

"Pat, you've got an exam."

"Huh?"

"Your exam."

"But miss, I can't pass. Even if I got 100."

"I want you here." Sue hangs up before he has a chance to protest.

She doubts he will come. He can't pass and she won't pass him. What Pat needs least of all is one more time when he does nothing all semester and pulls it out at the end. But if he has decided to fail, she's decided that she is going to make him *feel* his failure. You want to sleep through it all? Sorry. Wake up, Pat. The same for your mother.

Nelson isn't here either. His math teacher, Maria Cheung, searches the room with her eyes. She can't believe it! He hasn't missed a day all semester. How can he not be here! She rushes from the gym and calls his home. His brother tells her he over-slept, left five minutes ago, and should be there soon. Nelson arrives at 9:28, with just over an hour to do an hour and a half exam. He has forgotten to bring his calculator.

Just before Nelson appears, Sheri strolls in and sits down. No one notices. Every so often a hand goes up, a teacher walks back to it; otherwise, so many kids, such a big room, the silence is stunning. The rule is that no one can leave before ten o'clock, an hour into the exam; precisely at ten o'clock, Sophia, Sabesan, and several others leave. No one from the Enhanced class moves. At 10:15, Pat arrives. He doesn't even sit down. He is looking for Sue, he says. She told him to get here. He wants her to know that he did. Maria tells him Sue is in the staff room; he goes off to find her.

✦ ✦ ✦

At home, Rick Ray is marking history exams. He put the task off as long as he could – now the marks must go in. There's nothing more he can do, no place he or they can hide. It is their exam, but it's his exam too, reflecting his performance as a teacher. Will he pass or fail? Every semester, he fails enough to wince.

The history exam was in three parts. The first, worth ten marks, was fill-in-the-blanks. The kids were given twenty events, such as "Guglielmo Marconi received the first radio signal sent across the Atlantic Ocean" and "A socialist party, known as the C.C.F., was formed in Regina," and were asked to identify the historical time period for each, either "Turn of the Century," "World War I," "The Roaring Twenties," "The Great Depression," "World War II," or "After World War II," earning half a mark for each right answer. The class, Rick has discovered, has done terribly. Fahad got all twenty right, of course, Monika seventeen, Charlene sixteen, no one else more than ten. Pat got ten, Calvin and Sandee had nine, Karen eight, Chad, who wrote Rick's name on his paper as "Mr. Rae," three. Willy, who in General level wrote a different exam but had this same question, got zero.

The question gave too many options for lucky guesses, not enough information to intuit the right answer, the kids had to *know*. Some details might have come from Rick's lessons, most from the textbook, a few might also have been remembered from dinner-table conversations at home, from just having lived in this country all one's life. But many haven't lived here long, or had those conversations with people who might talk about such matters. And few of these kids ever read for pleasure. So according to Chad, Marconi received the first radio signal in 1956, and according to Willy and Karen, Chamberlain achieved "peace in our time" at Munich "After World War II."

Rick shakes his head. There is no substitute for reading. Not movies, not TV, not "educational" computer games. But what can a teacher do? Even the girls now. Once, with so few doors open to them, reading was their way to explore the world. Now, able to do more, like the boys, they read less. One day this semester, he stopped his lesson to his upper-grade class and declared "an emergency." Maybe you should just save yourself that few thousand dollars you're putting away for next year, he told them. Use it for something else. Because you're not going to be able to do university work. Not because you're not smart enough, but because you can't express yourself. You write the way you speak. Unself-consciously, fluidly, personally, emotionally: wonderfully in many ways, but on the page, words and thoughts demand discipline, structure, order – skills you just haven't learned. As non-readers, you have no reference points for proper written language. The spoken word offers too little time for details, and you need details to build thoughts, to express ideas. To intuit, imagine, create. Reading offers those details, and the time you need to absorb and play with them. It puts you in control, allows you to go at your own pace, slow down, pause, rewind, fast forward, and to fit between the written lines everything you know that those lines bring to mind. Reading isn't just a technique of learning, but a process for learning. It shapes what is learned and how, forces you to go slower, allows you to think, opens you up to discovery and pleasure, and turns all these into habits and needs. The medium is the essence of the message, but you have not mastered the medium and that's what is missing.

Rick didn't declare his "emergency" to discourage them, just to scare them a little. For a week, he took them back to basic sentences, verb tenses, paragraph structure, statement and argument, and it helped, but not much. What can he do when a fifteen-year-old bad reader walks through his classroom door? Tell him, sorry, you should have learned to read in grade one? Any learning you do in this class has to be on hold until you read better? That's not fair. The kid can still learn somehow. The world can be revealed in other ways. Rick can act out history, offer movies and games, but the kid's learning will still be limited. The results are all over these exam pages, unmistakable. How could these kids not know some of these answers? Sitting in his class seventy-six minutes a day for the last four months: what in God's name were they doing?

The class did slightly better on the second part, where, given names, places, or events, they had to answer ten out of twenty-five questions arranged in groupings of three, and show how each related to Canada's history: "Dust, grasshoppers, and gopher tails"; "Japanese-Canadians, Jews, and human rights." Each answer was worth three marks. Fahad got 28.5 out of 30, Monika 26, Calvin 13.5, Chad 7, Pat 0. He skipped the question entirely.

On the last part, the kids had to answer one question among many from each of the six time periods covered in the course. Paragraph answers were required; each question was worth ten marks. Explain why, they were asked, "Battles like Ypres, the Somme, and Passchendaele help us to understand both the valour and horror experienced by men in war," or, why "Inventions like radio, telephone, the movie theatre, and the automobile had obvious effects on the life styles of the 1920s." Here more than elsewhere on the exam, the kids needed a sense of history, and here Rick's kids did better than those in the other classes. "Despite the hard times," Fahad wrote, "many people found ways to escape from the boredom and suffering of the Depression. Many turned to the radio. Many went to the movie cinema to see stars like Shirley Temple and Theda Bara as well as characters like King Kong and Mickey Mouse. As another means of escape, many people turned to magazines like *Reader's Digest* to get their minds off the Depression. Games like Monopoly also gained fame as one could invest and build without losing a single cent of real money." Pat's best answer was to a question about ways to improve Canada's laws and/or government. "I think Canada needs to abolish the Young Offenders' Act," he wrote. "The Act gives kids a chance to easily get away with anything. I'm 16 so I know what it's like to be under the Act. I know kids robbing stores, stealing cars, asulting people . . . the list goes on, but they all say 'I'll stop when I turn 18' simply because they know they can get away with it until then. I think if we got rid of this stupid law Canada would be alot safer."

Pat had tried two of the other questions, then at ten o'clock, without even attempting the other three, he left. Chad left with him. "Damn, I should've made sure they weren't sitting together," Rick thought afterwards. But Willy stayed. He wasn't going to pass the exam and surely he knew that. Mickey's beckoned and so did his buddies, but he didn't leave. The last half hour, Rick walked past him several times, patting him on the back. "Keep working, William. Keep working." "I am, sir. I'm trying." When Rick marked his paper, he cringed at all the embarrassing gaps in Willy's learning. "You need to know more exact information to explain your answers," Rick wrote on his paper. He also wrote, "Good try, William."

In the end, Rick can't come up with any combination of marks and circumstances that will give Willy a pass. He got 37 on the final exam, 34 for the course. In the school's promotional meetings a few days before, Willy's name came up. "What are we going to do with this kid?" Principal Terry Chaffe asked in a tired, exasperated voice. To his surprise, and probably to their own, Willy's teachers spoke up on his behalf. "Oh, he's not that bad." "He's certainly not destructive." "If he hurts anyone, it's himself." But the best suggestion any of them had was to put

Willy in his stronger courses the first semester next year and, depending on how he does, into a special program the second. His teachers, it seems, realize he is academically terminal. Nothing more can be done; let's just see that he is happy. The psychologists who tested him recently think vocational school might be better, and this semester Willy did pass electronics. His teacher, Dan Henderson, was pleased. He had to keep encouraging Willy, keep "bringing out the pompoms," as Dan put it, always fighting to keep him in the classroom. "Look," he told Willy, "if I can't go out for a cigarette, neither can you." Often Dan had to take him aside and ask Willy questions privately, to see what he knew and how he was doing, because Willy would never ask questions himself. Dan had to show him he cared, but Willy worked. Sending him to a new school would separate him from his friends, and Mickey's, and people is what Willy does best. He likes being with people; people like being with him. Even smart, athletic people, achievers, people who will one day run their own little part of the world. And that's what will likely see Willy through. People will always look out for him because they like having him around.

Rick tries hard to find a way to pass Pat too, but he can't. Pat gave him nothing. He just wasn't ready to start the learning conversation. Maybe next year he'll do better, if there is someone else around who is willing to invest some time in him, who will take the chance. Phys-ed teacher Jim Long had Pat in his class this semester. The first week, in the kind of teacher-talk that goes around the staff room, Jim heard all about Pat and a friend of his also in the phys-ed class, two "bad news" kids. But Jim likes to find things out for himself, so he worked on both of them. He had the time a phys-ed teacher has, to talk, to joke, to get to know, and both Pat and his friend began to come around.

Then about midway through the semester, Pat caught on. You're trying to work on me, buddy up to me, make me change and be other things you think I can be. Until that moment, the two of them had been climbing the mountain together; suddenly it was as if Pat had jumped off the other side. Straight down. You almost had me, he seemed to be saying. But I don't want to be what you want me to be, whatever that is. For a while it seemed Pat also might bring his friend down with him, but his friend made his own breakthrough, because he had a sense of himself, Jim thinks, and Pat doesn't. Pat is nothing of his own, only the determined antithesis of what others in his life expect him to be. Before this semester, he had never failed a course; this semester he failed all four: 40 in history, 45s in phys ed and science, 19 in math.

Fahad had the highest mark overall, 96. Monika and Charlene were in the 80s, Ahmed, Calvin, Sandee, and Rodney in the 70s, Aisha and Karen, the 60s, Chad, Chandra, and Jamie, the 50s. Jamie passed! He got 22 on the final exam, but Rick did what he had promised himself he would do. Until the complication of his girlfriend's custody fight, Jamie never missed a day. Would it do him any good to fail? At what point is tough love just plain cruel? Maybe Jamie shouldn't be in school; maybe somebody should have told him to try something else. Maybe the school should not have accepted him. But it did, and it shoulders some of the responsibility for what happens to him, Rick thinks.

During exams, teachers are required to be around the school, often with nothing to do. So they hang around the staff room and talk, and sometimes questions that begged answers all semester find them. A teacher who had just finished teaching Jamie for the second time decided to look further into his story. Twenty years ago, at age six, she discovered, Jamie was diagnosed as "trainable mentally retarded." A younger brother and sister were later diagnosed the same. At eleven, Jamie was doing math at an early grade-two level, his language skills were those of a six-year-old. Later, he went to Britannia, a vocational school, when Terry was principal; after seven years out of school, after a series of jobs in a series of places, he ended up at Kennedy because no one checked his records. Now having passed math *and* history, he has two more credits than he had before.

✦ ✦ ✦

One-quarter of Maria Cheung's math class failed, Sheri, Dwayne, Sabesan, and Quentin among them. Sheri got only 25 on the final exam, 36 overall. Although she had decided earlier in the semester to change her life, she couldn't pull it off; too many of her old habits remained. Sabesan, who lacks Sheri's ability, shares her lack of application. Dwayne simply may not be able to do math at this level. Quentin offers so many challenges, it's hard to know which are most crucial. But now that he has his contact lenses, there is some hope for next year.

Nelson finished his wildly up-and-down semester with an up-and-down exam. Arriving twenty-eight minutes late, he still managed to pass, a 52, giving him 62 for the course, down 10 per cent from his mid-term mark. Sophia's final mark was 74, also down 10 per cent from mid-term; she had only 56 on her final exam, which she handed in half an hour before the end. Sometime after the first month of the semester, Sophia seemed to lose school as a priority. She would make light of a poor result or homework undone. "Ah, miss, I do it tomorrow." She would still follow every step Maria took at the blackboard, answering incessantly, annoyingly; her fingernails got longer, her clothes more stylish, she was growing up, adapting to a new life in Canada. Next year, she might swing back again. With a lively, curious mind and a need to know, she still might make it to medical school.

Three kids scored in the 80s, including the oldest of the three Indian girls whom Maria suspected of cheating, and Shiva, who didn't say anything all semester. But the star performer of the class was Anna. She had come to Canada from Bulgaria only a year ago. She appeared capable, conscientious, then halfway through this semester she seemed to change. In phys ed one day, teacher Theresa Chapman called the class together, but Anna kept on playing. Theresa yelled at her two or three times before she stopped. She thought Anna was just having a bad day. But this happened other days, and more and more it aggravated Theresa. Finally, she took Anna aside. Anna, she discovered, was deaf. Her parents hadn't told the school administration, because they were afraid she would be put in a special school. They knew she could do the work, they wanted to be sure she got the chance. Until the final exam was over, Maria knew nothing of Anna's condition. To her, Anna was just this quiet girl in the second row, second seat, who minded her own business, was there every day, and who topped her class with 98 per cent.

◆ ◆ ◆

For Sue Lishman's Enhanced class, the news is almost entirely good. Seven of the eighteen kids finished in the 90s, five more in the 80s; two failed, Pat and Casey. Leah recovered and finished with a 74, well below the 90 she got last year, but good enough to secure her exchange to Germany. The girls, in general, did better than the boys. Playing more sports, girls now get more practice at sorting out the puzzles that a game presents. The process of math seems less alien and daunting to them, the fruits more attainable. But not for all. Amanda, who got an 82, still thinks she "can't do math," and her 82 has only deepened math's mystery for her. Sue never did get to know Amanda well. It was the same with Veronica and Elaine, who sat next to her at the front of the room. They were all quiet, and good enough students for her to leave alone, and that's what they seemed to want. Their ambitions were elsewhere, mostly in art and English. Rohita's ambitions were everywhere. Rohita wanted a 90 – 90 is what Rohita *is* – and she got it. She is one of those kids Sue would like to pack in her bag and take to her new school. Rohita has been in Canada only four years, but she displays little of a newcomer's insecurity. Immigrant kids usually make their way first through their schoolwork; people and new cultures are harder to learn, so they keep to themselves, or follow. Rohita dares to lead. She is on the student council, on the *Kronicle*. During the student election, she asked Sue if she would help her hang a banner in the Caf. It was only afterwards that Sue thought to herself, I would never have dreamed of asking that of a teacher. Rohita is going to be student council president before she graduates, Sue is sure, and be one of the best the school has ever had. She may or may not be a gifted student, but she is a gifted kid.

Perhaps only one or two in this class are truly gifted in math, Sue thinks now, kids who can not only learn and apply the patterns she teaches, but find those patterns themselves. Sometimes she would give them difficult assignments with few instructions, just to see how far they could go themselves. She'd have a big lineup of kids seeking help at her desk, but Pat wouldn't be among them. He could see those patterns without anyone's help. He could be a nuclear physicist if he wanted, she thinks. *If he wanted*.

Donald is another story. She brought him up to a desk next to hers and tried to work with him, but he wasn't ready. He arrived at his goal of 75 too late in the semester to achieve it, and fell 7 per cent short. A 59 on his final exam didn't help. Worse, he failed English. By little enough that his teacher wondered if she shouldn't find a few marks and pass him. A year ago, she might have. He had had such a hard time coping with high school, and his sister's death, a failure might have been too much. Now he's doing better enough that his English teacher thought his English skills should matter too, so she failed him. Ahead, he has a big hump to get over. For so long, he has defined himself by his innate giftedness, and others have tolerated his social awkwardness because of it. As that giftedness comes to matter less, as promise is superseded by performance, what will fill its void?

How will he come to see himself? What new story will he write? Will he spin off to the quirky giftedness of the margins or find something more solid?

✦ ✦ ✦

Cathy Sylvester is pleased with her class's results. Four months ago, she would never have believed that could happen. They had seemed such a ragged group, only one or two real stars, one or two deadbeats, all the rest no better than middling. The spark was in the wrong place, in Nelson and the girls at the back, in them nothing destructive, but nothing to drive the class forward. She had always to keep on this class. Checking homework, marking labs, doing her walkabouts through the classroom, at their worst they were never that bad, at their best never that good, her job never too onerous and never done. Nobody finished in the 90s; only four failed. Nobody left her classroom with a "bad experience"; nobody's life was transformed. Over the semester, they had learned a little science, a little human nature, grown four months older and moved one credit closer to graduating. It could have been a lot worse.

Doug never regained the ground he lost during his week-long ski trip out west. His complicated life offered no time for second chances. The 67 he had mid-term, which had so dissatisfied his uncle, fell to 56 at the end. His lab partner, Rob, who didn't like school much but always did well enough to pass, who would think about the future when the future came, failed. He failed English as well. Next year will be pivotal for him. Tracy never even wrote her final science exam. Jennifer, who dropped to General level, went from 39 at mid-term to a comfortable 66.

About two weeks before the end of classes, Nelson went to Cathy. He wasn't satisfied with his marks, he said. He could feel himself failing. He had set as his goal 85 per cent on the final exam. Overhearing him, Doug laughed. Cathy gave Nelson a schedule, do a chapter a day, she told him, and he kept to it. He didn't get his 85, but a solid 73. The real breakthrough, however, was made by Jody, his "poolar screen" partner. At first she had seemed just one of "the girls at the back," loud, obnoxious, with an attitude as impenetrable as a wall, but she was determined to succeed. Before Jody, even the Fates crumbled. She got an 87.

◆ ◆ ◆

To Noel Lim, the story is all right here on his exams. The good student, the bad student, the good reader, the bad reader, what happens and why. One of the exam questions was a previously unseen passage, the other was from their course texts, *Romeo and Juliet* or *Forbidden City*. All but three of the twenty kids who wrote the exam did better on the sight passage, all but two passed it; twelve failed the second part. The sustained discipline demanded in the reading of a novel or play was more than many were willing to tolerate.

Three times during the exam James had summoned Noel back to his desk to ask about the instructions. Others had questions too. For these kids, an instruction is written with such intimidating precision. Every word matters. As "ballpark" readers, they aren't used to that. *What if I don't quite get it?* "Oh sir, sir . . ." And if they're not quite sure they understand, they lack the confidence to synthesize, express, create, too distracted by what they think they don't know. On the sight passage, the questions were numerous and specific, easier to understand; their answers easier to organize and express. The best students, Shiva and Mai, did well on both parts. For those on the margins of comprehension, the impact was great. Nelson got only six out of thirty on the second question. Asked how the behaviour of a character from their readings reflected societal pressure on that character, Nelson chose Mercutio. He started well then drifted into a character sketch. This is "*not* related to the topic assigned," Noel scrawled across his page.

Nelson printed his answers in his exam book, his lines rigid, grudging, the size and shape of his letters varying from the controlled beginning of a sentence to the galloping end. Many answers he put down first on the page in short form, then realizing the need for sentences, crammed in subjects and verbs later. When the question demanded specific details, he wrote concisely and well. Asked to give three details to show that "Jane" in the sight passage, was "pathetic," he wrote: "She can't handle drinking liquor and she drank too much. She has nothing to say that will interest people (she only talked about shopping, relatives, neighbours, house). She has no social grace or intellectual curiosity." When the question required more personal insight, his writing became vague and unstructured. Asked how students behave differently to cope with societal pressure, he wrote: "Some students these days smoke, and some of them do not smoke for themselves, they smoke just to gain popularity which is basically giving into peer pressure. I knew one person in grade 8 who smoked and never inhaled, that shows how some people think. If they don't smoke it will make them feel left out. Some students steal because other people ask them to, it just makes people feel like they are gaining popularity. That is usually what people do is try to gain popularity." "Very disorganized," Noel wrote.

Shiva, who never says anything, overexplained in his writing. James flowed onto his exam page. His letters were tall with round, full, generous loops, as if he loved the feeling of getting them down. Loved it too much, perhaps, as he sometimes lost his way: "In the story *Forbidden City* which is based on a young boy named Alex who gets stuck in Beijing after demonstrations get out of hand and Chinese security comes in and starts shooting and the government starts putting out new laws and orders." Noel came to enjoy James, the chances he took on a page. Most kids are satisfied with being safe and predictable. Noel gives them what he must, good marks; to the rare student who challenges himself, Noel gives enthusiasm, excitement, a tiny part of himself.

This grade-ten class wasn't the kind of group Noel likes best. Too many had too much else going on in their lives that got in the way of learning. Noel realizes that English is not life, and that life should be rich and complicated, external and internal. But language *is* part of that life, its exploration and pleasure. That's what he wanted his kids to know. Take a chance, "go out on a limb – no pun intended," he would always add, intending every pun he could make. All semester, he complained that his best students were "paint by numbers" types, preoccupied with being right, so boring and obvious. Many were immigrant kids, looking for, needing, every shortcut they could find to skills and grades. He knew that's what they were doing and why, and admired their effort, but language is more than efficient result, more than someone else's thoughts and feelings. It's a tool to explore and express your own.

On Parents' Night, Noel had told Pauline's sister that Pauline was still hanging on but might not be up to the demands of the course. Pauline had been in Canada from Vietnam for less than a year. An awkwardness remains in her language, but understanding now shows through. Asked about the societal pressures she has faced, Pauline wrote on her exam: "Every weekend when my friends asked me to go out, I had to ask my sisters. When I asked my sisters to give permission, the answers that I heard most of the time were 'NO.' But I didn't get angry yet. Until, one day, when I heard this same answer I started to get mad and argued with my sisters. I told them I didn't want to hear the same answer every day, and I asked them to stop controlling me. Then I ran up to my room and felt guilty over my actions. I hope my sisters trust me and let me go out with my friends." Pauline got the fourth-highest mark in the class.

Mai did even better. She is from Hong Kong and has been in Canada longer; by semester end, her writing had progressed from the routine perfection that so irritated Noel, to being flawed but interesting. She is finding in language something her own. She has also learned how to play the game, Noel has noticed, and he admires that. Moving to Canada from Guyana, he'd had to learn that game himself. When you're new to a country, there isn't time to fight every shadow – I'*m going to be what* I'*m going to be.* It's too many fights. The game is in the other guy's hands. Instead, you go to school, do well, go to university, learn to play the game better than he does, and the rest is yours. Just as in English – learn the rules of syntax, then you can go where you want to go, and people will let you. Mai has learned these rules, so has Shiva. James still has to play the clown, Nelson, the overeager child, Sheri, the angry black sister. Where does it get them, Noel wonders.

Take Sharifa, for example. She had done adequately on the sight passage of the exam, poorly on the questions about *Romeo and Juliet.* All semester, she had been an annoying presence in the back corner, whispering, giggling, meowing like a cat, making little drawings, writing vulgar sayings on the blackboard beside her. She had come into the exam with a failing grade. At the bottom of her last answer, with time running short, she had drawn a pear-shaped figure, almost all head, with two big eyes and a bigger single curl on top. Beside it, she wrote: "If you like this picture, give me 20 free marks. If you don't, I'll settle for 10." Beside it, Noel wrote nothing. Sharifa hadn't learned to play the game.

With the semester system now, there isn't the sense of finality there used to be about the end of a school year. Kids don't generally pass or fail their year, only individual courses. The stakes aren't the same, or they don't seem to be. A week from now, a few hundred of these kids will be at summer school. Some to pass what they have already failed, many like Nelson, who, with no job and nothing else to do, are in need of something to centre their social lives; or who want to improve their marks in courses they've already taken. Some, like Fahad, who are keen to graduate as early as they can, will take a new course. Many of these teachers, Sue Lishman included, will be teaching them. Year-round school, so unthinkable, so impossible to legislate for so many reasons, is slowly becoming a habit.

◆ ◆ ◆

Terry sits in his office, the thirty-first year of his teaching career is over. Most of the goodbyes have been said at staff get-togethers the last few days. There is no glow of summer freedom or relief on his face. He looks the same as he does every other day. And really he's not done until he turns out the lights, locks the doors, and sees that the parking lot is clear. Then it's home, to the golf course, to the cottage, next September already on his mind.

An historian by training, a doer by nature, he thinks back to look ahead. He had a good group of senior students this year. Steady, not outstanding. Academically, they were fine, but the school needed some sparkle that they lacked. The student council was only okay; the *Kronicle* was a wonderful bonus, but done mostly by grade-eleven students who can't set the tone for the school. The Terry Fox Run and Spirit Week raised lots of money but not enough kids took part. And they lost the Formal. That was a real blow. A more cohesive, spirited senior class could have kept it going, that's what bothered him. He has had such strong student leadership other years, he's been spoiled, he realizes now. Each year he tells himself he's going to get more involved with student council. Next year, he will.

Among his grade nines, he will have only five repeaters, and only twenty have been recommended for summer school. But there is a gang of fifteen or twenty kids that sprang up this year,

grade nines and tens, who concern him. Pat is one, Chad another.
They hang out together, hold each other up when no one and
nothing else does, but hold each other back when someone tries
to break away. One parent called to complain about the influence
of this group, threatening to take his kid out of school and put
him in another. That got Terry's attention. He will watch them
more closely next year, but in the back of his mind he knows that
the school can do little with kids like this. It's not that the work
is too hard, it's that they can't get down to learning. Year after year,
it's the same. The whole question disturbs, perplexes, frustrates
him. These kids must do better. A few hundred years ago, when
not much changed and there was little to learn, not much separated the learner and the non-learner. New technologies now
allow those who can use them to gobble up the informational
ground. The non-learner still walks from place to place, the learner
jets away, the gap between them is widening dangerously. For the
non-learner's sake, for everybody's, something must be done.

But Terry doesn't know what to do, except to try again. He
had his "Hard-to-Serve" committee this year. It met, talked,
suggested, and tried, but nothing really resulted. A few years ago,
he introduced an "Alternative Ed" program. Problem kids were
identified, some teachers freed from their timetables to stay with
them all day and teach them all their subjects. But some other
teachers complained. Why should these kids get special treatment? Why should they be rewarded for failure? (Why should
my classes become bigger so *theirs* can be smaller?) Terry soon
realized that he had the wrong teachers involved in this program, those on the margins who would do "that sort of thing."
Next year, he'll bring the program back, his "small 'c' conservative" critics on staff be damned. This time he will have high-
credibility teachers doing it.

He will also have the Board's new pilot project for older
problem kids. Four schools are involved, Kennedy is one of

them. Space has been rented in an office building nearby. The project serves only six kids a school, puts them together in one place out of the school, away from other kids and teachers, in behavioural quarantine. Yet six fewer problem kids can make a big difference. The program gives Kennedy and the other schools a way of saying to these kids, If you don't shape up, I've got another place for you. If you don't like that, quit. That is your right; my obligation is met. The result: six kids gone from Kennedy, six more who may drop out, ten more who may get the message and shape up. More than twenty of the worst kids gone or better: more hope for next year.

Next year, the biggest change will be with the grade nines. Semesters will be eliminated for them, they will take all their courses over the whole year, every second day. They will stay together in cohorts (classes), be taught by cohorts (teams) of teachers who will meet frequently to discuss curriculum and the kids, who will get to know them better. From there, who knows? The next few years will be critical, Terry believes. The old system is so entrenched. Instruction has been so subject-oriented that teachers have been able to be islands unto themselves. Just give me my kids, they say, and I will work hard with them. But they don't know how these kids are in their other classes, except the two or three problem kids a class whose names come up in the staff room. They don't know how their fellow teachers teach. They need to be forced out of the classroom, into each others' company. This cohorting system might help create new habits, start important new conversations among staff. "There is such an opportunity here," Terry believes, but he knows the power and resistance of systems. "This may pass without much happening. We'll just have to see."

As he sits in his office, the reality of the year end settles slowly into him. The feeling is not hollow, not full, not energized or demoralized, one rather of slightly agitated calm. "Overall, it's been a decent year," he says, though that suddenly sounds too easy to him, and he stops himself. "When you've been in a place for five years, you expect each year to be better, and get frustrated because it doesn't work that way. Really, it's a never-ending struggle." He smiles. "But that's okay."

Touch wood.

Epilogue

Beyond the Front Row

The problems of education seem like a hundred different threads in a ball, each of them equal, together a snarl. Where does one even begin. Yet if we were to pull at the loose ends of those threads, one by one, what might happen? Many threads will snag onto others, tangling the ball more tightly. Some will pull through, leaving fewer threads behind, but also a no-less-tangled ball. But a few threads, perhaps two or three, might tug at those around them, loosen them, connect to them, and the ball will begin to unravel. No government jurisdiction or school board has the money, no teachers, parents, or kids have the time, energy, patience, or good will, to deal with a hundred different threads. Which are the two or three that could make a difference?

It is hard to see which threads are central when you watch a ball unwind. No single thread seems significant, the implications of each are hard to imagine, sometimes the whole process seems hardly worth the effort. It's much easier to begin with a ball that is mostly unwound, then to go backwards and see how it happened.

The time, then, is T. L. Kennedy on the day of its fiftieth-anniversary celebration, Friday, October 31, 2003. This is how the school might look.

It hasn't been an easy route into this school and this classroom. During the mid-1990s, little seemed to change in education, the disrespect for teachers and systems continued, but in the wider world big shifts were occurring. Males, WASPs, the native-born, the educated, and the monied were beginning to share power. They did so with continuing great reluctance, but the rest of society would have it no other way. Habits millennia in the making were being broken. In schools, the transformation was hastened by a bulge of teacher retirements that passed through the system. Nearly 50 per cent of Peel's teachers reached retirement age before the year 2000. New teachers who had grown up with assumptions of equality and equity took their place. Many were the sons and daughters of immigrants who had arrived since the late 1970s, from India, Sri Lanka, Vietnam, and Hong Kong, from Guyana, and Jamaica. Dealing with kids who were more like themselves, knowing what was under every hat and turban, and what wasn't, these new teachers found the classroom less mystifying. The generation gap, which had once ensured order, then brought disorder, had been narrowing.

Also hastening the changes was the unhappiness that had hung over the system for some time. Greater democratization had brought kids to treat teachers only as equals, and had brought teachers to put up walls to protect themselves. Yet when this reaction had brought teachers only deeper sadness and dread, they realized that they would need to dismantle those walls, to get closer to kids, not make themselves more distant, to spend more time with them, not less. Doing so, they have discovered that their age, education, and experience, the badges which had come to matter not at all symbolically, *do* matter greatly in the day-to-day. The kids hear sense in their words now that they take the time to speak them. Earning and re-earning respect, teachers have found that many of the assumptions that make any place, any relationship, work, that once seemed gone forever, have returned.

The public attitude toward teaching has also been changing in recent years. Indeed, the last fifteen years of the twentieth century seem now like teaching's dark ages. It was a time of such insecurity. The family and the world economy had both been turned upside down, the signposts were all askew. Teachers who themselves could scarcely make out the present were being asked to prepare kids for a future they themselves couldn't imagine. The public's mood had turned sour. The first generation of kids to be university-educated had reached the age of authority in the 1980s and 1990s and had shown themselves unable to transform the world. An incessant message pulsed out daily from every TV and newspaper: *everything* is wrong. Eventually people began tuning out – and tuning in to things that seemed far closer to the reality of their own lives. Never as good as they once had thought they were, they began realizing they were never as bad, either. Nor does the future seem to them now so unliveable a place. Technological change, which had seemed so dizzying in the 1990s, happens day by day, they now realize, and most people have adapted to it, and have put away their worst fears.

A decade ago, it seemed as if the solution to education's problems was in new curriculum, new technology, new teacher training, new organizational structures for schools, in the big answers, because, if the solution wasn't there, where? Money was being redirected towards big-answer people – superintendents, educational experts, and specialists – who, separate from the classroom, in big-answer roles, had only big answers to offer. But in pulling on education's threads, allowing themselves to go wherever exploration took them, more and more educators have begun rediscovering the *whys*. The central thread which loosened the others turned out not to be any of the big answers. It was time.

At first glance, this classroom doesn't look much different from that of eight years ago. A big computer monitor sits on a desk at the front, with libraries of information at everyone's fingertips, ready to be called up, but the books and binders remain. There are still not computer terminals at every desk, and the same familiar mixture of excitement and fear is in the air. What *is* different are the dynamics of this room. Some kids are watching the monitor, some are doing other work, and the teacher is in their midst. The lesson is done, those at the front have punched up a program on the screen, something broader, richer, deeper, that goes beyond the lesson. The teacher, freed from their demands, has time to penetrate the front row to the rows behind, to reach the majority of kids who were always just there, the Dougs, Rodneys, and Sandees, who were barely passing, doing well enough to be ignored.

The teacher stops by their desks for longer now, talks more, listens more, spends more time going over the work that each kid has done. He seems to know these kids better, they seem to know him. Every day, he takes one of them to the back of the room, and they talk. In ten minutes with a kid, one to one, several times over the course of a semester, a lot can be said. The teacher can get beneath the skin of a student, discover what's keeping her from learning and what might make her change. Within weeks, the teacher can feel many of the kids respond, day by day doing just a little bit better. Better enough for long enough that the kids come to realize their improvement is no fluke, that they can dare to dream and try, without the pain of failure as their certain reward.

Not everybody needs these talks, or not in this way. In a class of twenty-two, maybe fifteen need them, not more. Five talks a week, a talk with each kid once every three weeks, six times a semester, that's a lot of conversation, a lot of getting to know and of understanding. And the more a teacher knows about a student, the more he wants to know. There's nothing terribly interesting about that sullen lump in the middle row; there's something possibly fascinating about that same kid, who stutters when he talks, plays piano, and loves his dog. Ten minutes every three weeks, a minute a day in passing, thirty seconds in the hall and perhaps a few more seconds in the hall with the kid's other teachers, especially now that grade-nine "cohorting" has spread to all but the senior grades.

The random mixing of kids course by course is gone; kids now stay together in classes, or "cohorts." Cohorting of kids has brought cohorting of teachers, cohorting of teachers has brought cohorting of classrooms. A school within a school within a school. For kids and teachers, a world shrunk to human dimensions. Everything seems smaller, the school, the classrooms. At Kennedy the rooms aren't arranged by subjects any longer – the science classrooms here, the math there – but by kids. The grade nines and tens in this part of the school, the elevens there. Kids go out one classroom door and through another nearby; teachers watch them go and come. With time and a reason, talk happens naturally between kids and teachers. The teacher knows a kid's other teachers without having to contact the office, without having to take the extra step that breaks the chain. With time and a reason, talk happens between teachers, too. They hear remarkable stories about their students from their other teachers, further pieces add to a suddenly more interesting puzzle they want to know more about. Teachers are learning to teach small.

Homeroom teachers have also been brought back, offering a few more minutes of teacher-kid contact a semester. Cohort teachers meet regularly. At first in meetings, they would run down their list of kids as if on a roll call: name, a few words, next. Now that they know these kids better, they talk more, and an hour that once seemed to them like two, has turned into ninety

minutes that rarely seem enough. Once teachers used to stake out
their teaching ground, senior kids or grade tens, wherever their
interests took them. Once, with more information to learn, the
priorities were courses, for teachers as experts. Now that cohorts
of kids stay together more than one year, teachers stay with them
more than one year. They teach them grade-nine *and* grade-ten
science. From this experience, teachers have been reminded
again of what they've known all along: it's kids they are teaching, not subjects. It's *learning* they are teaching them, not history
or math, which are mere instruments for this learning. And it's
a *feeling* about learning they are trying to get across most of all.
They want every child, when faced in the future with a book, a
piece of technology, an adult, a child, a man, a woman, a black,
a white, a genius, a dolt, a group, or only one other, to feel comfortable. To feel that he *can* learn, and *wants* to learn, from all the
imaginable sources of his learning. That's what "learning how to
learn" and "lifelong learning" really mean, what parents really
want when they drop their child off on that first day of school.
Help see him through, they ask, so that one day he might see
himself through.

Teachers have less time set aside for their colleagues now,
more time for kids. Teachers know they will seek out other
teachers if they have a teaching problem, on their own time if
necessary, but that they might not seek out kids if kids have a
learning problem. They have come to see "prep time" differently.
They still have one period a day to prepare their lessons, but now
more teachers spend most of that prep time in their classrooms,
not behind the closed doors of the staff room or department
rooms. They prepare their lessons where kids can find them. It's
mostly the good students who drop by, of course, but good students need their time, too. With a hunger to know, these kids will
hunt down teachers wherever teachers are. If they have to give
up part of their lunch period to do it, they will. The average

student, whose bodily hungers are too distracting, must be cap-
tured in class. There has been one casualty, however, of teachers
spending more prep time in classrooms: the card games. But card
players, like good students, have an irresistible hunger. They find
time to play at lunch.

Even PD, Professional Development, days have changed. Once
they were treated so casually that teachers almost lost them in
the public spending squeeze. Now one day a semester, classes
stop, teachers remain in the school, and kids and their parents
come in to talk. Teachers call and make appointments with those
parents whom they most want to see. Some teachers also make
house calls: to understand how families live who are often
different from their own, to learn one more piece in the puzzle
of their students' lives. What better professional development
than that?

This whole-family focus started several years ago, and has
been picking up steam. If the mountain wouldn't move to them,
teachers realized, they had to move to it. They had whined long
and loud about never seeing the parents they most needed to see
on Parents' Night, about the kids of those parents never coming
to see them after class, until they finally accepted that neither
was going to happen. They also came to realize how unequal
the system is, in practice. Buy a new computer for the school,
and it's there for 1,470 kids to use. But who uses it? Give a class
seventy-six minutes of your time, it's there for all of them. But
who uses it? Teachers had always thought it was the bad kids,
interrupting a lesson, taking away from class time. Then one day
a teacher brought in twenty-two stopwatches, one for each kid,
and started each watch as each kid took the floor. They discovered that it's the good students who monopolize a classroom,
their hands always up, never without a question or an answer.
Teachers had once considered that what these kids asked and said
was simply part of the lesson, trickling down to and benefiting

the rest of the class. But in reality, not much trickles down; even less seeps in. And who uses the library? Who is on the *Kronicle*, in the choir, on the yearbook staff? The same few kids. On paper, everything had seemed stacked in the bad students' favour – the special programs, the counsellors', the vice-principals' and principal's time – until someone decided to add it up. It wasn't even close.

The teachers now realize that it isn't enough merely to put a chocolate cake on the table, then to withdraw from the room, allowing those with the most ravenous hunger to take all they can get. Everyone should get some. In trying to right the imbalance they have set aside those ten minutes a day in class, arranged appointments on PD days – and created some after-school time as well.

An Ontario government report on education in the mid-1990s recommended that teacher training be extended from one year to two. The purpose was to give every prospective teacher more months in the classroom, more experience, more confidence, before facing their own first classroom. In practice, this extended training has given them additional time of a different and more important sort. The student teachers them-selves triggered the change. With two years of training, practice-teaching placements had become longer. With no quick escape to each next assignment, every problem they faced struck home. In their first experiences in a classroom, they came face to face suddenly with the kid who didn't want to learn. They were stunned. They had been good learners all their lives. They loved learning: what's wrong with these kids, they asked. Back at the faculties of education, they prodded staff with questions. Staff decided that perhaps they should spend more time preparing these teachers to deal with kids who *weren't* just like them, who *didn't* love learning, who ran for cover at the first hint of it. Kids who would make up the majority of every class these teachers had in their teaching lives.

Now part of a teacher's training is to follow these kids home. To talk to their parents, and to them, to learn their whys, to understand their stories. During each teaching placement, a new teacher visits two families a night, four nights a week, Fridays excepted, after dinner when everyone is home, parents they would never see on Parents' Night. They say to these parents: your kids are away from school too often, and are too often late when they do come. They don't do their homework. Then they tell these parents why this matters. They ask parents to remember what it's like to sit down at a table when someone is already in the midst of a story, or to arrive for a movie ten minutes late. That's what it's like for your son or daughter, these young teachers say, when they aren't in school, on time, with their homework done. They get behind and lose the story. They don't know what's going on, and after a while, they don't want to come at all. They fight you every step of the way, out of bed, out the door. But you *can* help them. It doesn't matter if you feel stupid in math – most people do – or think you've forgotten more history than you ever learned. Do what you *can* do, what as a parent *only* you can do: Get your kid to school, on time, every day. Ask about his homework, be around, care. The five minutes you didn't know what to do with with your kids, like fishes and loaves, will turn into thirty minutes that fly by. The difference that will make – you won't believe it.

At the end of six weeks, new teachers have been in every home of every student who needs them most in every class they teach. Teachers have always known that they needed parents on their side, now they are learning how to get them there.

Many of these young teachers, now in their first jobs, have continued the habit of home visits. Slowly, the habit has rubbed off on older colleagues. These colleagues don't often make house calls, but instead of going home each day at 4:00 p.m., they leave half an hour earlier. The kids they most need to see aren't there then anyway; if time runs out on the others, those others will find the answer themselves, they know, and still be back tomorrow. Then, about 7:30 p.m., the teachers make two or three phone calls, ten minutes a call, spending the same thirty minutes they saved in the afternoon – except it's a different thirty minutes. The payoff for them is not just in reaching kids and families they otherwise wouldn't reach, but comes from a motivation more universal. They do it for the same reason they want kids to do their homework. They know as teachers that if they put in that extra half hour a night, the next day will be better. *They* want to have fun in the classroom, too.

Last year, an important threshold was finally crossed: three Kennedy teachers walked into Mickey's. They didn't stay long, and they and other of their colleagues have returned only twice since, but their gesture was noted, and now they have one more thing to talk about with their students. Mickey's still belongs to the kids, just as the staff room still belongs to teachers, but not neccessarily, not always, if something matters more. Now, at Mickey's, where the kids who don't like school still go, the most popular video game is "virtual-reality school."

"He who can, does. He who cannot, teaches." George Bernard Shaw's quip seemed too much the literal truth to critics in the 1980s and 1990s. It was a time for doers. God was dead, life without eternity felt urgently short. There was so much more to know, and so little time to know it. The new answers were complicated and elusive. They took training. The hero became the expert, somebody better than everyone else at something. That took time, more and more of it. The functions of life became specialized. In business, in personal lives, people did what they were good at, hiring others for the rest. Personal hierarchies were created, information passing up the line. But it was the information of other doers, absorbed in their own expertise, with its own language; it was their information, not yours. Input improved, output did not. People began to realize that in politics, in business, in family matters – in a democracy – hierarchies don't work. Structures, relationships, needed to be flattened. Doing was not enough. The lessons of doing had to be passed on. To be received, not just given, conveyed in the receiver's language, on the receiver's time, with the receiver as object, not subject, with the receiver at the centre. Those who have learned that lesson are able to spread information to more people to use in more and different ways, and now thrive. "Us-ism" and self-interest go hand in hand.

Teaching is the act of putting someone else at the centre: the student, the son or daughter, the employee, the citizen. During the last years of the twentieth century, we lost our instinct for teaching. In the need to become experts, we had no room at the centre for anyone but ourselves. In the messages we delivered, in the tone we delivered them in, it was "Student, teach thyself" – and it didn't work. Structures – political, corporate, family – need the learner at the centre. Habits of hierarchy still remain, but political and corporate leaders, parents and friends, now realize their need to be good teachers. He who can does. He who does must also teach.

This past decade, the focus of education has shifted back to the classroom. The important people in the education debate no longer inhabit corner offices or appear on television screens, they are teachers and kids. People have come to realize again that a school works in the classroom – or it doesn't work at all; that education may be about teaching and teachers, but really it is about learning and kids; and that education reform may be for *all* kids, but really it is for the majority of kids in every class who are doing just adequately or worse. People have also come to realize that traditional education reform, which focused on new technology, new curriculum, and new organizational structures, was really for front-row kids with front-row needs. The changes it brings keep kids contemporary with the world, but cannot touch a kid's fundamental story, that lifelong relationship he or she has with learning. After years of pulling on so many threads, people have come to realize that the central thread is time. It is only with time that stories that need changing can be rewritten. The classroom is now a better place because we are learning to teach to beyond the front row.

Acknowledgements

This book is the result of the help, encouragement, and inspiration of many people. During a time when nearly every word expressed about education was angry and critical, I asked the Peel Board of Education to accept the presence of a stranger in one of their schools. It would have been far easier for the Board to say no. That it said yes was due principally to the trust of Bob Lee, Peel's Director of Education at the time, and to the support provided by Dawn McDowell, Peel's former Director of Communications. There also needed to be a principal who would take me in, someone with enough enthusiasm for the project to overcome the complications that would certainly arise. Throughout, Terry Chaffe remained respectful of his obligations as principal, never losing sight of personal propriety, yet he always looked for ways that would allow me to fully experience the school: in the staff room, in counselling offices, in the vice-principals' and principal's offices, in meetings outside school with principals and superintendents, and – mostly – in the classroom. He encouraged his teachers to open their doors to me, and, ultimately, it is from them that I asked for, and received, the greatest indulgence. In a classroom day after day, whatever *is* will show itself. Maria Cheung, Noel Lim, Sue Lishman, Rick Ray, and Cathy Sylvester, among others, understood the book's intent, accepted the risk, and became essential collaborators in its writing. So did the kids. They put up with another adult body in their classrooms, tolerated my questions, and accepted me. The book, above all else about them and for them, needed them. I am very grateful for their friendship.

In writing the book, I have had the benefit of much good advice and guidance. From those who, with much more than professional interest, have read all or part of various drafts; from Doug Gibson, who offered his unfailing encouragement; from Anne Holloway, my editor, who gave to the book her clear, demanding, and patient eye.

I have had many great teachers in my life, inside the classroom and out: my mother and father, Margaret and Murray Dryden; my brother, Dave, now a school principal; my sister, Judy; Mrs. Freeman, Mr. Cassie, Mr. Jackson, Mr. Thom, Mr. Picard, Walter LaFeber, Ralph Nader, Scotty Bowman, Jon Segal; my wife, Lynda, once a teacher herself, who day after day offers her family her humane view of the world; and our kids, Sarah and Michael, who have been willing to endure my many meanderings down roads unmarked, and treat them as "adventures," and who provide the fuel that propels us on to more new adventures than we ever could have hoped for. All these people have made learning fun; they are the book's inspiration.

In memory of Sheldon/Nelson
(November 6, 1978 – October 9, 1995)